John McDonald

Secrets of the Great Whiskey Ring

Containing a Complete Exposure of the Illicit Whiskey Frauds Culminating in 1875

John McDonald

Secrets of the Great Whiskey Ring

Containing a Complete Exposure of the Illicit Whiskey Frauds Culminating in 1875

ISBN/EAN: 9783337259068

Printed in Europe, USA, Canada, Australia, Japan

Cover: Foto ©ninafisch / pixelio.de

More available books at **www.hansebooks.com**

GEN. JOHN McDONALD.

SECRETS

OF THE

GREAT WHISKEY RING,

CONTAINING

*A COMPLETE EXPOSURE OF THE ILLICIT WHIS-
KEY FRAUDS CULMINATING IN 1875,*

AND THE

CONNECTION OF GRANT, BABCOCK, DOUGLASS, CHESTER H.
KRUM, AND OTHER ADMINISTRATION OFFICERS, ESTAB-
LISHED BY POSITIVE AND UNEQUIVOCAL

DOCUMENTARY PROOFS,

COMPRISING FAC-SIMILES OF CONFIDENTIAL LETTERS AND TELEGRAMS EMA
NATING FROM THE WHITE HOUSE, DIRECTING THE MANAGEMENT
OF THE RING. ALSO PHOTOGRAPHS OF GRANT, BAB-
COCK, BRISTOW, GARFIELD AND THE
FAMOUS SYLPH.

TO WHICH IS ADDED

*THE MISSING LINKS IN THE CHAIN OF EVIDENCE OF JAMES
4. GARFIELD'S IMPLICATION WITH THE DISTRICT
OF COLUMBIA RING AND CREDIT
MOBILIER BRIBERY.*

BY GEN. JOHN McDONALD,

*Formerly Supervisor of Internal Revenue for the District comprising Mis-
souri, Arkansas, Texas, Kansas, Indian Territory, and New Mexico.*

CHICAGO:
BELFORD, CLARKE & CO.
1880.

PREFACE

NEARLY five years have elapsed since my conviction as a member of the Great Whiskey Ring of 1875, or, more properly, of the Ring the exposure of which occurred during that year. Five years is but a short while to those whose current of life flows with the melody of prosperity and contentment, but to him whose memory is seared by the basest ingratitude man ever showed to man ; whose sacrifices for those in power above him have ruined a life, in the debris of which his eyes can never unbend their fixed gaze at his own bitter humility, it is ages.

In this introduction to my thorough exposure of the whiskey frauds culminating in 1875, it is my desire to qualify a most unenviable position ; one which I have no disposition to shrink from, however false appearing those sleuth hounds fresh from a gluttonous feast of public blood ; those abusers of trust who cry "thief" loudest in order to deflect the gaze of justice from their own villanies, seek to make it. I do not approach the bar of public opinion at this day, laying bare the hideous deformities of recreant high-place officials, for the purpose of vindicating myself. Far from it. Denying nor affirming nothing as to my own guilt, the law has spent its force upon me ; I have paid the penalty, and further claims against me no man has ; I am, therefore, entitled to a considerate hearing in what I have to say.

Thoroughly appreciating how prone the public will be to throw discredit upon my statements, I have determined to omit much that is unsupported by written or other corroborative evidence, and confine myself to charges which I can prove by overwhelming testimony. Every step, therefore, is cautiously made, and if there is a singe libel contained in this book I am amenable to the law, the burden of which few men have felt more heavily. Each declaration is made as if I were under oath, and in order that the true story shall appear unabridged I have dealt liberally only with the facts in which I have been as equally unsparing of myself as of all others implicated with me.

During the rigid investigation of the U. S. Grand Jury, when nearly every man in the nation believed that many of the highest officials in Washington were beneficiaries of the whiskey fund, I was asked a thousand times to disclose the secrets I was believed to possess. Indeed, I was promised immunity from punishment if I would become an informer; but those secrets were not revealed, for reasons easily understood : I was an appointee of President Grant, and as his friend and the recipient of his favors, certain obligations were created which I was not forgetful to regard. Gen. Babcock was the President's private secretary, and there will be few to contradict me when I say that he was, in a great measure, the President's chief adviser, especially in cases were his private matters were concerned. I regarded Babcock's instructions as those emanating from the highest authority, and however my obedience to their orders may be considered, they were the excuse for my actions. Having become identified with the purposes of my superiors, sharing their benefits and entrusted with their confidence, when disclosures were made and the hour of sacrifice was at hand, I could not assume the character of a base ingrate to escape a punishment which, missing me, would involve the entire nation in the deepest disgrace. If I were convicted I knew that the tenure of my punishment would be limited to the disposition of him in whose hands the pardoning power was vested ; having received his promise of an immediate pardon I put on the sackcloth of disgrace and, from the high position I had so many years maintained, I descended to the most humiliating, stigmatical depths—a felon's cell. For seventeen months I wore the garb of infamy, that leprous, foul, polluted character which gnaws at sensitive nature "like a worm in the bud." I not only suffered this restraint of liberty with its unending night-mare of moral death, but lived on to see the honest accumulations of many years of patient labor wasted because I could not protect it, and from an ample fortune upon my entrance into political life I was reduced to penùry when released. Those in power forgot me and their promises ; they feared to issue me an immediate pardon because of the pressure of public opinion, which might become intensified against them at such a bold interference to defeat the sentence of the court, and I was therefore permitted to languish until my forbearance would endure no more ; then I *demanded* my pardon, under threats of exposure if it were not immediately granted, and I was released at once.

To those who will cavil at my course, the question will be suggested, "Why are these disclosures made now, when the time for their effective use, in the courts, has passed:" Grant's re-nomination would have afforded a more plausible pretext for the publication of these disclosures—viewed from a strictly partisan standpoint, and unfortunately a great many persons can discover no merit in anything which may be devoid of political complexion. The purpose of this publication now has a broader base to rest upon than mere personal vindictiveness or political influence. It is to expose the villainies of an administration the very mention of which should excite a righteous indignation and befoul the atmosphere; but though the crimes of Marius, who sold offices in the public places of Rome, were as virtues, compared with many of the corrupt acts of Grant's administration, yet there is a very large percentage of American citizens whose eyes cannot penetrate beyond the military glory with which Grant is clothed; who parade his statesmanship and would reward his crimes with an honor no other American ever held or sought. It is with an earnest and will considered belief that Gen. Grant will be a disturbing factor in the politics and purity of the nation so long as his infamies remain hidden, which furnishes one of the reasons for this exposure, and with this contribution to the literature of uncovered venality goes forth the hope that the supporters of the Grant administration will find the proofs herein which will cause the blush of shame to mantle their cheeks for having lent their aid to perpetuate infamies of such magnitude as were constantly developing while Gen. Grant was our Chief Magistrate, who, as will be conclusively shown, was an active participant in the frauds laid bare in this work.

I have included the venal acts of Gen. James A. Garfield, because of his position now as candidate for the Presidency, and to forwarn the nation against abuses in office which he will certainly inaugurate if elected.

I have no affiliation with the Democratic party further than my desire to see the return of honest principles, and above all, "honest acts," which will reclaim the nation from the disgrace visited upon it by corrupt officials, among which class the public will include

JOHN McDONALD,

Formerly Supervisor of Internal Revenue for the district embracing Missouri, Arkansas, Texas, Kansas, Indian Territory and New Mexico

CONTENTS.

CHAPTER I.

CHAPTER II.

CHAPTER III.

CHAPTER IV.

CHAPTER V.

CHAPTER VIII.

CHAPTER IX.

CHAPTER X.

CONCLUSION.

The Missing Links Convicting James A. Garfield of a Corrupt
Connection with the Credit Mobilier and the District of
Columbia Ring.

————

CHAPTER I.

The great whiskey frauds culminating in 1875,
are a part of the history of American politics. No
ring was ever before formed embracing such a gigantic scope and including among its chief instigators
and membership, such distinguished Government
officials. The original intention of the organizers,
adopting suggestions from the highest authority in
the land, was to make the ring co-extensive with
the nation, with headquarters in all the large cities,
for the purpose of raising a campaign fund with
which to advance the interests of President Grant
in his aspirations for a second term. So far as my

B

personal knowledge extends, the money received from the distillers and rectifiers was used according to the original intention of the members, until Grant's re-election, when, the purposes of the organization having been accomplished, but with the management of the colossal fraudulent undertaking thoroughly in hand, it was decided to continue the appropriation of the revenue and to make the members of the ring the beneficiaries of the fund. During congressional and municipal campaigns, however, a part of this fund was always used in the interests of the Republican candidates.

HOW I BECAME SUPERVISOR.

In the years 1868-69, I was engaged in Washington City collecting war claims against the Government and buying up Quartermaster's informal vouchers. I conducted this business with much success, but in September of the latter year, being a passenger on the ill-fated train on the Erie Railroad which burned at Mast Hope, Pa., with such destruction to life and property, I lost my trunk containing over $9,000,000 of these claims. My individual loss approximated $300,000, to recover which, I went to President Grant for the purpose of obtaining from him a note of introduction to Jim Fisk, then Manager, and Jay Gould, the President of the Erie Railroad Co. Grant declined to give me the note, as did also Gen. Sherman, to whom I made a like request, giving as their reason, that such an exhibition of personal interest in claims of such nature as these represented, would be improper. During my conversation with the President, I mentioned the fact that several of my friends in St. Louis had requested me to make application for one of the Supervisorships, an office created by Congress, July 20th, 1868.

I did not tell him that I wanted the office, because the appointing power was with the Secretary of the Treasury, but referred to the desire of my friends merely as a casual, social remark.

President Grant responded at once, saying: "Well, McDonald, I would like to give you one of those places, and if you will accept, all you will have to do is to return to St. Louis and procure some recommendations, make your application and forward your papers."

Having received such a decided and unexpected promise, I begun to think seriously of accepting the position, and returned to St. Louis at once. Directly after my return William McKee, of the *Missouri Democrat*, also suggested to me that an application for Supervisor would certainly be granted. I talked with a few of my friends in St. Louis, concerning recommendations, etc., some of whom interested themselves in my behalf, and, in a few days, I had prepared a very large list of recommendations, which, together with my application, I carried in person to President Grant. He examined my papers with great care and then had them filed with Commissioner Delano, and on October 5th, 1869, my commission as Supervisor of Internal Revenue was issued.

A false impression has long prevailed respecting the character of my indorsements, created by newspaper assertions that I was opposed by the members of the Merchant's Exchange and the best people of St. Louis. In order to disprove this false claim, I herewith copy a few of the great number of my recommendations, many of which were unsolicited.

St. Louis, August 30, 1869.

General U. S. Grant.

Dear Sir: Colonel John McDonald, of this city, is an applicant for the office of Supervisor of Internal Revenue. I know him to be man of great energy, a true Republican and a devoted friend of your administration. I believe he will discharge the duties of the office faithfully and honestly, and therefore commend him to your most favorable consideration. Very respectfully, your obedient servant,   E. W. Fox

On this letter were the following endorsements:

I cheerfully join in the above recommendation.

Jas. E. Yeatman.

I have known Major McDonald for several years. He was one of those who promptly responded to the wants of his country, and was active in getting up the 8th Missouri regiment, one of the fighting regiments of the war, and served in that regiment as Major and was in some of the hottest of the fights. He deserves well of his government.

Wm. M. McPherson.

General Sherman's Endorsement.

Washington, D. C., Sept. 8, 1869.

Major McDonald served under my immediate command in 1862–3, with great honor and credit to himself. He is a very active business man of an extensive acquaintance. I am personally acquainted with all the parties to this document, and certify them to be of the very best in St. Louis, and they know the matters of which they write. Major McDonald is entitled to the most favorable attention of the departments of the government.   W. T. Sherman, General.

EXECUTIVE DEPARTMENT,
JEFFERSON CITY, September 2, 1869.

HON. COLUMBUS DELANO, Commissioner of Internal Revenue.

DEAR SIR:—I have not the pleasure of an intimate acquaintance with Brevet Brigadier General John McDonald, who desires to be Superintending Inspector of Internal Revenue at St. Louis. He is very strongly endorsed by persons of *very high* respectability whom I *do* know. I doubt not, from such recommendations, he would make an efficient public officer and give character to the position. I am very respectfully, your obedient servant,   J. M. McCLURG.

U. S. SENATOR McDONALD.

LITTLE ROCK, ARK., Nov. 20, 1869.

HON. C. DELANO, Commissioner of Internal Revenue.

DEAR SIR:—Gen. John McDonald, lately appointed Supervisor of Internal Revenue, and assigned to Arkansas, is here on duty. I am highly gratified with the appointment and assignment, and I have every reason to believe that it will redound to the interests of the public service. This State needs the watchfulness of a firm, honest and energetic man to look after revenue matters, and I feel assured from the tone of McDonald's circular to collectors and assessors that he is the right man and means business. Your friend and obedient servant,   A. McDONALD, United States Senator

MR. DELANO TO THE PRESIDENT.

TREASURY DEPARTMENT, OFFICE OF INTERNAL REVENUE,
WASHINGTON, Sept. 9, 1869.

DEAR SIR:—Gen. John McDonald presents excellent recommendations for Supervisor of Missouri, Kansas, etc., vice Mr. Marr, the incumbent. He proposes to see you and present his papers. Judging from what I know of Mr. McDonald, as well as from his endorsements I presume he will make an efficient and faithful officer. Senator Drake urges strenuously

Marr's retention and I dislike, in view of this fact, to make a change without your approbation and advice.

I am very sincerely, etc.,   C. DELANO.

To PRESIDENT GRANT.

McKEE, FISHBACK & Co.

OFFICE OF MISSOURI DEMOCRAT, }
ST. LOUIS, Sept. 5, 1869. }

GEN. GRANT, President United States,

DEAR SIR.—Gen. McDonald is an applicant for Supervisor of Internal Revenue for this district. We do not wish to multiply words in his favor. We have known him for years. He was a brave soldier, a true Republican in the day of our trouble. He never faltered in his duty. He is eminently qualified for the position he seeks. He has energy, ability and integrity, the requisites you require in public officers. His appointment will give general satisfaction and particularly oblige your friends here and none more than ourselves.

Most Respectfully,

McKEE, FISHBACK & Co.

LIEUTENANT GOVERNOR STANARD.

ST. LOUIS, Sept. 1, 1869.

HON. COLUMBUS DELANO, Commissioner of Internal Revenue,

SIR.—It affords me more than usual pleasure to recommend for appointment to the office of Supervisor of Internal Revenue of this district, Gen. McDonald. He is an able, efficient and upright man, and I believe him peculiarly fitted to discharge the duties of the office. That his appointment will give general satisfaction I have no doubt, and certainly it will add strength to the party here.

Very Respectfully,

E. O. STANARD, Lieutenant Governor of Missouri.

This was endorsed as follows: I concur with the gentlemen in their recommendation of Gen. McDonald.

NATHAN COLE, Mayor of St. Louis.

IRWIN Z SMITH, Judge St. Louis County Court,

JAMES S. FARRAR, Judge St. Louis County Court.

STATE SENATOR GEORGE H. REA.

SECOND NATIONAL BANK, }
ST. LOUIS, Sept. 7, 1869. }

HON. COLUMBUS DELANO, Commissioner Internal Revenue,

SIR.—The bearer of this, Gen. McDonald, is well known in this city as a man of sterling integrity, a hard worker and possessed of good business qualifications and great energy. Any appointment given him would give general satisfaction in this city.

Truly Yours,

GEORGE H. REA.

EX-GOVERNOR FLETCHER.

ST. LOUIS, Aug. 31, 1869.

DEAR SIR.—My old friend Brevet Brigadier General John McDonald, will be an applicant for appointment of Supervising Inspector Internal Revenue at this place. Permit me to say that I have known him long and well; he is a gentleman of remarkable energy and fine business qualifications, and possessed of a quick perception and ready ability of reaching conclusions from combinations of facts, which eminently fit him for the place. Gen. McDonald was one of the first among the young men of Missouri to respond to the call of the country in 1861, and was a favorite officer in one of our fighting regiments. As a soldier he deserves well of the country, and as a business man he is well fitted to do good service in the civil department.

Very Respectfully your obedient servant,

THOS. C. FLETCHER.

HON. COLUMBUS DELANO, Supt. Internal Revenue United States.

The endorsements on this recomendation were as follows;

Having entire confidence in the fitness of Gen. McDonald for the position referred to, I shall be much gratified to hear of his appointment, and believe he will give general satisfaction.

JAS. B. EADS.

I cordially indorse every word of the within.

FRANCIS RODMAN, Secretary of State of Missouri.

ROOMS RADICAL UNION,
EXECUTIVE COMMITTEE.
CITY AND COUNTY OF ST. LOUIS, No. 11 NORTH FIFTH ST.

ST. LOUIS, Sept. 4, 1869.

HON. C. DELANO, Commissioner of Internal Revenue,

DEAR SIR : — I know Brevt. Brig. Genl. John McDonald well, and most cheerfully say that a more satisfactory appointment to the office of Inspector of Internal Revenue at St. Louis could not be made. McDonald has the requisite integrity, ability, energy and tact necessary to fill the position with credit to this administration. I speak of what I know ; having been four years President of R. U. Ex. Committee my opportunity to form a correct judgment has been good. I think, sir, you will find McDonald an officer who will obey orders promptly and do all in his power to honestly collect the Revenue so much needed by our government. McDonald can command any endorsement required. I hope you will appoint him to the office.

I am dear sir, respectfully, your obedient servant,

ALFRED CLAPP.

P. S.   I am not now the President of the above R. U. Ex. C.   A. C.

FROM HON. PETER E. BLAND.

ST. LOUIS, Aug. 31, 1869.

HON. COLUMBUS DELANO, Commissioner of Internal Revenue.

SIR : — Permit me to recommend my friend Genl. John McDonald for appointment to the office of Supervisor of Internal Revenue in this district in case of the removal of the present incumbent. Genl. McDonald's political record is too well known for remark, and his promptitude, efficiency and general ability, peculiarly fit him for discharging the duties of that office in a manner satisfactory to the government and beneficially to the just interests of all concerned.

Very respectfully and truly yours,

P. E. BLAND.

In addition to the foregoing letters were also the following which I omit for want of space:

Capt. John Scudder.

Geo. P. Plant, President Merchants Exchange.

Capt. Bart. Abel, and a large number of other members of the Merchants Exchange.

U. S. Senator Rice of Arkansas.

Congressmen Logan H. Roots and Bowles of Arkansas.

Gov. Powell Clayton, Arkansas.

Senator Pomeroy, of Kansas, and many others.

A stronger endorsment than this no man ever forwarded to Washington as I have been frequently told by those occupying the highest positions in official life.

The opposition made to my appointment, and brought directly to the notice of the President, was the following telegram:

St. Louis, Feby. 16, 1870.

Hon. Geo. S. Boutwell, Sec'y of the Treas., Washington.

If the contemplated change of Supervisor in this district is not fixed, I would suggest that the character of the new appointee should be investigated here and at Memphis.

Chester H. Krum, Atty. U. S., etc.
C. W. Ford, Collector.
C. A. Newcomb, U. S. Marshal.

St. Louis, Oct. 7, 1869.

Hon. Geo. S. Boutwell, Secretary of Treasury, Washington, D. C

Please withold commission of McDonald until you hear by mail. We regard it as highly prejudicial to the interests of the Government.

C. Schurz, U. S. S.,
D. P. Dyer, M. C.,
Jno. W. Noble, U. S. Att'y.,
C. A. Newcomb, U. S. Marshal.

[COPY OF LETTER.]

EASTERN DISTRICT OF Mo., }
U. S. Attorney's Office. }

St. Louis, Oct. 7, 1869.

HON. GEO. S. BOUTWELL, Secretary of the Treasury, Washington, D. C.

SIR: We have to-day learned, by the telegrams of our daily papers, that John McDonald, of this place, has been appointed Supervisor of Internal Revenue, and assigned for duty to this district. We beg leave to assure you that the reputation of this man, and his associates, are such that he can bring no moral support to the Government in the enforcement of the Internal Revenue Laws, and that it is quite certain that his qualifications, natural or acquired, are such as render the appointment an unfit one to be made.

We believe that, by his being placed in so important an office, the collection of the revenue will be retarded, and the combinations which have heretofore existed against the Government, will be re-established.

C. SCHURZ, U. S. S.,
D. P. DYER, M. C.,
JNO. W. NOBLE, U. S. Att'y.,
C. A. NEWCOMB, U. S. Marshal.

[COPY OF TELEGRAM.]

HON. GEO. S. BOUTWELL, Secretary of Treasury.

I unite with Senator Schurz, and others, against the appointment of John McDonald for Supervisor.

G. A. FINKELNBURG, M. C.,

[COPY OF TELEGRAM.]

To HON. GEO. S. BOUTWELL, Secretary of Treasury, Washington, D. C.

I unite with Senator Schurz, Dyer, Finkelnburg, and others, against the appointment of John McDonald as Supervisor of Revenue.

R. T. VANHORN.

Being greatly concerned about my heavy loss in the Erie disaster, I went to New York from Washington for the purpose of taking steps to recover from the Erie Company a compensation for my losses. After persistent efforts I obtained a small sum, and, leaving the claim in an unsettled condition, I returned to St. Louis, only to find that I had not been assigned to duty, and nearly all the territory had been occupied by other appointees. A bitter fight was made against my assignment by Drake, Newcomb, Schurz, Van Horn, (who afterwards became most instrumental in having Missouri added to my district in order to displace Supervisor Marr, then in charge of the state), and C. W. Ford, then collector at St. Louis, whose letters will be referred to hereafter. On the 12th of November, 1869, I took possession of the Supervisor's office, having charge of the district embracing Arkansas and Indian Territory, with headquarters at Little Rock.

Before leaving Washington to take charge of the district, instructions were issued to me to investigate gigantic frauds which it was reported were being perpetrated by tobacco manufacturers in the Indian Territory. I spoke to President Grant of the strength of the tobacco combination, and told him that in proceeding against these manufacturers, I would need the assistance of himself and the revenue department. His reply was: "Proceed without fear and be assured you shall have the last hearing."

I lost no time in pushing the investigation against the Indian Territory revenue evaders, and the har-

vest of fraud was so bounteous that, in about one
month's time, I had four large manufactories, together with large and various lots of unstamped
tobacco, libeled and in court.

Commissioner **Delano** sent me several telegrams
ordering a release of the goods thus seized, which
I disregarded, by not reading, for the reason that I
was confident I had a clear **case** for the Government, **and** therefore thought it would be criminal
to stop at such a stage of **the** proceedings, a position which afterwards brought great credit upon
the administration.

The Republican **party** in Missouri, **at the** time
I became a revenue officer, was harrassed by
dissentions, and the especial virulency of the
Missouri Democrat sowed the seeds of a growing discord among the adherents of the administration.

The President **was** greatly annoyed at these
apparently **irreconcilable** differences among his
friends, **and, to** restore harmony within the party,
he sent for **me,** and after a lengthy discussion of
these difficulties, he decided to attach the state
of Missouri to my district **and** make my headquarters at St. Louis.

This order was as follows:

TREASURY DEPARTMENT, }
OFFICE INTERNAL REVENUE. }
WASHINGTON, Feb'y 14th, 1870. }

SIR:

The **state of** Missouri **has been detached** from the district
of Supervisor Marr **and** appended to yours. Your district
will, therefore, now embrace the states of Missouri and Arkan-

sas, and the Indian Territory, and your headquarters are fixed at St. Louis, Missouri.

Very Respectfully,

J. W. Douglass,

Gen. John McDonald,   Acting Commissioner.
Supervisor, Little Rock, Ark.

The President had confidence in my ability to pacify the disturbing elements, and frankly confessed that it was essentially necessary for me to direct my best efforts in this direction, as his success for a second term lay chiefly in the demand for his re-nomination coming from the West. The change pleased me because St. Louis was my home, and headquarters in that city would be much more agreeable for many reasons.

Immediately after assuming charge of the revenues of Missouri I had a conversation with Wm. McKee, senior proprietor of the *Missouri Democrat*, in which he admitted that his opposition to the President was caused by Grant's persistency in appointing persons to office in St. Louis contrary to his (McKee's) expressed wishes, and against the best policy of the party in the state. He was especially bitter against Ford, the collector, and asserted that he was entitled to the benefits bestowed upon the party by his paper. Several other conversations occurred between us in which contingencies were provided for.

In the early part of April, 1870, I took a trip South and remained absent for some time; upon my return, among the communications awaiting my attention was the following, enclosed in a letter of instructions from Acting Commissioner Douglass:

St. Louis, Mo., April 4th, 1870.

DEAR SIR:

You had better examine Mr. Ford's affairs at once, as well as L. Card's distillery; if you do so, as it ought to be done, you will find something which will *astonish you.*

R. D. SIMPSON.

(Private.)

In this connection it is proper that the reader understand the fact that nearly every distillery in the district was, at that time, libeled and shut up, and the revenue was coming in at an exceedingly slow rate; but I at once acted upon the suggestion of this letter and thoroughly investigated Mr. Ford's books, and also the distillery. During the progress of this investigation, which was made without the suspicion of Mr. McKee, the following editorial appeared in the *Missouri Democrat* of August 12th, 1870.

AN OPEN LETTER TO THE PRESIDENT.

When you said "Let us have peace!" Mr. President, and the people, taking that phrase as their battle cry, elected you, we at once began to labor for the policy thus marked out— Political disabilities still kept alive in this State the passions of war, and, that the State might have peace, we advocated their removal.

Every form of prejudice, and passion, was at once appealed to by those who resisted that course. We were accused of a design to betray and destroy the party, when, in truth, we had only advocated the very policy upon which a Republican President had just been elected.

The liberal policy triumphed in the Legislature; first in the election of a Senator, and finally in the submission of Constitutional Amendments, removing a disfranchisement no longer required or justified by public safety. But notwithstanding this deliberate decision of the representatives of the party, there were

men who refused to accept. The advocates of your policy they
denounced as "infamous," as "traitors," and the like. The
attempt is now being industriously made, in every part of the
State, to control the Convention of the party against that
policy which will give the State a perfect peace. And, satisfied that they cannot prevail by the honest vote of the party,
a deliberate effort is made to swindle the majority of the Radicals out of their rights: first, by the election of delegates in
meetings not called for that purpose; and, second, by a repre-
sentation which enables 35,000 Radicals, in sparsely settled
counties, to overpower and vote down in Convention 50,000
Radicals in the more populous counties. All these things are
done to control the party in this State against the policy of
which you are the author, and which men have been encouraged to advocate by your high authority.

In these schemes, Mr. President, there are busily engaged a
few of the men who hold federal offices under you. They were
selected, in part, for their supposed fidelity to the party, and
to the liberal principles which it advocates. But they use the
official position and influence thus given to them in desperate
efforts, not only to defeat that policy which originated with
yourself, but to defeat it by swindling the majority of the
party out of its legitimate power to out-vote a minority.

It seems to us, Mr. President, that the few individuals
referred to, as they are engaged in making war upon a vital
feature of your administration, and by methods calculated to
divide and disrupt the party, may very fitly be deprived of
official influence and position that strengthen them in their
undertaking. We commend the subject to your consideration,
Sir, and shall take occasion to mention, in a less public manner, the names of these disturbers of the party, and opposers
of the policy of your administration.

Meanwhile, with, or without, any aid, the majority of the
Radical party will carry the liberal policy forward to a complete and glorious triumph. The result is not in doubt The
amendments will be indorsed by the Convention, and adopted

by the people. The question is rather this: Whether the administration shall be more or less fully identified with the iberal policy, which the President himself originated and proclaimed. The people will support the administration. They would also be pleased to see the administration support itself.

The full intent of this editorial was not doubtful. McKee was anxious for the removal of several revenue officials distasteful to him, and particularly C. W. Ford, the Collector, who was such a warm bosom friend of the President's that only extraordinary influences could accomplish his removal. Hence the editorial was in the nature of a threat, a part of which was carried out by Mr. McKee in the organization of the Liberal party in Missouri, the following fall.

A very sudden change now transpired, which transformed the elements of discord into the happiest reconciliation. In the investigation I prosecuted at Ulrici's distillery (formerly run by Card & Lawrence, as referred to in Simpson's letter of information,) a most glaring fraud was unearthed, viz. the discovery of 48,000 bushels of grain, which had been used for distillation and unaccounted for to the Government. The magnitude of this fraud was equal to stealing directly from the Government the sum of $117,600, and I at once accused Mr. Ford of guilty knowledge in the disposition of that money. After a season of skillful evasion Mr. Ford admitted the frauds, and exhibited the deepest humility and remorse of conscience. I reported to Mr. McKee the result of my investigation, and from that moment he was anxious for the retention of Mr. Ford in the Collector's office, and expressed his sorrow at having published in his paper the editorial just referred to and printed in full.

For some time before this McKee had made suggestions to me about organizing a ring among the revenue officials in St. Louis, to derive profits from illicit distilling, but Ford prevented a consummation of this intention; and after Ford was detected, in connection with Concannon, his deputy, in defrauding the Government, he still refused to treat with McKee, because of the antagonisms which had existed between them. The matter was then laid before President Grant, together with an explanation of McKee's opposition to the administration. Soon afterwards Ford signified his willingness to meet and arrange details with McKee, which, (I can state with only circumstantial proof,) was caused by instructions from the President to Mr. Ford

Having come to an understanding, arrangements were completed by which McKee, Ford and myself were to control all the federal appointments in Missouri, the Senators of that time, (Hon. Frank Blair and Hon. Carl Schurz,) not being in sympathy with the administration, and were consequently ignored by the President.

The revenue was honestly collected and returned until the fall of 1871, when, at the suggestion of Mr. McKee, one Conduce G. Magrue was imported from Cincinnati to manage the illicit distilling, and to arrange for the collection of the assessments to be made on the distillers and rectifiers. Magrue's qualifications for this position were of the highest order, as he had successfully conducted two or three enterprises of like character before. His introduction to St. Louis was, ostensibly, as an agent for some patent paving company in the East.

The Ring would have begun operations much earlier than it did, had it not been for the fact that every distillery in St. Louis was libeled, with the single exception of Ulrici's, at which Ford's crookedness was first discovered. A removal of these libels, necessary to a release that would permit the distilleries to run again, required the labor of several months; not that there was any opposition to their release, but because of the delay in accumulating the evidence and advancing the cases, in the department, for final disposition. I went to Washington myself and remained there until I had procured the release of all the libeled distilleries. During my stay in Washington, I received the following letter from John A. Joyce, my private secretary, who was well acquainted with the purposes of the Ring and that the President was to share its profits:

St. Louis, Mo., Oct. 15th, 1870.

DEAR GENERAL:

I have had a talk with McKee to-day with regard to the situation in Missouri. I know that down deep in his breast is a *warm spark* (ironical) for the President. That spark can be fanned into a flame that will burn brightly until 1872, and culminate in a grand ovation for the *hero* of the war and light his way to the White House.

It is no use disguising the fact, the *Missouri Democrat* is a great power in this State, and we must secure it for Grant now and for 1872.

*   *   *   *   *   *   *   *   *   *

I hope your interview with the President will be satisfactory to all concerned and that he will turn a kind ear to what you may relate. *You are his friend.*

Be sure and fix our St. Louis cases, for they will materially advance the interests of the administration. Yours in haste,

JOHN A. JOYCE.

Enclosed with this letter was a slip upon which was written in lead pencil the following:

"I send you this letter for the purpose of good. If you see the President and have a chance, take it out of your side-pocket and let him read it. Think and act."

There was, I repeat, an understanding between the President, McKee, Ford, Joyce and myself that a Ring should be formed, the proceeds from which should constitute a campaign fund to advance the interests of the administration, hence the manner in which Joyce writes, also the following:

ST. LOUIS, Nov. 28th, 1870.

DEAR GENERAL:

Yours of the 24th, was received this, Monday morning. I am pleased to know that Sec'y Delano, John & Co., (referring to the Secretary's son and others) are as ever your warm friends.

By this time I presume you have had a talk with the Chief at the White House, and learned whether Drake has succeeded in pumping any vitriol into the mind of the President against the supervisors.

If Gen. Cowan is made commissioner we will not, I presume, suffer thereby, as he will have every reason to be our friend. * * * * * * * * *

I read the article in the St. Joe. *Herald* to Capt. Ford, and he was highly delighted to know that a Brown (B. Gratz) paper had taken that shoot, and was curious to "know how in the world did you get him to publish it." I informed him that you had a way of doing things, and gave Bittinger (the editor) to understand that it was to his interest to support the administration. * * * * * * * * *

I hope your interview with the President will be of a satisfactory character, and that you will return to your district stronger in his estimation than ever.

*   *   *   *   *   *   *   *   *   *

This office is running as smooth as a sunbeam, and my only anxiety is that you will, this time, make *talk* and *promise* (sic) count " greenbacks," for what is a man in this world without a good supply of the " filthy lucre " *obtained honorably* and *honestly.*   I am ever yours,

JOHN A. JOYCE.

A thorough understanding of this latter letter can only be obtained through a knowledge of the current events of that time: Col. Bittinger was a U. S. Gauger and was also one of the editors and proprietors of the St. Joseph, Mo., *Herald,* an influential Republican sheet which had followed the dictation of the *Missouri Democrat* and espoused the Liberal movement whose candidate and champion was B. Gratz Brown, in 1872 the candidate for Vice President, with Horace Greeley. President Grant, being ambitious for a second term, saw the necessity of reclaiming the *Herald* and *Democrat.* How he obtained the support of the latter will be more fully related hereafter. I was the instrument used by the President in each case to pacify and win over these recalcitrant sheets. Being well fortified with instructions, I saw Col. Bittinger, and, finding him plastic to essential overtures, promised to place him in a position by which he might be a beneficiary of a fund created through illicit distilling in St. Joseph. In addition to this promise to permit the St. Joseph distilleries to run crooked, I also agreed to secure for him an appointment as consul to one of the important cities of

England. C. B. Wilkinson, also one of the proprietors of the *Herald*, had a claim against the Government amounting to nearly $10,000, in his settlement upon going out of the office of Collector in about 1865. This claim (I was told by Wilkinson) had been ignored, although the influence of Ben. Loan, Van Horn, Asper, Senator Henderson, Jim Craig and Senator Drake, I believe, and many other influential politicians had been exerted for its allowance. I also promised to collect the claim, and to give the paper certain federal patronage, if the *Herald* would renounce its liberal course, and come out strong for the administration. My offers were accepted, and when I went to Washington I told President Grant of my arrangements, and drew his attention to the condition of Wilkinson's claim. I further told him that Mr. Wilkinson was especially anxious to secure this money, as he would then be enabled to increase the power of his paper.

The President replied: "There will be no trouble about that, for I will see Mr. Boutwell and have the matter attended to."

Upon my return to St. Louis, I reported to Mr. Wilkinson the readiness of the Government to settle the claim, and in two weeks thereafter I appeared in Washington with Wilkinson, and took him to the Treasury Department.

Upon meeting Mr. Boutwell, the Secretary, Wilkinson announced the object of his visit, whereupon the Secretary replied: "Yes, I have already been spoken to about that matter; if you will come back about two o'clock we will fix your claim," and calling a messenger he sent out for the Comptroller and the papers in the case.

Wilkinson kept the engagement, and at the appointed hour he received a draft on the Assistant Treasurer at New York for the full amount of the claim.

Thus the engagement with the *Herald* was consummated, and to the more thoroughly seal the compact and utilize Bittinger and Wilkinson the latter was, in February 1873, appointed collector of the revenue at St. Joseph, and the "machine" there went into full operation under a new regime. The district had been running crooked, however, for some time before, but now the earnestness of the illicit distillation was pronounced and bold. Con. Magrue having arrived in St. Louis in September, 1871, everything was then fixed for the manufacture of illicit whiskey throughout the district.

The foregoing is a succinct statement of the successive steps leading to the organization of the Whiskey Ring at St. Louis; but the same history has been partially written before, with greater minuteness, by Wm. Grosvenor, formerly editor in chief of the *Missouri Democrat*, when that paper was the property of Mr. McKee. Mr. Grosvenor was, owing to a peculiar relation (not criminal) with the St. Louis members of the Ring at the time, well qualified to write a true history of its superficial operations and, barring three or four material errors which I will correct, his statement is a true one. It is as follows:

"Prior to Grant's inauguration there had been a Whiskey Ring in St. Louis — officials under Andrew Johnson had made money; favored distillers had spent money freely to sustain the party which Johnson aided. But the ring of those days was, in comparison, a laughing affair. It served to excite the cupidity of certain Republicans who sought the control of certain offices after Grant was elected. Nearly all were disappointed. Grant had formerly lived at St. Louis and had there a set of friends to reward, a few of whom had been active partisans. Mr. McKee, senior proprietor of the *Democrat,* then the leading Republican organ in that part of the country, demanded the appointment of Col. Constantine Maguire as collector, with the expectation that his brother, Henry McKee, would be deputy collector. Now the deputy collector has charge of the distilleries. But Grant appointed Col. Ford unknown as a Republican, who had loaned money to Grant when he was in great need, and who subsequently acted as his confidential adviser in the disposition of his private means. Well known Republicans were recommended for supervisor of internal revenue in that district. Grant appointed Gen. John McDonald, a man who had held intimate relations with him when Grant was in command in the Mississippi Valley and who was understood to have made some money in cotton operations below Memphis at that time. When it was known that McDonald was likely to be appointed there was a general opposition alike by business men and Republicans; the Union Merchants' Exchange protested; prominent citizens and the newspapers protested. What business men had known of McDonald did not lead them to think him a suitable person for such an office. Leading Republicans protested. Members of Congress from Missouri, then all Republicans, led by Carl Schurz and Drake, who were at bitter warfare personally, all united in protest. But while this opposition was most threatening, McDonald remained in St. Louis, saying openly: "They need not trouble themselves; I know Gen. Grant better than any of them, and I shall be appointed, no matter who protests." He was right. McKee was indignant and bitter. He had not been able to control the collectorship, and from that time spoke of Grant in terms which it would not be decent to repeat. Early the next year the controversy respecting a removal of disfranchisement began, and the *Democrat's* readiness to split the Republican party on that issue was almost wholly due to McKee's vindictiveness toward Grant and desire to show his power. He and his active partner, Mr. Houser, had been among the most bitter disfranchisers, and could in no way have been led to take position against disfranchisement but for desire to control the federal offices in St. Louis. Grant, fully advised of this, and supposing that no higher motives governed Schurz and other Republicans who opposed continued disfranchisement, made war on the Liberal movement, quite unnecessarily, for nine-tenths of those who supported it cared nothing about the offices, and had at that time no feeling of antagonism towards him or the Republican party. The result was the Liberal victory of 1870 in Missouri. McKee felt that the power of his paper had been shown, and began to talk freely of a National movement against the Republican party, of which his paper was to be the chief organ, and Gratz Brown, his former associate in the *Democrat*, the presidential candidate. Then began the Whiskey Ring.

Early in 1871 McKee said to me, at that time editor of the *Democrat*, that reasons had been presented to him for changing the course of the paper ; that the opposition to Grant ought to cease; that there were very important arrangements on foot which would be highly profitable to all of us if we could be on good terms with the federal officials. Naturally insisting upon more light, I was told by him at last, after many significant winks and nods, that the matter in question concerned the revenue service, and that we could just as well make $100,000 each if we would let him arrange it and say nothing more in the paper against Grant. I declined to change my political opinions so readily, and was presently notified that my services as editor were no longer needed. I

demanded reasons, but was peremptorily refused any **explanation.** This was in February, **1871.** The paper did suddenly wheel around to the support of Grant, and in **March the first** general assessment of whiskey distilleries was **made.** According to testimony given at St. Louis, a regular share of the money collected from distilleries was, from **the** first, paid to John Leavenworth, since deceased, for delivery **to** Mr. McKee. How far the promise of this share in the **profits of** illicit distilling influenced the sudden conversion in **the** political opinions of McKee and his paper others can **judge.**

The first assessment was made, professedly, **to raise a cam**paign fund, for the city election in **April, 1871.** As soon as the *Democrat* changed its course, a great effort was made to put an end to the liberal organization, and **unite all former** Republicans in support of **the** administration, and a victory in St. Louis was reached, **as proof that** the re-union had been effected. **How much of** the money raised, professedly **for this purpose, was actually** paid for campaign expenses, is **not known. But** more than one distiller has **told me how he was induced to contribute,** and how, if he **objected to fraud,** he was forced **to choose between** participation with the Ring or bankruptcy. **Col. Ford** was at that time collector, and Mr. Concannon, who **has since** made his **peace** with the **Govern**ment, by testifying, I believe, was deputy **in the collector's** office. **If** distillers, or rectifiers, declined **to act with the** Ring, care was taken, first, to entrap **them in some apparent** or technical violation of **the** law, which, **by pre-arrangement** among officials, was detected at once—**in some cases, before** the distillers or rectifiers had time **to discover that the** "crooked" stuff was on their premises. **Then their establish**ments were **seized, and they were** told to see **Mr. Ford. When** they saw Ford, they were told to go to Concannon. When they went to Concannon, they were told that there was a little difficulty, which they could arrange by seeing John Leavenworth. **When** Leavenworth had explained matters, they perceived that **if** they did as he desired them, there would be no trouble; if not, they would be prosecuted and convicted for violation of law, and bankruptcy would be inevitable. How many men in St. Louis were forced into the Ring by this and other ways, and how many went into it voluntarily, probably, nobody will ever know. Leavenworth is dead; Ford is dead, and others who had part in the earlier transactions are no longer accessible. But Megrue, then an official, in whose room, in a building on the corner of Fifth and Pine streets, it is said, the spoils were at first divided every week to the several parties in interest, has testified to transactions in his time. After his departure, and Leavenworth's death, one Everist, for whom officials are now searching, and J. N. Fitzroy, who has recently pleaded guilty and testified, acted as confidential collectors and disbursers of the funds. Thus it is probable that abundant proof will show to whom money was paid. For whom, may, in some cases, be a more difficult question to answer.

Ostensibly, the funds were originally collected for party purposes. During the Presidential campaign, in 1872, when Republican leaders were alarmed, a dispatch was sent by one of them, a very prominent Senator, calling for a new assessment on distillers, unless this dispatch itself was forged by some member of the Ring, as a pretext for unusual demands. But neither that year, nor any other, was the conduct of Republican campaigns, in St. Louis, or Missouri, such as to warrant the belief that any large sums was at the disposal of the committee. On the other hand, the sums collected were very large. One after another, distillers and rectifiers became aware that the greater part of the funds collected from them was consumed for other than party purposes. But in 1872, the excuse was made that it was necessary to establish a reliable Grant organ. Early in that year, the *Democrat* had been forced to sale under order of court for dissolution of partnership, and McKee, and Houser, had been bought out by Mr. Fishback. Whether he would restore the paper to the liberal position it had taken in 1870, was not known, but he was not

deemed " a reliable Grant man." The Ring needed an organ
—McKee reeded a paper as a reason for contined payments to
him. Accordingly, the *Globe* was established by McKee and
Houser, and it is stated that the payments to Leavenworth,
for McKee, were nearly $1,000 a week, amounting to over
$44,000 within less than a year. Even this large sum was but
a small part; it is said one-fifth—of that portion of the profits
which distillers were required to pay. Many gaugers and subordinate officials were paid extra salaries by the distillers themselves, but about forty per cent. went to the higher officials.
How this portion—the fund of the Ring, proper—was divided
at different times, the testimony will probably show. It is alleged that one portion went to the supervisor, another to the confidential agent, and another to McKee for himself; another to
him, professedly, to deliver to Ford, the collector; another to
"the man in the country," a phrase supposed to refer to somebody in Washington; for at an early day, the Ring must have
secured some powerful influence at the Capital—that the
supervisor had considerable influence, either with Grant himself, or through somebody else, was obvious when he was
appointed. Col. Ford, the collector, had so great an influence
with the President, that his appointment as Secretary of the
Interior, when Delano was about to vacate that office, in 1873,
was confidently expected by the Ring, and, I believe, was actually determined upon by the President at the time of Ford's
sudden death. It is not known to me whether any evidence
proves that money set apart and paid for Ford, ever reached
him, and he may, perhaps, have supposed that the only collections made were for political uses. But, however strong Mc-
Donald and Ford may have been, there was needed, and there
was secured, somebody at Washington to give the Ring early
warnings of the treasury investigations, and to stop all complaints from reaching the Secretary or the President, for
the couduct of the President, since the exposure, makes it impossible to believe that he was in any sort of complicity with
the Ring. Yet complaints were forwarded, sometimes to the

Secretary, and sometimes to the President himself, without result. If investigations were ordered, either the person selected and sent out, was one whose eyes and ears could be closed by a bribe, or the Ring was warned by telegraph before he had left Washington, and had ample time to put everything in readiness to receive him with equanimity. That complete immunity was thus secured at an early day, is certain. Mr. Avery, the chief clerk of the treasury, is under indictment for complicity, and there is testimony that $200 per week was set apart for him. But he was not the only person at Washington whose constant aid was needed, and, if statements of the division of funds are correct, the amount sent thither was much greater than he was said to have received.

It is stated in recent dispatches that telegrams and documents sent from Washington to members of the Ring have been placed before the grand jury now in session. Of course persons having part in this dangerous business did not sign their own names; fictitious signatures were used at both ends. But the original telegrams, if obtained from the office by legal authority, may be in recognizable handwritings, and rumor says that at least one person nearer the President than Mr. Avery, will thus be proved to have been telegraphing to the Ring with a fictitious signature. It was at one time openly alleged by distillers that Commissioner Douglass was in the Ring, but, if they had been told so by officials in St. Louis that alone would prove nothing, and I know of no other evidence concerning him. What the Ring needed at Washington was not influence with any department. When Mr. Douglass suggested, and Secretary Bristow ordered a transfer of supervisors to different districts, a measure which would certainly have uncovered fraud, Gen. McDonald declared in the most confident manner that the order would be immediately recinded; he jumped on the cars, went to Washington, saw the President and telegraphed back that all was right. The order was recinded. What representations could have led the President to believe it wise or necessary to revoke such an order, it is hard to guess. But the Ring openly boasted that it had a power at Washington which could not be resisted nor broken. Moreover, the members undoubtedly believed it themselves. That is the mysterious part of the whole business. No man who watched the proceedings of these people can possibly doubt that they were absolutely fearless of exposure, and perfectly convinced that their power was greater than that of Secretary Bristow himself. Repeatedly they boasted, even after the exposure had begun, that they would have him out of the cabinet in a few days. At one time they named the day on which Delano would become Secretary of the Treasury. They did not go about like men who had anything to hide. Diamonds, for which official salaries would not account, were worn openly and purchased several thousand dollars' worth at a time, without attempt at concealment. Officials with moderate salaries lived with their families at hotels, expending obviously more than their known incomes, and yet made open purchases of costly summer residences. If whiskey operators or discharged revenue officials threatened to make exposures at Washington, they were kindly invited to " expose and be——" not blessed. One at least tried it, made a dead failure, came back to St. Louis, and was told that he had better keep his mouth shut in future, or he would get sent to the penitentiary for defrauding the Government.

When McDonald, now indicted, went to Washington, he was received by the President and rode with him on the avenue. When the President visited St. Louis, McDonald was usually in his company, and as late as October, 1874, when the President visited the Fair grounds, in the presence of 50,000 people, McDonald was by his side. It was currently reported at the time, that, having praised a horse at the Fair, the President received it the next day as a present from his friend McDonald; that he permitted the officials there to have a carriage manufactured expressly for him, and to pay his bills at the hotel. How many of these stories were falsely set afloat by members of the Ring, in order to strengthen their claim of great influence with the President, I cannot say. But one thing is certain, this Ring had some peculiar power at Washington, and the investigation will not be complete until the nature of that power is thoroughly made known. The President owes it to himself to have that thing exposed, if nothing else. As it stands the matter is both ugly and mysterious. The Ring actually had great power at Washington; boasted that it had absolute power, and apparently believed it, and yet members of it have been convicted. I confess that these things lead me to suspect that somebody, known to be influential with the President, traded on that influence, received money for it, and made members of the Ring believe that the President himself winked at the conspiracy. The Ring was broken two or three times, and payments stopped. Once there was a quarrel about the amount of assessments. It made quite a noise in St. Louis, and everybody expected a general explosion. Presently it was settled by some new arrangement, and everything went on peacefully again.

In the fall of 1873, there was a cataclysm of some sort, so violent that for a time the *Globe* published bitter anti-third-term articles. If this Ring kept books it would be safe to wager that about that time the usual weekly settlements were interrupted, and in point of fact, there was a notorious run about Busby's distillery, and daily expectation of disclosure. In due time harmony was restored, and the *Globe* recovered its loyalty. The sudden death of Col. Ford, the collector, caused a brief disturbance. But the Ring urged the immediate appointment of the same Colonel Maguire, whose selection for that office McKee demanded in 1869. He was appointed; Fitzroy became his deputy, and from that time forward the loyalty of the *Globe* was intense and glowing. Indeed, so violent was its attachment to Republicanism, pure and undefiled, that in 1874, when four-fifths of the Republicans in the State desired to join with the independent Democrats in the support of a no-party anti-Bourbon ticket, McKee agreed to support the movement only on condition that he should name the candidate for State Treasurer. When that was impossible, the *Globe* denounced the plan as treachery to the party, and McKee himself, with others in the Ring, went to the State convention and tried to organize a bolt, and the nomination of a strict party ticket against the formal decision of a party convention. Failing in that, he used his paper throughout the campaign in savage hostility to the independent ticket, and helped the Bourbons materially. Republican ward meetings were packed by companies of men gathered up from distilleries, under the lead of revenue officials. Republican candidates for the legislature, who would not pledge themselves to vote against the re-election of Senator Schurz, were openly denounced by this Ring and its organ, and defeated wherever it was possible. Doubtless this opposition helped to insure the election of a former Confederate general. For this most important service to the Republican party, after leading members of the Ring had been indicted, they claimed that they were entitled to executive favor. This behavior of the Ring in the campaign of 1874, led to its destruction. Men who had no knowledge of its existence, except by general rumor, set themselves to find out something about this influence which had marched men from distilleries to Republican ward meetings. When the Merchant's Exchange statistics for 1874 were published, some men compared the receipts and shipments of whiskey with the official report of the quantity produced in the city. It was at once apparent that the quantity consumed and shipped was greatly in excess of the quantity received and said to be manufactured. The excess represented a loss of revenue, in St. Louis alone, of $1,200,000 yearly. This suggested a new mode of detecting the fraud—namely, an examination of the bills of lading, or other commercial reports of receipts and shipments. It soon became evident that fraud could be fastened upon individuals. Mr. Fishback, proprietor of the *Democrat*, communicated confidentially with Secretary Bristow. Without the knowledge of those who had been accustomed to warn the Ring of doings at Washington, the Secretary commissioned

Mr. Coloney, commercial editor of the *Democrat*, as special
officer of the revenue.   Thus armed with ample authority, Mr.
Coloney proceeded first to collect, as if for the newspaper, a
complete statement of every bill of lading or shipment during
the year, not of whiskey alone, but of all important articles, so
that his object was not suspected.   But the comparison of
these shipments, from operators in whiskey at St. Louis, with
official reports at Washington, gave conclusive proof against
nearly all the illicit establishments, and led to the general
exposure of whiskey frauds all over the land.   Thus a few
commercial statistics upset the most powerful conspiracy ever
formed against the revenue service in this country.   When the
long labor of tracing and comparison had progressed far
enough to insure the conviction of the leading distillers and
rectifiers, the Secretary sent on from Washington special
agents to make seizures.   But in doing so, he found it necessary for the first time to make known to a few trusted officials
the work he had on hand, and that very night the telegraph
took from Washington to Gen. McDonald at St. Louis the
announcement: "Lightning will strike on Monday."   For
about two months before Mr. Fishback had been offering to
sell his controlling interest in the *Democrat* to Mr. McKee, of
the *Globe*.   All offers had been disregarded.   Mr. Bowman, as
attorney for the *Globe*, had made efforts for amiable settlement, and through him Mr. Fishback had been led to name
terms which he would accept, but for weeks those terms had
been treated as totally inadmissable by the owners of the Ring
organ, and Mr. Bowman, not imagining that anything could
occur speedily to bring the parties together, had left town for
a few days.   On Monday lightning did strike.   The distilleries
were seized by special officers from Washington.   Even then
the Ring was perfectly defiant, and predicted that in a very few
days every establishment would be released, and Secretary
Bristow removed from the Cabinet.   But the next morning's
Democrat contained a dispatch of several columns from Washington stating the nature of the evidence which had been

collected. Then, for the firt time, the Ring saw that it had to fight hard.

That morning there was a hurried meeting of the Ring, and books were consulted. That very afternoon Mr. Fishback's proposition was accepted, and the *Democrat* passed into control of the Ring. That same night editorials, congratulating the President and Secretary upon the exposure of the fraud, being in type of the *Democrat* office, were sent to Mr. McKee, of the *Globe*, for approval, and the proofs were returned by him with an order not to publish them. From that day nothing was admitted to the *Democrat* in the nature of further exposure or comment favorable to the government. So much in haste was the Ring to complete the purchase, that it could not wait the return of the attorney who had acted for the *Globe* in the matter, but others were at once employed to draw up the necessary papers. The *Democrat* was speedily consolidated with the *Globe*, and ceased to exist."

One of Grosvenor's mistakes is in his assertion that "the first assessment was made professedly to raise a campaign fund for the city election in April, 1871."

The first money derived from illicit distilling was in September, 1871, the month Magrue appeared in St. Louis to put the machinery of the Ring into operation. I cannot give the minute details of the collection and disbursment of the illicit fund for the reason that there was no rule established for the government of the Ring members in their operations. One month an assessment of $20,000 may have been levied on the distillers and rectifiers and during the next month five times that sum may have been called for. Much depended upon the demand for money made by Gen. Babcock for division among the administration conspirators, and the demand for local purposes.

In addition to this the Washington segment of the Ring was in the habit of sending agents into my district for the sole purpose of blackmail.

I can have no doubt that Hogue, Brasher, and others who appeared here as revenue agents were sent by Babcock, and Rogers the deputy commissioner (whom I conversed with and received almost admissions of the fact), for the purpose of scaring the St. Louis distillers into the payment of large sums of money for their silence. More than $100,-000 was paid out of the fund in this way and that some of this money went into the White House has always been my positive belief.

Grosvenor alluded to the fact that in the fall of 1873 an explosion occurred which well nigh disrupted the Ring and seriously disturbed the loyalty of the *Globe*. The statement is correct and here I will explain the cause: As previously stated, Grant's collusion with the Ring consisted in his utilization of corrupt money to secure his re-election. After this purpose was accomplished I was anxious to see the Ring organization dissolved because its ramifications were so extensive, and included such a vast number of men of every character that I was in constant dread of public exposure.

Time and again I talked with McKee and the other managers urging upon them the danger of our position and the bad policy of continuing the corruption after our purposes were accomplished. I laid the matter before Grant who referred me to Babcock whose judgment he relied upon. McKee, in the meantime became very much offended at my determination to break up the Ring, and finding the administration rather according to my wishes he brought the pressure of his paper against me and was loud in his demands for my removal, being unable to accomplish which he attacked the third-term idea. At length, by seductive argument, the administration concurred in McKee's opinion that the Ring could be run successfully by creating a fund to advance Grant's third-term aspirations. When this view became pronounced I at once accepted the purpose as a self-sufficient one and harmony again prevailed among all the members of the Ring.

An explanation of this extract in Grosvenor's letter, "During the presidential campaign of 1872, when Republican leaders were alarmed, a dispatch was sent by one of them, a prominent Senator, calling for a new assessment on distillers," is as follows: A few days before the demand was made Senator Morton came to see me, while on his way to Hot Springs, and although he was badly crippled he ascended the stairs to my office by the aid of his crutches and spoke to me in words of great friendship, saying that he had not climbed a pair of stairs for a long time before and that he did so in this instance out of compliment to me. We only talked of politics in general, but a few days afterwards Henry T. Blow came to me and said: " The Republicans over in Indiana need our aid very badly and require money to help them through the campaign." I gave Mr. Blow $1,000, and understood through Mr. McKee that $30,000 was collected and sent to Indiana by Mr. Blow.

Mr. Grosvenor, while editor of the *Democrat*, learned some of the secrets of the Ring through the suspicious actions of Mr. McKee and at length, in order to pacify him, Joyce gave him under pretence of a loan the sum of $500, to cease exercising his curiosity, and soon thereafter he was notified that his services, as editor, were no longer required. His letter bears the impress of a disturbed mind having some jealousies to vindicate, but under the circumstances he writes with an unusual regard for facts which, however, are bad enough to afford him much satisfaction in airing.

The Grosvenor letter carries the narrative far beyond the regular order, and creates a hiatus in events which compels me to return and gather up the broken threads.

I desire, here, to impress upon the reader a very essential fact which I trust will not be forgotten nor misconstrued: In producing corroborative evidence I must use the proofs furnished by my co-conspirators and such fragments as may be gathered from the statements of parties engaged in the prosecutions, or newspaper writers whose facts have been gleaned from interviews with indescreet members of the Ring. The copious reference I make to the letters of Col. John A. Joyce, my private secretary and confidant, is pardonable I hope for these reasons.

In order to show the unanimity and complete accord of mutual understanding between President Grant, Babcock, Douglass and others at Washington with the members at St. Louis, the following letter is produced, written while I was in Washington seeking the compromise that would permit the libeled distilleries in St. Louis to resume operations.

St. Louis, Nov. 22, 1870.

Dear General:

By attending to the following suggestions the interest of the Government will be advanced.

1st. Have the Department compromise the Curran and Thompson cases, sure!

2d. See Avery and have him remember that Bittinger is to remain in office—and fix for him to get the other position hereafter.

3d. Be sure and fix the Leavenworth matter.

4th. Have General Sanford set right.

5th. Fix things so that your "say" under section 49 will remove and transfer storekeepers and gaugers.

6th. * * * * *.

7th. * * * * *.

8th. Above all things remember while in Washington that talk and promises will not pay and that theory does not amount to a row of pins unless put into practice.

9th. Let me know what's what.

10th, The future looks bright, and if you only get down to business while at the Capital all will be well.

11th. Gunther starts on his round for the benefit of Alex McDonald, to-morrow. We must strain every nerve to elect McD. to the Senate.   Yours,

J. A. J.

This letter requires comments that will show the full meaning of the writer, John A. Joyce. In the beginning he refers to advancing the interest of the Government in an ironical manner. His true meaning is, "advance the interest of the Ring."

The explanations seriatim are as follows:

1st. Ford and McKee were especially anxious to have the Curran and Thompson distilleries resume, and to run crooked.

2d. Avery was chief clerk of the Internal Revenue Bureau, and all appointments had to go through his hands. The desire of Joyce was to have Avery allow Bittinger to remain gauger until other arrangements, previously explained, were consummated.

3d. McKee had recommended the appointment of John and Zeb. Leavenworth, the former as gauger and the latter as storekeeper, and it was particular for the Ring's purposes to have these two men appointed.

4th. Sandford was a relative of President Grant's wife by marriage, and it was at Mrs. Grant's desire that I asked for him an appointment as a special clerk in my office, to look after tobacco stamps, etc. The allusion to him by Joyce was merely to call the matter to my mind.

5th. This meant to obtain unlimited authority from the department, which I did, Douglass furnishing me with orders, and remarking at the time: "I know you fellows out there are doing something for political purposes, but I don't want to know the details." I had previously spoken to President Grant and Babcock asking them to speak to Douglass and have him give me the authority I required to make our purposes successful. They each told me they would, and the gratuitous remark of Mr. Douglass led me to believe they had kept their promises.

9th. By this he exhibits his desire to know if the President and his nearest officers in the departments are favorable to the combination for illicit distilling, and what he must expect.

10th. Is the same idea.

11th. This statement furnishes another proof that the Ring was a political combination. McDonald was at that time Grant's favorite, but events occurred after this which caused us to leave McDonald, and throw our support to Clayton, under his written promise to support Grant's administration, which elected him.

The next letter from Joyce, betraying the motives of the Ring and who its members were, reads as follows:

St. Louis, Mo., Dec. 1st, 1870.

DEAR GENERAL:

* * * * * * * * *

By this time I presume you have seen the President, and talked over the consolidation of districts, and that a conclusion has been reached as to Missouri.

I had a talk with Ford yesterday and read him part of your letter. He is highly delighted at your success in the Thompson and Curran cases. These gentlemen happened in to-day, and I gave them the good news. This move of yours will do the administration great good and tend to a reconciliation o the contending elements here.

Col. Van Horn was in this morning, on his way to Washington. He and Burdett are at the Planter's House. I told Van Horn a few things, and I know he will set Burdett right, if his machinery needs adjusting. You will see them both in Washington in a few days. Van was much interested in the consolidation matter and was much relieved when I told him that "things were all right in his neighborhood." Van went away feeling good and determined to pull any kinks out of Burdett that got twisted in the late mill.

* * * * * * * * *

Yours as ever,

JOHN A. JOYCE.

The consolidation of districts, referred to a reduction of the number of collectors and assessors, according to an act of the previous Congress. My letter, to which Joyce makes reference, was a notification of the fact that I had succeeded in releasing the Thompson and Curran distilleries, and had completed our combination with Grant, Babcock, and those at the Washington end of the line.

The attitude of Mr. Ford towards me, while it might have appeared more properly in an earlier part of this book, is not now wholly out of place, and if pardon is necessary, I ask it for including this array of circumstances here.

After my first appointment as supervisor, but before Missouri had been attached to my district, during the opposition of Krum, Newcomb, VanHorn, Dyer, (then a member of Congress,) all of whom subsequently urged my re-appointment, Mr. Ford attacked me with extreme virulency. He addressed two letters to the President, appealing to him in the name of a life-long devoted friend, not to have any thing to do with me. His denunciation embraced all the imprecations he could command, and all the indignation of his nature was emptied upon my head. Receiving no reply to the first letter, two weeks afterwards he wrote a second, excusing the extraordinary tone of that communication by his disinterested devotion to his most valued friend, the President, but warmed up to his task and poured out fresh vials of abuse upon my character, befouling me in the most ingenious manner.

Mr. Ford was aware of the effort then being made to enlarge my district (which only included Arkansas and Indian Territory) so as to embrace Missouri, and he having been engaged filching from the Government was afraid that my transfer to St. Louis would result in his exposure. This reason was clearly demonstrated afterwards, for after I had uncovered his frauds and provided means to prevent a public disclosure of his acts he became my warmest friend, and in 1872 he wrote the strongest letters to the President urging my re-appointment.

The following letter will also furnish another reason for Ford's change of attitude towards me:

(STRICTLY CONFIDENTIAL.)

> OFFICE OF THE MISSOURI DEMOCRAT, }
> McKEE, FISHBACK & Co., PROP'S., }
> ST. LOUIS, February 13th, 1871. }

FRIEND McDONALD;

Joyce informs me he leaves to-day for Washington. I send by him a few lines to call your attention to the conversation we had before you left. I have seen Ford but have had no conversation with him. He expressed the greatest suprise at your influence with heads of departments, and was delighted with the manner in which you went into Thompson, talked to members of Congress, etc. You have convinced him (Ford) of a very important fact and he will have full confidence hereafter.

I am very sorry your consolidation plan fell through. Our enemies could have been wiped out completely if you had succeeded.

* * * * * * * * * * * *

Don't forget our newspapers here. They must be supported and the Government is able to do this.

* * * * * * * * * * * *

Joyce will report fully.

> I am yours in haste,
>
> WM. McKEE.

I received this letter through Joyce while I was in Washington. Its plain language requires little explanation. In the first paragraph where he says he has seen Ford but has had no conversation, proceeding at once to give expressions of Ford, is only an apparent contradiction. His meaning is that he did not converse with Ford concerning the arrangement made for manufacturing illicit whiskey. While Mr. Ford treated me with much defference after my discovery, hopelessly involving him in the whiskey frauds, and was willing to talk with me about our interests in the illicit whiskey combination, yet I could plainly see that both he and McKee did not place implicit confidence in my assertions that the White House was possessed of all our secrets. To satisfy them thoroughly upon this point I made arrangements through Babcock and Joyce to have them meet me in Washington for the purpose of having a personal interview with the President. I wrote to Joyce to see McKee and Ford, and convey to them the wish of Babcock and myself, that they should appear in Washington at their earliest convenience. In proof of this I give the following extract from one of Joyce's letters.

St. Louis, March 3d, 1871.

Dear General;

* * * * * * * * * * *

I have not seen Ford or McKee in regard to going to Washington, but will have an interview with them to-day if I can.

Have you had Babcock write them to proceed to Washington? etc.

* * * * * * * * * * *

Yours etc.,
John A. Joyce.

Neither of these responded to my invitation so I returned to St. Louis and, urging them to accompany me, in April, I think, we proceeded to Washington together. Before our arrival Babcock, being notified of our coming, made arrangements for McKee and Ford to dine at the White House. This they did, but I was not one of the party having declined so as to allow the President, McKee and Ford to talk the matter over free from the restraint which I was afraid my presence would impose. They returned to me at the Ebbett House about seven o'clock p. m. and informed me that they had passed a most agreeable time with the President, though they had not spoken to him upon politics but had made an engagement to meet him again, in company with myself, at eight o'clock p. m. At the appointed hour we visited the White House, when, after saluting Mrs. Grant, in company with the President we retired to the Blue Room and spent a long while thoroughly canvassing the political issues in the West, and particularly our scheme for creating a campaign fund. The President distinctly informed both Mr. Ford and Mr. McKee that he had intrusted certain matters to me, that he understood everything, and that whatever we wanted would be forthcoming upon request. Mr. McKee then told the President that the quartermaster in charge of the Government stores at St. Louis might be dispensed with and the interests of the party promoted by the appointment of a more influential working Republican. The President replied: "Well, name your man and I will see Belknap and have him appointed." Mr. McKee then named Maj. E. B. Grimes, who was then stationed in the extreme West, as the successor.

The following day McKee, Ford and myself called on Secretary Belknap, who upon our enterance remarked: "What do you fellows want; another quartermaster at St. Louis, eh? I understand that you are in control of matters out West, and what I can do, which I presume is not much, will be done with promptness."

McKee and Ford returned to St. Louis highly delighted with their visit, and fully satisfied that they had harbored a most unjust suspicion against me, which they tried to atone for by giving me their implicit confidence thereafter.

McKee and Ford are both dead, and therefore unable to give their testimony, either in corroboration or denial of this plain, unvarnished statement. I am sorry that the record of men who have made their final accounting with life, must be used to their discredit, and but for the truth of history which circumstances force me to disclose, no power could induce me to unseal my lips. To the living, however, there is due a certain regard for their peace of mind, and to sacrifice the living for the dead would be as unholy as to make a peace offering of the innocent. What I here declare is a solemn assertion resting upon my honor and the pride that is still left me, not a mite of which have I ever forfeited. In future chapters I will give letters concerning both these men, furnishing positive proof of my statements.

The following letter furnishes what I will call very strong presumptive proof of the general understanding had between the President, Babcock, Joyce and myself in the management of our peculiar interests in St. Louis; this leter bears the same date as the one last quoted:

St. Louis, March 3d, 1871.

DEAR GENERAL :

* * * * * * * * *

Now I want you to put in your best licks for our mutual friend, Avery, who is in every sense fitted for the vacancy. I believe you have influence enough with Col. Thomson and Pleasanton to have him appointed. If you can't do the thing yourself you can find a *Man* who can. Avery is our friend and we want as many of his sort as we can get. You might have Gen. Babcock speak to Pleasanton in Avery's behalf.

Ford wants you to come back, etc.

* * * * * * * * *

Yours truly,

JOHN A. JOYCE.

There was an understanding in the appointment of Avery which is plainly apparent in the above letter, and which subsequent events abundantly proved. The phrase "You can find a *Man* who can" referred to President Grant.

In the disclosures, and connections of individuals with the Ring, the name of John W. Douglass has only been mentioned as a faithful executive officer, performing all the duties as Commissioner of Internal Revenue. It will astonish many when I declare that he, too, was well acquainted with the Ring organization, and was, in fact, appointed to his position through our influence, and that he rendered efficient aid in promoting our interests.

The following letters will furnish the necessary evidence connecting him with the Ring. They explain themselves, the first being written to me while I was in Washington:

St. Louis, Aug. 16th, 1871.

Dear General:

*   *   *   *   *   *   *   *   *

I had a talk with Ford this morning. He wrote a strong letter to the President in behalf of Mr. Douglass. I have just finished a letter to Douglass, in your name, inclosing a copy of Ford's letter, and I know that Douglass will be tickled away down into his boots.

*   *   *   *   *   *   *   *   *

Yours, etc.,

John A. Joyce.

The following letter I received after my return to St. Louis:

Treasury Department,
Internal Revenue Bureau.
Washington, Aug. 21st, 1871.

My Dear Sir:

Your letter of August 16th has just been received with very great pleasure. I feel truly grateful for its complimentary congratulations. I am also much obliged for your kindness in offering to give me your warm and valued support in the Senate. I hope you are not mistaken in the good opinion you hold.   *   *   *   *   *   *

Please thank Mr. Ford for his letter to the President and for the kindly interest in my behalf, also to Col. Joyce, etc.

*   *   *   *   *   *   *   *   *

Very truly yours,

J. W. Douglass.

Hon. John McDonald.

The following letter, when thoroughly understood, establishes the guilty knowledge of Commissioner Douglass, and also the venal understanding of Brasher, the revenue agent.

(private.)   CINCINNATI, Oct. 21st, 1871.

Gen. McDonald:

Dear Sir: As I desire, particularly, to spend a short time in Kansas, I should be very glad to be ordered to report to you for special duty, without at all interfering with your present arrangements. Com. Douglass will order me to you as soon as he learns it will be agreeable to you, If my coming will occasion you any inconvenience, I shall be glad to hear from you to that effect, that I may make my arrangements accordingly. I presume you have heard from Mr. Douglass on this subject.

Very truly yours,

B. P. BRASHER.

The import of this letter is readily explained. The distillers had just begun their illicit work, and the appearance of a revenue agent would, naturally, create much alarm; in addition to this, in the earlier existence of the Ring, the distillers did not know that the Washington officials were participants in the combination, but presumed that the criminal knowledge was confined to St. Louis members. "Hoping that this visit would not interfere with my arrangements," had reference to this fact. Another matter was provided for by the words, "If my coming will occasion you no inconvenience," etc., in that, there might be enemies, who had discovered some irregularities; some discharged employe, or others, who had obtained such knowledge, who, seeing a revenue agent in my district, might insist upon an investigation.

The result of his application was a permission to visit Kansas, where he remained some time, presumably occupying his time practicing the best manner of enjoying an elegant leisure.

I herewith append a correspondence, the date of which is out of place here, but its immediate application as a proof of Douglass' thorough knowledge of the whiskey frauds being perpetrated in my district, is conclusive, and, therefore, proper in this connection:

St. Louis, Mo., June 11, 1874.

Hon. J. W. Douglass, Commissioner of Internal Revenue, Washington, D. C.

* * * * My client, who was engaged in manufacturing whiskey, during the years 1871 and 1872, and who having those years distilled over $500,000 worth of whiskey, of which amount some $300,000 was "crooked whiskey," and, of course, unreported to the Government, states that this was done through the agency of a ring at that time composed of government officers, as follows: C. W. Ford, Jno. McDonald, Joe. Fitzroy, James H. Concannon, John A. Joyce, John Leavenworth, Henry Hardaway, Charles Hardaway. Douglass Thrope, Andy Megrue, and Theodore Hemans.

In this Ring was Wm. McKee, now of the *Globe*, and one Maj. Con. Megrue, at this time in Washington, in the interest of the new Ring, now in successful operation. McKee was then in for the reason that he was the only man who could be trusted to reach Mr. Ford, which service he successfully performed, and received his weekly reward. The money from distilleries was collected every morning, and in the afternoon was apportioned out to each member of the Ring in Con. Megrue's room, No. 8, over "Billings' Bank," south-east corner of Fifth and Pine streets.

It will serve no useful purpose at this time to give you all the particulars that justify me in the conclusion that the entire matter may be exposed, and the guilty parties brought to justice; and, therefore, I submit a synopsis of what he can prove, if permitted so to do. This, after making due allowance for the purchasable power of the old and new Rings. (1.) The main facts as above stated. (2.) The quantity of whiskey shipped from St. Louis during 1871, 1872, and 1873, was fully three times the amount manufactured and taxes paid in St. Louis. (3.) Will show that the amount of grain distillers purchased for manufacturing whiskey, was four times the amount as represented on Government books.　(4.) That whiskey represented as dumped in St. Louis, has been shipped direct from the distillers to Cincinnati, Baltimore, New York, and New Orleans.　(5.) That for the stubs on the gaugers' reports, in St. Louis, as half-barrels and kegs, the duplicate stamps on the barrels will show a full barrel of proof whiskey. (6.) That when Gen. Lowell suddenly made his appearance here (I think in the spring of 1872), he worked with such celerity that Bevis, Frazer & Co. had barely time to save themselves, by tapping 100 barrels of whiskey in a slush hole underneath their store; and Peter Curran, another house, dumped an entire mash.　(7.) That a special agent of the department, one B. Penn Brasher, came here twice, and his eyes were closed by the receipt, the first time of $7,000, and the second of $5,000.　(8.) That in almost every instance, they were successful in closing the mouths of the Government officials sent here, and the time of their arrival was known a week in advance.

As to who is in the new Ring, my client says he has not learned fully, but knows of its existence, and speaks of the same as an established fact.　Concannon, McDonald, Fitzroy, and Joyce, of the old Ring, agree, however, as he says, that Con. Maguire must be in, as, without his assent, the business could not be carried on for a week; and he supports this by an explanation of the working of the department.　He is, also, wary of District Attorney Patrick, but the grounds do not, in my mind, outweigh his unexceptionable reputation for honesty and integrity in this community.　I have thought it advisable to mention the fact, however, as you know the difference between affirmative and negative action.

My client will expose the old Ring, and break the new, if the government will just give him complete indemnity for past offenses, which he says he was led into committing by the old Ring, at a time when he was wholly ignorant of their operations, and of the business, the Government to give him the necessary authority to work up the case, and the aid of an additional detective.

D

It is proper here to explain that the usual course would have been to communicate direct with Commissioner Delano, but the confidential clerk, who opens his mail, my client says, was in the old Ring, and it is probable he is in the new arrangement.

If, upon reflection, and in view of the statements made, as they have been given to me by a client, who, of my personal knowledge, during the years named, was engaged in the business of distilling, and whose word I have reason to place confidence in, you deem the matter of sufficient importance to lay the same before Mr. Delano, in person, I will be under obligations.

I wish to add that, inasmuch as two of the parties, Ford and Leavenworth, are dead, and the former's character has never before been questioned, and I entertain a high personal regard for him, it is desirable to avoid having his name mentioned, except so far as may be necessary to protect the Government.

P. S.   Since writing the above, Concannon has resigned, and Megrue has returned to the city.   I will further add that my client, if absolved, will, upon request of Commissioner Delano, lay the matter before him in person—the expense of the trip to be that of the Government.

I need not mention that it is most desirable to keep these matters secret until the Government has fully investigated the matter, as any other course would defeat the ends of justice. Aside from this, I do not want to do any injury to any of the parties, or do them any injustice.   This can only be avoided by keeping the matter quiet until the Government is ready to make arrests.

Truly yours,
Jesse B. Woodward.

St. Louis, Mo., Aug. 19, 1874.

Hon. J. W. Douglass, Washington, D. C.

Dear Sir ; — I returned yesterday, and find that there has been considerable change in the situation since I was in Washington.   Fitzroy has ostensibly been thrown out of the combination but his successor, Theodore Hemans, in point of fact is simply his pupil.

Concannon complains to us if the department had a skillful agent here to protect him he would tell all he knows. He has been open in his expressions to Mr. Downs, and is exceedingly anxious to break the new Ring, although such action may uncover the operations of McDonald, Maguire & Co.

Mr. ―――― is in straits in respect to his property, and if protected will, I am assured, expose not only the old but new combinations as well. He is a man of good character and his testimony will go far toward the conviction of the old and new Ring.

The distilleries that are running are working at this time their full capacity and with the knowledge of Maguire & Co. They are open and defiant, and say that they have their support in the administration at Washington and will not be injured.

Please advise me if the government proposes to move in the premises. If the government will act, I will guarantee that the guilt of those named can be established by competent testimony, and brought to a realizing sense of the law which they so flagrantly violate.

If desired, I have reason to believe that two of the leading Journals in this city will open the ball upon my suggestion, and bring these government officers to their feet. This is event the administration does not care to take the responsibility of moving first in the premises.

Trusting to hear from you soon I remain your obedient servant.   JESSE B. WOODWARD.

TREASURY DEPARTMENT, }
OFFICE OF INTERNAL REVENUE, }
WASHINGTON, Sept. 5, 1874. }

SIR :

Your letter of the 19th ult., in regard to " Ring " affairs, as you designated them, was duly received.

You remember that when I saw you here I said to you that the matter should be referred to the United States District

Attorney.   You objected to this, urging that his interest was such that you would not trust him with the management of the business.   I replied that I had to use the present prosecuting officers provided by the government and would be obliged to do so until they were changed for others, and that your course was to show the proper department that the present district attorney was unfit, and thus endeavor to secure a better one, and that your unwillingness to lay the evidence, whatever it was, before the district attorney, rendered this officer powerless to act.

On the strength of your former letters I sent a special agent to you in St. Louis to get information, but he returned, having seen you, and investigated the allegations for several days, without obtaining anything upon which to base official action.

Whenever you can feel assured that the instruments provided by law for the detection and punishment of these crimes alleged are trustworthy, I shall gladly co-operate with you ; until then I do not see what more this office n do in the matter.   Respectfully,

J. W. DOUGLASS, Com'r.

ST. LOUIS, Sept. 15, 1874.

DEAR SIR :

Your letter of the 5th inst. (1 B. 77) received, and in view of what has passed, I feel compelled to explain that Mr. Hinds stated to me that he was expected to return in one week, which arrangement would give him but two or three days in St. Louis ; that he knew nothing of the internal revenue law in respect to distillers and, therefore, refused point blank to make any personal investigation, for the reason that he would be unable to determine as to whether a particular case was a violation of the law ; that he did not know what he was sent here for, as by reason of his unfamiliarity with the law and modes of stealing, he could be of no service.   For fuller exposition I copy a letter to me now in my possession as follows : " When Mr. Hinds, agent for the government, came here, I was with him nearly all the time, and gave him information where irregularities were being carried on, both in stills and rectifying houses, and urged him to go with me and see a certain house that was then mashing four times the amount of grain their permit allowed ; that the gauging was performed by boys, the gauger being absent and holding a position in the office of the *Globe* while ostensibly filling that of the government.

I requested him to submit to an interview with the internal revenue officer in respect to these and other frauds. This he declined, assigning as a reason for his refusal, that he knew nothing of the law, and if irregularities were developed he would do nothing ; that he had no instructions or authority to make any examinations of houses, and he hardly knew what he was sent here for. He told Hon. Erastus Wells the same, and on leaving stated that he had all the information he thought necessary to have."

In this connection permit me to call your attention to the fact, that information of Hind's arrival here was received by me from an attorney for the whiskey ring, which attorney gave me his name and the purpose of his visit, and described him accurately. This fact being brought home to Mr. Hinds he expressed great surprise, and I will do him the justice to say that I have no thoughts that the information came from that source.

It is quite singular that the members of the Ring boast openly of their acts, and say they are too strong, solid, to be broken, and further, that you are a member.

I have not asked, and do not ask, that Mr. Patrick be removed ; what I ask is that, without his or the Ring's knowledge, one or more experienced detectives, familiar with the whiskey business be employed, and that no case be submitted to him until the chain of evidence is complete. Then he will be compelled to prosecute or fall. I can designate two men, and, if employed, I will guarantee not only the exposure but conviction of the first government officials of this city.

Truly yours,

JESSE B. WOODWARD.

Our efforts to have Douglass appointed Commissioner of Internal Revenue were successful, and everything was then secure for practical operations and, as previously stated, in September following the distilleries throughout the district begun to run crooked.

The next letter indicating the direction of the zephyrs, in the beginning of the illicit distilling, reads as follows:

St. Louis, Sept. 19, 1871.

DEAR GENERAL:

*   *   *   *   *   *   *   *   *   *   *

I had a talk with McKee and Ford this morning and they are pleased with the *last* move.

*   *   *   *   *   *   *   *   *   *

Mr. M. left for New York last evening after satisfying all at this end of the avenue.

*   *   *   *   *   *   *   *   *

Get all the facts you can regarding Schurz, and bring them home for campaign consumption.

*   *   *   *   *   *   *   *   *   *

Yours in the Faith,

JOHN A. JOYCE.

The last move referred to as pleasing Ford and McKee was the appointment of Douglass, there being a thorough understanding between us all with Douglass that he was to perform his duties with special regard to the interest of the Ring.

The party referred to as "M." was Con. Magrue, who had just then assumed the management of the Ring.

Carl Schurz was an enemy of Grant's and one of the obligations of the Whiskey Combination was to fight him to the death if possible.

CHAPTER II.

The wheels of the Ring were kept well oiled, and
nothing interfered to mar the smooth tenor of our
purposes until Congress, by an act passed during
the preceding winter, and which took effect August
1st, 1872, legislated all the Supervisors out of office.
Up to this time the law provided for the appointment of twenty-five Supervisors by the Secretary of
the Treasury, but after this new law went into effect
another act passed Congress providing for the appointment of ten Supervisors by the President,
subject to confirmation by the Senate. The change
therefore consisted in a reduction of the number of
Supervisors, and transferred the power of appoint-

ment from the Secretary of the Treasury to the President.

About six weeks previous to the expiration of my office by limitation of the act referred to, I went to Washington and had an interview with the President. At this meeting I told him that in the appointment of the ten Supervisors under the new act, if he consulted my wishes, he would leave me out. I explained to him the pressure that would be exerted for the place, and assured him that my desire was to enter the campaign actively in his behalf; that out of office my influence would be greater and I could work more persistently.

The President's reply was that his preference would be to have remain in the service.

Leaving the matter in this shape, I returned to St. Louis, and when my office expired, the President, finding himself overrun with applicants for Supervisor, and the political pressure of officials being almost irresistible, yielded to my wishes and omitted my name in his list of new appointments. Immediately thereafter, however, I was appointed as one of the Commission, composed of Gov. Edwin M. McCook, then Governor of Colorado, Hon. Jno. D. Long, of Maine, and myself, to treat with the Ute Indians for a relinquishment of their reservation in Colorado to the Government.

While absent performing my duties as one of the Commission, there was a general demand made for my re-appointment, engineered by Mr. McKee and others. The prime cause for this desire was in the ambition of the old members to continue the operations of the Ring. Through these efforts the State

Central Committee of Missouri, of which Hon.
Henry T. Blow was chairman, prepared and forwarded to President Grant a series of reasons why
I should be re-appointed. Among the large number
of written requests was the following, the signer
of which bitterly opposed my first appointment, and
who will figure more prominently in this history
hereafter:

EASTERN DISTRICT OF MISSOURI,
U. S. ATTORNEY'S OFFICE,
ST. LOUIS, July 26th, 1872.

HON. GEO. S. BOUTWELL, Secretary of the Treasury.

SIR:—Having seen, in the telegraphic news of yesterday,
that Supervisor John McDonald has not been retained in office
under the recent consolidation, I take this occasion to express
my regret that it has been deemed expedient and proper to
make a change in this Department.

Soon after having been appointed to my present position, an
effort was made to add Missouri to the district of Supervisor
McDonald. I opposed this change, and joined in a remon-
strance. But the change was made, and since that time I have
had abundant opportunity to satisfy myself that it was for the
benefit of the Internal Revenue service.

Supervisor McDonald has been, to my personal knowledge,
an active and efficient officer. He has placed me under
obligations for valuable aid rendered me in the discharge
of the duties of my office. He has always been ready and
willing—more than that—solicitous to secure a prompt and
vigorous enforcement of the Revenue Laws in the Judicial district. Aside from the fact that Supervisor McDonald has been
a competent officer, it is equally true that his large acquaintance
in this State renders him especially valuable to the Republican
party, as a powerful adherent for the coming campaign.

I trust that this communication will not be regarded as
officious, but as truthfully stating not only my own views, but
those of many influential men, with whom I have conferred

since the announcement of the change in the Supervisor's office.

Without the request or suggestion of the Supervisor, I have given him this letter as a sincere expression of my conviction that the proposed change can secure no beneficial result.

I have the honor to be your obedient serv't,

CHESTER H. KRUM, U. S. Attorney.

After this paper reached the department, President Grant wrote on the back of the endorsement the following:

" Respectfully forwarded to the Secretary of the Treasury:

The dispatches and letters received in favor of Sup'r Mc-Donald are so numerous, and from people of such standing and responsibility, that I do not know but that his name had not better be substituted for retention in place of Emory's, or any other who you may think can be best spared.

U. S. GRANT.

Aug. 1st, '72.

In blue ink the following:

Vice COBB, H. S. R.

[A fac-simile of this endorsement is found on the opposite page.]

The extraordinary language and bad grammar used in the President's note, on the back of Krum's endorsement, will excite comment, but the note is in Grant's own handwriting, and the errors are therefore his own.

Among the other requests for my re-appointment was the following telegram:

ST. LOUIS, July 25th, 1872.

To GEN. JNO. McDONALD, Ripon, Wisconson.

Ford gone West. The thing is done. Telegram sent President.   (Signed) J. A. JOYCE.

This telegram was a notification that Col. Ford had sent a personal request to the President to have me re-appointed.

Respectfully forwarded
to the Sec. of the Treas,
The dispatches and letters
received in favor of Sup.t
McDonald are so numerous,
and from people of such
standing and respectibil-
ity that I do not know
but that his name had
not better be substituted
for retention in place of
Emory's, or any other when
you may think can be
best spared.

U. S. Grant,

Aug. 1st/72

see Cott

appd

The demand for my retention bore immediate fruits and before my return from Colorado my appointment, as Supervisor over an enlarged district, was made.

During my stay in Denver I received the following letter:

St. Louis, Aug. 22d, 1872.

Dear General:

I received yours of the 17th inst., wherein you give glowing ideas of what we may be worth in the future.

* * * * * * * * *

The President, upon the return of Cobb to Washington, thought best to continue us in the service, and I have direct information that he has signed your commission as Supervisor. But the Treasury Department has not sent official advice as yet. There is a hitch somewhere even now, but from a telegram I received from our mutual friend B. (Babcock) at the White House, I gather that all will come out right.

* * * * * * * * *

Our little trick is so, so, and our prospects may be better. Keep your shirt on and we may be happy yet. Put me down for a gold mine, a silver gulch and a diamond quarry—in fact anything to beat Greeley. Yours, on the rush,

JNO. A. JOYCE.

This letter contains no doubtful language. It simply refers to Babcock's influence, which I knew would be used for my re-appointment to advance his own interests. None of this influence, however, was needed. It was all merely ornamental, for the President, being "one of us," was as anxious as Babcock, McKee, Ford, Maguire, and the other chief members of the Ring were, to keep me in a place where I could render them such effective service.

Another evidence of Douglass' connection with the Ring is found in the following letter from Joyce:

WASHINGTON, D. C, Dec. 5th, 1872.

DEAR GENERAL :

Got in the city at two o'clock this afternoon. After putting on a clean shirt went to the Internal Revenue Bureau. I had a kindly and general talk with Douglass, privately, about Brasher. He said that B. was sent to St. Louis to do some special work, and that you and Ford might let him have his own way. Douglass said he was your friend and should tell you all in time. I guess that Boutwell, Douglass, and other folks whom I might name, want to pin something upon somebody for their own information.

* * * * * * * * *

Douglass said that he would not force B. upon you.

Yours,

"JOHN A."

Brasher was a revenue agent, who performed the duties of detective; with this information the letter and Douglass' relation to us is understood at once.

The appended letter furnishes another link in the chain of documentary evidence connecting Gen. Babcock with the Ring organization:

LAWRENCE, KAS., April 25th, 1873.

DEAR GENERAL :

I arrived here this morning in company with Gen. Grant and party. The mayor and citizens of Lawrence met us at the depot and the Presidential party rode around the city. I was in a carriage with Miss Nellie Grant, Miss Kimball, of St. Louis, and Major Dunn. Gen. Babcock and his brother went together. Gen. O. E. and the subscriber had a splendid chat on the train. He is our friend to the end.

* * * * * * * * *

Yours, etc.,

JOHN A. JOYCE.

Gen. JOHN McDONALD, St. Louis.

The reference to Gen. O. E. means Babcock, his christian name being Orville E. Shortly before this I had dismissed from the service "Chat" Hardaway, a storekeeper, and several members of the Ring became alarmed lest he should divulge some of the secrets. Joyce's conversation with Babcock was with relation to this dismissal and its possible results. McKee tried to force me to re-instate Hardaway and, for some time, matters as sumed a serious aspect. I wanted Babcock to stand by my action, and, in the conversation referred to, he assured Joyce that he would, and in this instance he kept his promise.

The Whiskey Ring did not confine its operations to St. Louis, but was in full activity in all important cities. In New Orleans there was a gigantic Ring under the immediate supervision of James N. Casey, Collector of the Port of that city, who was President Grant's brother-in-law. Herewith is inserted a letter from Col. Casey with the true explanation added:

CUSTOM HOUSE, NEW ORLEANS, }
COLLECTOR'S OFFICE, May 15th, 1873. }

GENERAL :

An old boyhood friend of mine, W. R. Jouett, is in the distillery business, and may have need of your kind offices at times, as a personal favor to myself; if the occasion arises and you can extend him any courtesy or favor, I ask that you will do so, and I will find means to reciprocate.

Very truly yours,

JAMES N. CASEY.

Gen. JOHN McDONALD,
    Supt. Internal Revenue.

Although our St. Louis branch of the illicit
organization drew its fund from a number of distillers, yet they were not all included in the Ring at
this time. Jouett was running crooked, but he
was subject to the Storekeeper, and therefore had
to be so circumspect in his operations that he could
turn out only a limited quantity of illicit whiskey.
I never allowed any distillers to approach me, and
several of them did not know that I was conscious
of their crookedness, among whom was Jouett.
This letter of Casey's was written, as Casey informed me personally afterwards, in response to a
request made by Jouett asking him (Casey) to intercede with me for an inside position in the Ring.
This inside position would allow him to run his
distillery day and night without his being subjected
to the dictation of subordinate officials or the fear
of evil consequences. The request made upon me
by Casey came from a source which I would not
disregard, for Casey's word bore the seal of high
authority.

Nothing transpired after the date of the last letter quoted, important to record here, until the
death of Col. C. W. Ford, the collector, which
occurred at the residence of T. B. Blackstone,
in Chicago, October 24th, 1873.

Among the telegrams I sent to the friends of Col.
Ford, notifying them of his death, were the two
following:

CHICAGO, Oct. 25th, 1873.

HIS EXCELLENCY, U. S. GRANT, Washington:

Hon. C. W. Ford died at the residence of Mr. Blackstone at
six o'clock last evening; his remains go to Monroe, Mich., this

evening at five o'clock. *I have made provision for the safety of his private papers* and effects. I will be in St. Louis Monday.

McDONALD.

CHICAGO, Oct. 25th, 1873.

J. H. CONCANNON, Internal Revenue Office, St. Louis:

Col. C. W. Ford died at six o'clock last night. His remains go to Monroe, Mich., this evening. I have instructed McMasters to take charge of his personal effects and *papers*. You will take charge of the collector's office as acting collector.

McDONALD.

Being fully aware of the fact that there had been correspondence between the President and Col. Ford concerning the management of the Whiskey Ring and the distribution of the campaign fund, I telegraphed to the President in this manner in order to dissipate any anxiety which might be felt of these letters falling into the hands of other parties.

Col. Ford very frequently read to me letters which he had received from the President, and told me that he was always particular to destroy those that would compromise his friend, which, I presume, he did. But I knew that the President would feel more secure upon my assurance that these letters would not fall under the gaze of any other person.

Concannon was first deputy collector, and had been a sharer of the illicit whiskey fund for a long while; in fact he divided with Ford the money derived from the first crooked operations of the Card and Lawrence distillery, where I made the discovery of Ford's dishonesty when I took charge of the district. I therefore had nothing to fear in appointing him acting collector.

The operations of the Ring continued without

interruption until November 15th following, when Constantine Maguire took possession of the Collector's office by virtue of his appointment made about two weeks previously. This appointment was the result of an underderstanding consummated immediately upon my return from Chicago, and under the following circumstances:

McKee had suggested the name of Maguire on receiving information of Mr. Ford's illness. The day, therefore, that I returned, a meeting was held between McKee, Joyce, Maguire, and myself in my office, at which certain pledges were obtained from Maguire and his appointment then decided upon.

At our dictation the following telegrams were sent ·

ST. LOUIS, Oct. 25th, 1873.

To GEN. E. O. BABCOCK, Executive Mansion, care of President Grant :

Poor Ford is dead. McDonald is with his body. Let the President act cautiously on the successorship.

(Signed.) JOYCE.

In reply to this was the following:

WASHINGTON, Oct. 26th, 1873.

To JNO. A JOYCE, St. Louis:

See that Ford's bondsmen recommend you.

B. (Babcock.)

In response to Babcock's telegram the following was sent:

ST. LOUIS, Oct. 27th, 1873.

To GEN. O. E. BABCOCK, Executive Mansion, care Pre's. Grant.

The bondsmen prefer the man they have recommended. An expression from the President to his friends here will secure everything. Let the President do for the best. Depend upon McDonald and myself to stand by his actions to the last.

(Signed,) Jno. A. Joyce.

The three following explain everything:

St. Louis, Oct. 28th, 1873.

We have the honor to recommend Col. Constantine Maguire for collector of Internal Revenue of the first district of Missouri.

(Signed,) John A. Joyce,
Wm. Patrick.
C. A. Newcomb,
John McDonald.

St. Louis, Oct, 28th, 1873.

Gen. O. E. Babcock, Executive Mansion, Washington,

See dispatch sent to President. We mean it, mum.

(Signed,) Joyce.

Washington, Oct. 28th, 1873.

Wm. H. Benton, Wm. McKee and John M. Krum.

Your request in regard to the collectorship will be complied with.   (Signed,) U. S. Grant.

These three parties addressed by the President were well known to the secrets of the ring. They were Ford's bondsmen and for a multiplicity of reasons that will hereafter be developed, were anxious to have Maguire appointed. A very strong protest signed by a large number of prominent persons in St. Louis, such as James G. Yeatman, Robert Campbell, etc., was made against the appointment of Maguire, but no attention whatever was paid to it. In fact President Grant, in his deposition, taken as evidence in the Babcock trial, stated that he had no remembrance of seeing the protest, but added, that he presumed it was on file at the department.

In Joyce's dispatch when he uses the insinuating words, "we mean it, mum," the significance is very apparent. By this he conveys to Babcock the fact that Maguire had been sounded and has been initiated into the first degree of the Ring, with promises of proving a faithful member.

The dispatch signed "B" was from Babcock.

The appointment of Maguire effected no change in the conduct of the Ring; everything remained in a tranquil and yet vigorous condition.

In the early part of November three revenue agents, Brasher, Yaryan and Gavitt, came to St. Louis according to an advance notice I had received of their intention, and made an examination of the books of the distillers. They, of course, found great irregularities, and positive proofs of the immense amount of illicit whiskey being manufactured, but instead of submitting a full report of the actual facts informed the department that they had discovered many technical violations of the law, which, while it lay the distillers, rectifiers and wholesale dealers, liable, yet they recommended that no stringent action should be taken, but that they should be informed that in future similar violations would result in an enforcement of the penalties prescribed.

After agreeing upon the nature of the report Brasher should submit, the three agents left St. Louis, Yaryan going to New Orleans, Gavitt to Michigan, I think, and Brasher to Washington. Subsequent events indicated that Yaryan had understood that Brasher would make a true report of affairs, but that Brasher had submitted a false report in order to prepare the way for successfully black-mailing the distillers in a short time thereafter. The facts are, that in the latter part of the same month, Brasher again visited St. Louis by order of Commissioner Douglas. This order was given for the purpose of investigating all the books of the Collector and illicit dealers, so that they might be straightened up and thereby be proof against a possible congressional investigation.

The real personal object of Brasher's second visit was to blackmail the distillers and rectifiers, which he accomplished, in the following manner: He went through the distilleries and rectifying houses, the proprietors of which he informed that, having discovered gross violations of the revenue laws, and that reports of these violations had already been sent to the department, his duty was to make a thorough report of the actual facts. This created a stampede and so alarmed the illicit operators that immediate steps were taken to suppress the report, which had already been prepared. Notwithstanding the fact that at this time there was a general belief among the distillers and rectifiers that the President, Babcock, Douglass, and other Washington officials were affiliating and benefitting by the Ring, yet Brasher succeeded in dissipating this idea and aroused their fears to such a pitch that they made a score of offers to Brasher, to buy him from making such a report as he had proposed. After remaining in St. Louis more than a month Brasher consented to change the entire tone of his report and exempt the distillers and rectifiers, pronouncing their crimes more technical violations, provided they would pay him the sum of $20.000, $10.000 of which sum should be paid upon transmission of a copy of the reformed report to Commissioner Douglass, and a duplicate of the same sent to me. The other $10.000 was to be paid when the report should be placed on file at Washington.

Brasher set to work at once and made a draft of a report such as suited the distillers and rectifiers, of which the following is a copy:

St. Louis, Mo., 9th January, 1873.

Sir:

I have the honor to report that since my return here I have been engaged in making a thorough examination of the distilleries of "Bevis & Fraser," "R. W. Ulrici," "P. Curran," and "M. Thompson," together with the rectifying establishments of "Bevis & Fraser," "Garnhart & Co.," "Bollman & O'Hara," "McCartney & Co.," "H. L. Downs," "Lange & Benecke," and "Derby & Day," and in comparing their books with those of the United States Storekeepers, and the records in the offices of the Collector and Assessor of Internal Revenue in this district, that the result of this investigation has failed to disclose that condition of affairs, which was presumed to exist, from the statements made to me by persons claiming to possess most direct and positive information of the fraudulent distillation of spirits in this district, or from the irregularities which appeared on the examination, based on this information, made in November last.

I find the books of the distillers, rectifiers and United States Storekeepers to agree with the records in the offices of the Collector and Assessor of Internal Revenue, and that they show the spirits distilled and rectified have been reported properly, and the taxes collected thereon.

It appears that the state of confusion, existing here in November last, in these establishments, and, also, to a certain extent, in some of the revenue books, all of which seemed to

corroborate the charges of fraud, was the result of the unusual
excitement attending the political campaign, then just ended,
in which, I am informed, these parties and the revenue officers
particularly took a very active part, to the consequent neglect
of their business and duties respectively. It would further
appear that, in addition to this derangement of business generally, the clerk in charge of the books of the rectifying house
of "Bevis, Fraser & Co." was sick and unable attend to his
duties.

As the information furnished me, as to the existence of fraud,
depended, and I was assured, with no possibility of failure,
on the books of these different establishments and the records
in the Internal Revenue office for verification, and my inform-
ants having no further evidence to offer, I can but conclude
that, whilst the irregularities, on the one hand, justified
the suspicions of fraud, on the other hand corrections of
the Internal Revenue records disproves it. In conclusion,
however, I desire to remark that though it appears these irregularities were simply the result of negligence they, nevertbe-
less, fully justified the investigation and that it remains with
you to consider them, and the remedy which will prevent their
recurrence in the future. I wish to acknowledge having received
all the assistance asked for, from the different revenue officers
of the district, during the investigation.

Very respectfully,

B. P. BRASHER, Revenue Agent.

HON. J. W. DOUGLASS, Commissioner of Internal Revenue,
Washington, D. C.

The amount agreed upon was paid, the first
$10,000 being given to Brasher, in a room at the
Southern Hotel, by John Leavenworth and Alfred
Bevis, as they themselves informed me. The remaining sum was paid soon after. I was not informed of this impious act for sometime after it was
accomplished, but as soon as I learned the facts, I

went to Washington and repeated them to Commissioner Douglass, whose reply was that he had long tried to get clear of Brasher, but the Ohio influence, through which he was appointed, was so great that his retention in the service was a necessity. The real cause, however, was the knowledge he possessed of the Ring and its supporters, as subsequent proofs contained herein will show.

In the spring of 1874, Yaryan returned to Washington, and called at the department, and requested the chief clerk to show him the report made by Brasher. He read it carefully, but with the greatest astonishment, to find instead of the report communicating the facts of gigantic frauds, by illicit distillation, it had dwarfed the crimes into mere technical violations. His astonishment, however, was doubly intensified, when after concluding its reading, he turned the report, only to find that it bore the following endorsement in Commissioner Douglass' own handwriting:

"Brasher verbally reports that Yaryan agrees with him that no action should be taken."

A scene ensured during which Yaryan denounced Brasher, and told Mr. Douglass the real condition of affairs at St. Louis. The matter was afterwards carried to Solicitor Wilson, but it was hushed before assuming any undue proportions or had led to any trouble.

CHAPTER III.

The arrangements were now so complete and no
special political necessity appearing for the use of
the funds collected from the distillers and rectifiers,
the Washington end of the line begun to let their
wants be known. I made a regular report, generally each month, to the President, of the manner in
which the whiskey money was used.

Owing to the very useful position W. O. Avery, Chief Clerk of the Internal Revenue Bureau, occupied, and for advancing us information, he was made the first beneficiary of the fund in Washington. About November 15th Joyce sent Avery a letter containing $500, it being, I repeat, the first Washington remittance. Not receiving an immediate acknowledgement of its acceptance Joyce sent the following telegram:

St. Louis, Nov. 23, 1873.

Col. W. O. Avery, Washington.

Did you get my last letter with enclosure?

(Signed) Joyce.

To which he received the following reply:

Washington, Nov. 24, 1873.

John A. Joyce, Revenue Agent, St. Louis.

Letter with enclosure received.

(Signed) W. O. Avery.

In January a revenue agent visited us at St. Louis and made some examinations. I was not in the city at the time and after he returned to Washington I was in doubt as to the report of that visit. In all our apparent security there was still a dread lest the knowledge of our operations should reach Bristow; and in order to ascertain the object and result of the agent's visit, I sent Joyce on to Washington to secure the necessary information. Shortly after his arrival in that city I received the following dispatch:

Washington, Jan'y. 21, 1874.

Gen. John McDonald, Planters House, St. Louis.

Everything looks well. Send on report. Feel hunkey.

(Signed) John

On the next day Col. Joyce wrote me the following letter which explains this telegram:

EBBITT HOUSE, WASHINGTON, Jany. 22, 1874.

DEAR GENERAL :

Well, it is after eleven o'clock, and just before retiring I will give you my day's rambles in very brief style : I saw and *talked* (sic) with Douglass, Clayton, Babcock, the President, Belknap, Rogers and Avery. You can just imagine what I said to each, and can bet your last nickle that I got what I wanted. The White House people were very pleasant, and Douglass was all peaches and cream.

* * * * * * * * * * *

Brasher has no authority to visit St. Louis, and if he troubles you or yours, put him where he "will do the most good." I am going to ride with Bab. (Babcock) to-morrow.

* * * * * * * * * * *

Just *keep our kettle boiling* (sic) and don't let anything interrupt the good cause of patriotism.

* * * * * * * * * * *

Yours always,

JOHN A. JOYCE.

After Joyce's arrival in Washington he went direct to the President and others, as admitted in his letter, and from them ascertained that the agent sent into our district would not report anything prejudicial to our interests. The report referred to in the telegram was the result of an investigation I had made respecting a matter called to my attention by the department, and I was desirous of ascertaining the result of the revenue agent's visit before submitting that report.

In March Joyce, who was then a revenue agent, was ordered to proceed to San Francisco for the purpose of investigating reports made concerning distillers and rectifiers in California. I was in

Washington at the time Joyce received his instructions and, learning through Commissioner Douglass that Hogue, a revenue agent, would visit my district, in order to have Joyce fix up everything so as to avoid any appearance of crookedness should Hogue make a critical investigation, I sent the following telegram:

WASHINGTON, March 9, 1874.

JOHN A. JOYCE, St. Louis.

If sickness in your family prevents you from going West, Hogue may pay you a visit. (Signed) MAC.

In addition to my telegram Avery sent the following:

WASHINGTON, March 11, 1874.

Did you receive Mac's telegram. Your friends will doubtless make you a visit. (Signed) W. O. AVERY.

To which the following reply was received:

ST. LOUIS, March 11, 1874.

COL. W. O. AVERY, Internal Revenue Bureau, Washington:

Telegrams received. I start for San Francisco Saturday night. All perfect here.

(Signed) JOYCE.

Before leaving, however, he sent the following dispatch:

ST. LOUIS, March 14, 1874.

GEN. O. E. BABCOCK, Executive Mansion.

Start for San Francisco to-morrow night; make D. (Douglass) call off his scandal hounds that only blacken the memory of poor Ford and friends. Business.

(Signed) J.

By this he meant that if there was a searching investigation made it would result in exposing Ford, —who was not suspected by the public until after his death,—and all the members of the Ring.

Having posted his Washington friends Col. Joyce started for San. Francisco on the 15th of March and remained absent from St. Louis two or three months. Hogue and Brooks, the revenue agents of whose coming we had been notified, arrived in St. Louis in the latter part of April but remained only a short time, as they soon discovered there were no traces of crookedness.

No illicit whiskey was made in my district during Joyce's absence in the West, but upon his return from San Francisco he proceeded to Washington, in obedience to an order from Com. Douglass to make his report on the Pacific Coast investigation, and during his stay in Washington matters were arranged for resuming illicit operations. Following is a dispatch showing result of Joyce's visit to the Capital.

WASHINGTON, July 1, 1874.

GENL. JOHN McDONALD, St. Louis.

Things look all right here. Let the machine go.

JOYCE.

The following letter furnishes an explanation of the telegram:

EBBITT HOUSE, WASHINGTON, July 4, 1874.

DEAR GENERAL :

*   *   *   *   *   *   *   *   *   *

I was a little surprised to-day by Genl. B. telling me that that little thing we gave him was a fraud.

*   *   *   *   *   *   *   *   *   *

I have a good many things to tell you when I get back. I had a splendid talk with the President.

Billy is Chief Clerk and Holt will take his place. Things are working nice. You want to push things at that end of the line. We have lots of friends here.

*   *   *   *   *   *   *   *   *   *   *

Yours to the end of the row,

JOHN A. JOYCE.

The allusion contained in this letter, to "that little thing," referred to a diamond shirt-stud, which we gave to Babcock during his visit to St. Louis, the preceding spring. This, one of our many presents to our Washington friend, weighed nearly four carets, and cost $2,400. There was a flaw in the stone, however, which I had not discovered, and the General, not being very well pleased on that account, I took the stone back and purchased another and finer one for him.

"The things he had to tell me, and his talk with the President," consisted of assurances which permitted the Ring to operate freely, without danger of prosecution. The reference to "Billy" and "Holt," was an announcement that Billy, or W. O. Avery, had been transferred from the position of chief clerk of the Internal Revenue Bureau, to that of chief clerk of the Treasury Department, which for former position was supplied by the appointment of Col. Holt. Both of these men were thoroughly identified with the Ring's interests, as the appointments were both made at our special request. With this change, and new understanding, Joyce was justified in issuing his request to "Let the machine go."

A report obtained currency some time in the latter part of August, that St. Louis would soon be visited by another revenue agent, and hearing nothing from Washington, I had Joyce send the following telegram:

St. Louis, Aug. 26th, 1874.

Col. W. O. Avery, Chief Clerk Treasury Department, Washington.

Are friends coming west? See H. (Holt), and give me soundings. (Signed) "A."

To this dispatch there was no answer, and fearing that Avery's induction into an office in which his superior (Sec'y. Bristow), was then making efforts, or, at least contemplating measures that would expose the Whiskey Ring, had resulted in a contra-riwise influence, and that he was afraid to give us the information we desired, Joyce sent him a letter, in which the following sentence occurred: (The exact date of this letter I am unable to give from memory, and we rarely retained copies of either letters or telegrams) "If you have any doubt of the propriety of sending this information, see Gen. Babcock, or, if he is not in the city, see G." This meant for Avery to repeat his wishes to Babcock or President Grant, and they would furnish the necessary information to us.

Upon receipt of this letter, Gen. Babcock being absent from Washington, Col. Avery took it to the President, who, after reading the contents, wrote the following endorsement on the back of the letter.

"Joyce and McDonald are reliable and trustworthy. Let them have the information they want."

(SIGNED.)   U. S. GRANT.

One of the prime motives which actuated Col. Avery in going to the President for his endorsement, was to obtain a color of authority for revealing secrets of the Department. He was thoroughly known to the fact that the President was cognizant of all the tricks of the Whiskey Ring, and was, in fact, a member of it; he also realized that his position was a new one, with which he did not yet have that familiarity that would hide all his acts, and his first duty, he felt, was to obtain the confidence of the Secretary.

The reports of intended raids, from revenue officers, continued to circulate, which resulted in several communications passing between Joyce and the departments. Hinds had left Washington, and his absence created a suspicion that he was about to visit St. Louis. All fears were allayed, however, upon receipt of the following telegram:

WASHINGTON, Oct. 18th, 1874.

J. A. JOYCE, St. Louis:

Your friend is in New York, and may come out to see you.

(Signed.) AVERY.

Joyce replied to this as follows:

ST. LOUIS, Oct. 18th, 1874.

COL. W. O. AVERY, Treasury Department, Washington:

Give me something positive on the movements of friend. Act surely—prompt.

(Signed.) "A."

In obedience to the request contained in this telegram, Avery saw Babcock, with relation to the intentions of revenue agents coming to St. Louis, and on the next day Gen. Babcock sent the following telegram:

WASHINGTON, Oct. 19th, 1874.

J. A. JOYCE, St. Louis:

Put your house in order. Your friends will visit you.

(Signed.) MAC.

This telegram was proven, upon his trial, to be in Babcock's handwriting. It was intended to send Hogue into the district, but, owing to illness, he did not come.

On the first Monday in October, 1874, the St. Louis Fair opened, with President Grant, Secretary

Borie, and Gen. Babcock in attendance. Grant and Babcock were my guests, at the Lindell Hotel, that fine hostelry having then been but recently opened. Soon after his arrival in St. Louis, and while engaged with him in conversation at the Lindell, I reminded the President that, on his previous visits, he always had the use of Col. Ford's team to drive while in the city, but, I added, since our friend is dead, I presume you have been at a loss for the use of such horseflesh as you have been accustomed to driving. I then told him that I had a team, which, while it was not the fastest in the world, was fair to drive.

He responded: " Well, Mac, I never knew you to own a bad horse, and if you have a pair of serviceable roadsters I'll use them to-morrow, by driving them down to my farm, and if they have speed I will gladly accept the use of them while here."

On the following day I had the team hitched up and drove them around to the hotel for the President. Before he got into the buggy, I said to him: You may find them a little slow at first, but you can touch them up a little with the whip, and when you get well out on the Gravois road, tighten the reins, and I don't think you will have any trouble getting four minutes out of them.

He then stepped into the buggy, with Secretary Borie beside him. They drove out to the farm, twelve miles from St. Louis, and remained absent until evening. I received the team after his return, and taking them to the stable, a short time afterwards, in company with my wife, I called socially at the Lindell, and met there Col. Joyce

GEN. U. S. GRANT.

and his wife, Mrs. Grant, Mrs. Borie, and a number of others. Secretary Borie came up to me, and, placing his hand familiarly on my shoulder, remarked: "General, I never had a finer ride in my life than to-day, behind your horses, and the President is in exstacy over them."

Just then President Grant greeted me and said: "Mack, I never saw better horses; why, when we got out on the road they would'nt take the whip, for when I drew the lines they went like a shot out of a gun. You should have seen Mr. Borie; he drew his feet under the seat, pressed his hat over his eyes, and, while he clenched the buggy-bow with one hand and the seat with the other, he would every moment ask me if I did'nt think the horses were running away." In a moment afterwards he added: "I would like to own those horses, and if you will sell them I will give you $1,000 for them." I replied: General, I don't want to swindle you in that way. But I used the word 'swindle' in an ironical manner, for $5,000 would'nt have bought them.

He then told me that he had seen some very fine horses at the Fair, owned by Mr. Dorsey, of Kentuckey, a pair of which he thought of buying at the price fixed by the owner, $1,500.

We joked about the horses for some time, but, before leaving him that evening, I told the President the team was at his service during his stay in St. Louis, and that I hoped he would find much pleasure in them. His delight was manifested by their almost constant use, on several mornings going to the stable himself after the horses. Seeing that the team was a source of so much pleasure to the President, I at length told him that he should have those horses, and for him to think no more of buying a team. I ascertained that he had no handsome buggy, so I took it upon myself, as I told him, to procure a rig such as I would buy for my own ornamental use as well as for effective service.

He thanked me, and declared that nothing would please him so much as such a tribute of my friendship.

Before the President came to St. Louis to visit the Fair, I asked him, in Washington, if he intended exhibiting any of his stock. He replied that he had tried to add to the success of the Fair by lending his presence and entering his stock, but that the Association had never awarded him a single premium, so that hereafter he did not propose to enter any of his stock again.

I told him that there was nothing personal in the action of the Fair Association, and that it was his duty, having so large a stock-farm in the immediate vicinity of St. Louis, with so many interests in the city, to aid the Fair, and that he ought to enter his prime stock every year.

The result of our conversation was his promise to attend the Fair that year and to enter his "Young Hambletonian."

When I returned to St. Louis I called on Arthur Barrett, who was then President of the Fair Association, and repeated to him the complaints of the President. Mr. Barrett replied that the reason President Grant had not been given a premium was because his stock had been entered in competition with that which was superior, and the committees did not wish to show partiality to anyone. After talking with him awhile he told me that I might be placed on the committee that would award the premiums on stock, and, if I wished to assume the responsibility, the President's stock might secure a premium.

I secured the position as a member of that committee, and when "Young Hambletonian" was entered I told one of the members that there was only one thing I wanted done, obtaining the consent of the committee to which, I would favor anything else they wished. This one thing was to give the first premium to the President's stallion, and, although there were several pre-eminently superior horses in competition, the other members of the committee endorsed my act and awarded the blue ribbon to "Young Hambletonian." The reason for me showing such remarkable and unwarranted preference to the President, in the light of subsequent events, is plainly apparent.

The following article appeared in the next morning's *Republican :*

* * On all occasions there will be found plenty of people to carp and grumble, and the award of the first premium to Grant's "Young Hambletonian" yesterday was no exception. It was largely hinted about the grounds that the influence of the administration had been powerfully brought to bear to secure the premium, and there were some astute forecasters of political events who saw in it much of this third term mystery; while the New York *Herald* man—if there was one on the grounds —undoubtedly detected a clear case of Cæsarism, and posted off to inform his editorial master, the Westonian Bennett, that "the '*Herald*' sensation had again become a '*Herald*' prophesy."

The character of the gentlemen comprising the commitee which made the award is an ample refutation of the charge that the first premium was secured by those appliances which are sometimes brought to bear to depose a chairman of a foreign relations committee of the Senate, or to pull an Arkansas governor out of a state house. At the head of the committee was Gen. John McDonald, supervisor of internal revenue for this district, while associated with him were a number of gentleman who, though they do not hold any federal offices, are still fully as capable of being impartial in any case where the administration is concerned as Gen. McDonald possibly can be. There is no doubt that the award was made with all due deference to the circumstances of the occasion. In other words, it is perfectly clear that the influences which impelled the committee to make the award they did were exercised in the most perfectly proper manner, and without the least regard for anything that was foreign to the object in view.

The President and his party returned to Washington on the last day of the Fair and shortly after their departure Col. Joyce and myself went to Hoblitzelle & Cousland's and purchased from them a complete outfit consisting of harness, two blankets for each horse, and a buggy whip, the cost of the latter being $25. We had a gold breast-plate made for each horse, on which the President's name was engraved. The buggy was purchased from Jas. A. Wright, and was the finest he had in stock. All the bills for the harness, buggy, etc., I paid in President Grant's name. In a few weeks after his arrival in Washington I chartered a special car in which I sent the horses and the handsome outfit to Washington with the compliments of Col. Joyce and myself. While en-route the horses were in the special charge of Nat. Carlin, who was at that time superintendent of the President's farm.

Gen. Babcock, the President's private secretary, sent us a very flattering letter acknowledging receipt of the team and rig, which letter I either gave to Judge Krum, the attorney who defended Gen. Babcock, and have never been able to recover it, or burned it, among many others.

CHAPTER IV.

Col. Joyce, even after his appointment as revenue agent, remained in my district and continued to act as my confidential secretary. He was a shrewd, and thoroughly reliable man and withal one of much cunning and spontaneous resource. I entrusted him not only with all my secrets but left the arrangement of all the details furthering the interests of the Ring, in his hands. He was especially intimate with Gen. Babcock, and during the visit of the Presidential party in October, Col. Joyce and Gen. Babcock were almost inseparable. They canvassed future contingencies and the need of money by the White House officials.

Very soon after the departure of the President from St. Louis, rumors came to us that a raid was contemplated by revenue officers. Col. Joyce at once wrote Gen. Babcock concerning the rumor but receiving no immediate reply he indicted the following dispatch:

St. Louis, Oct. 25, 1874.

Gen. O. E. Babcock, Washington.

Have you talked with D? (Douglass) Are things right? How? Answer. (Signed) J.

The report being false Gen. Babcock did not answer by telegraph but sent Col. Joyce a letter in which he assured him there was no present danger of official interference.

In the latter part of November reports were again circulated that revenue agents Brooks and Hogue were en-route to St. Louis to make a searching investigation. With the alarm such reports invariably excited, Col. Joyce sent the following telegram:

St. Louis. Dec. 3, 1874.

To Gen. O. E. Babcock, Washington.

Has Secretary or Commissioner ordered anybody here?

(Signed) J.

Secretary or Commissioner referred to Bristow and Douglass.

To this the following reply was received:

Washington, Dec. 5, 1874.

To John A. Joyce, St. Louis.

Cannot hear that anyone has gone or is going.

(Signed) O. E. Babcock

On the same day this latter dispatch was received I started for Washington, but on the preceding day Col. Joyce had collected the sum of $5,000, from

the distillers and rectifiers which he requested me
to deliver to Gen. Babcock, in accordance with the
understanding had between them, when the latter
was in attendance at the St. Louis Fair.   This
money, as I saw it counted, was in bills of the de-
nominations of $1,000 and $500.

I reached Washington on the morning of December 7th, and directly after office hours went to the
White House.   The first person I met there was
Gen. Babcock, whom I found seated at his desk in
the Secretary's room, and, after passing the usual
greetings I took the money from my pocket and
handed it to him, with the remark: Here is $5,000
which Joyce collected from the boys for your benefit just before I left St. Louis.

He took the package and placed it in his pocket
without counting the money, with many expressions of gratitude, remarking that he understood
the source from whence the money came.

During this time a committee from the two
branches of Congress were waiting upon the President to inform him of the opening of Congress, and
their readiness to receive his official communications.   When the committee left the Executive
Chamber, the President followed one of the Senators to the head of the stairs and there took leave
of the committee. I was standing in the ante-room
awaiting an opportunity to speak to him, when he
turned about and seeing me, extended a cordial
greeting.

He asked me how long I would remain in the
city, and to call upon him each day while in Washington.

GEN. O. E. BABCOCK.

I replied that my stay would be but a few days.

He then spoke freely concerning the team and rig I had sent him, saying that his gratitude was unbounded, and pronounced the horses the finest, by far, in Washington.

Said I, General, I have some papers in connection with the team which, with my explanation, I wish to give you. He asked me to come on the following day at noon, saying he would be at leisure then.

I told the President that I had the papers with me and if he could spare a few moments I would give them to him then. He assented, and together we walked into the Executive Room where I handed him all the bills, which were in his name, for every article Col. Joyce and I had purchased in completing the buggy and outfit, each bill being receipted in full. At the same time I asked him to give me a small sum of money so as to enable me to say, if the question were asked, that I sold the team to him. He handed me a $50 bill which I declined, assuring him that a much less sum would answer my purpose. He next gave me a $10 note and I returned him $7 in change, leaving me with the sum of $3 for a $6,000 outfit. One-half of the actual expense of the team, buggy and harness, and the cost of transportation was paid to me by Col. Joyce who united with me in making the present.

Having disposed of the receipts and made the President apparently secure from the prying curiosity of newspaper correspondents, who always saw in these gifts stepping-stones to political preference, we changed our conversation to a discussion of political matters in the West. I told him that I had just given Gen. Babcock $5,000, which, I remarked, is a part of the proceeds of our campaign fund in St. Louis. He assured me it was all right, as he had intrusted Babcock with the details of western matters, and whatever we did with him (Babcock) would be quite satisfactory to all, and added: " I will see to it personally, however, that you get all the changes you want."

I then explained to him what an uncompromising " old hog " (as I used the term) McKee was proving himself to be; that we were compelled to give him from $500 to $1,200 every week in order to pacify him and keep his paper for us in the coming campaign. His reply was: " Well, you must do the best you can and depend upon me to do all for you at this end of the line you may require."

While we were thus engaged a messenger came and informed the President that his team was at the door waiting for him. He asked me to walk down stairs with him and take a look at the horses. I did so, and showed the hostler how to draw the curb rein to make them drive properly. While we were looking at the horses, Commissioner Douglass came by and spoke to us, but after passing a few remarks, he walked on. President Grant then requested me to get in and take a drive with him, which I did, going out nearly to Blandensburg, and, returning, making a circuit of the city and driving through all the principal streets. During our ride the conversation recurred to political matters, and chiefly upon his prospects for a third term. He mentioned the names of several parties who, he thought, would possibly be candidates. Among these were Gov. Morgan, of New York, Morton, Conklin, Logan, and Blaine, the latter being then Speaker of the House. He criticised each of these and appeared satisfied that his chances were much better than were those of the parties discussed.

Upon our return from the ride I went back to the White House with the President, and, while the colored attendants were brushing our clothes, a messenger-boy informed me that Gen. Babcock was in his office and wished to see me. I left the President in the reception room and went up stairs, where I met Gen. Babcock alone. He first asked me if I had talked freely with the President in relation to appointments out West and the arrangements generally in my district. I replied that I had, and that the President promised to make any appointments or changes of officers I desired. I asked him what Brooks and Hogue were doing or were going to do. His answer was that he did not know, but would find out on the following day and advise me. He assured me that he was not going to allow them to go to St. Louis on a "blackmailing trip," as, said he, "we want all the money you can raise now ourselves." Another subject on which we conversed related to Garfield's connection with the District of Columbia Ring, which will be referred to fully hereafter.

Babcock's carriage came for him while we were talking, and he asked me to ride over to the greenhouses with him, which I did. I selected, by his permission, a number of rare and valuable plants, which he had shipped to my wife at my country seat, Sunny Side, Wisconsin. He then drove me to my hotel, and after parting with him, I sent the appended dispatch:

WASHINGTON, Dec. 7th, 1874.

Col. JNO. A. JOYCE, St. Louis:

Had long ride with the President this afternoon. B. and H. are here. You will hear from me to-morrow.

(Signed)   JOHN.

On the next day I called to see Commissioner Douglass, and told him not to send anyone into my district, for a visit now would injure us very much. I also saw and talked with Babcock, H. C. Rogers, deputy commissioner, and Avery. I very plainly told Rogers that I thought he, Brooks, and Hogue were in collusion to blackmail St. Louis distillers, and that if he sent revenue agents into my district I should report him at the White House. The result was that they promised me no agents should go to St. Louis, and assured me there were no grounds for suspicion. Having received this assurance, which was very necessary, as at that time every distillery was running day and night turning out illicit whiskey, I sent the following dispatch:

WASHINGTON, Dec. 8th, 1874.

J. A. JOYCE, St. Louis:

Dead dog. The goose hangs altitudinal. The sun shines.

(Signed)   JOHN.

My fears of this blackmailing visit were caused by the following letter, which was handed to me by Col. Holt, who asked me to let Gen. Babcock read it:

NEW YORK, Nov. 21st, 1874.

To H. C. ROGERS, Deputy Commissioner, Washington:

MY DEAR SIR:—I am summoned to appear in cases in court in Philadelphia on Monday, the 23d. The cases will probably be disposed of on that day, so that I can be at Washington on Tuesday, I think. If possible, please have Hogue there at that time, and may I ask that any Western cases may be put in such a shape that we can take charge of them, and so make the trip profitable to the department and satisfactory to ourselves.

(Signed)   JAMES J. BROOKS, Special Agent.

I took this lettter to Commissioner Douglass and showed him how the scheme to rob us out West was developing; then I handed it to Babcock, and by him it was shown to the President. On the 10th I left for St. Louis, leaving everything in the hands of Babcock, instructing him to telegraph me in case he succeeded in preventing the coming of the revenue agents, or if Bristow persisted in sending them. Immediately upon my arrival home the following dispatch was sent by Babcock (a facsimile of which is given):

WASHINGTON, Dec. 13th, 1874.

Gen. JOHN McDONALD, Supervisor, St. Louis:

I succeeded. They will not go. Will write you.

(Signed)   SYLPH.

A great deal of speculation has been indulged in by the public concerning the signature "Sylph." The explanation is very important, and even at this day will, doubtless, be read with much interest.

On Wednesday evening, during the visit of Gen. Babcock to the St. Louis Fair, he and Col. Joyce were walking down Fifth street, on their way to my office from the Lindell Hotel. When they

278 – 9, 5 And

Washington D.C.

Gen John A McDonald
At Louis Mo   I succeeded they

will not go I will write your   [signature]

Oct 6 3 —

were between Olive and Pine streets, Gen. Babcock
observed a beautiful young lady approaching them,
and was most agreeably surprised to see Col. Joyce
tip his hat to her in graceful recognition. It is true
that the General was popularly appreciative, because she was unquestionably the handsomest
woman in St. Louis. Her form was petite, and yet
withal, a plumpness and development which made
her a being whose tempting, luscious deliciousness
was irresistible. Most beautiful of face, with eyes
of deepest azure, in whose depths the sun-beams
seemed to gather, and the fires of love from flames
of flickering constancy, seemed ever and anon to
melt into love itself. Her hair was like threads of
gold and silver blended, and when she loosed her
locks they fell like the shimmer of sunlight, and
quivered like the glamor the moon throws on
the water. She was the essence of grace, distilled
from the buds of perfection, and with a tongue on
which the oil of vivacity and seduction never ceased
running; she was, indeed, a sylph and syren,
whose presence was like the flavor of the poppy
mingled with the perfumes of Araby.

After passing the "Sylph," Gen. Babcock, with
enraptured eyes and anxious breath, impatiently
enquired of Col. Joyce who the exquisite beauty
was, remarking at the same time: " She is the most
bewitching and beautiful creature I ever saw; for
heaven's sake, let us turn the corner and meet her
again, so that you can give me an introduction."

Col. Joyce has an almost national reputation for
his bric-a-brac quotations, and an apt and elegant
passage from some popular poet or orator is always

waiting to slip from his tongue. Upon this occasion he could not restrain his nature, and with an illumination on his countenance, as a preface to his reply, he repeated a poem, written by a pastoral Kentucky poet, the first lines of which are as follows:

Her Sylph-like form, her beauty and her grace,
She floats like a seraph on the light wings of space," etc.

The General was very much pleased with the rythmical recitation, but his impatience grew more intense.

The Colonel, to relieve his companion's anxiety, answered him by saying: "My dear General, keep strictly cool; it would not be the proper thing to meet the lady again and introduce you on the street, but if you will excuse me a short while I will see her and arrange an appointment by which you can greet the Sylph within the next hour or two." With this, having secured the approval of the General, Col. Joyce turned and followed the woman while Babcock continued on to my office.

Directly after dark, Col. Joyce and the "Sylph" stepped into Freund's restaurant, on the corner of Fifth and Pine streets, immediately under my office, and called for a bottle of wine and while drinking and chatting, according to an understanding conveyed to Gen. Babcock, the anxious Private Secretary dropped in and was warmly greeted by Col. Joyce, who, with an *eclat* for which the Colonel was distinguished, arose from his chair and bowing gracefully, said: "Miss Hawkins, this is my particular friend, Gen. Babcock, from Washington. Sit down, General, and have some wine with us." Then there was a cheerful flow of conversation for

SYLPH.

some time until a ripe acquaintance was established after which, by invitation of Col. Joyce, who had a key to my office and also to my private rooms, the party went up stairs and shortly afterwards the Colonel returned to the street, leaving the General and his luscious companion together in my rooms. I met Col. Joyce on the sidewalk as he descended from the stairs and, as I knew nothing of the General's present occupation, I was easily persuaded to take a bottle of wine with the Colonel at Gregory's, and thus I was unconsciously prevented from intruding upon the devotions of two loving souls.

The full name of this woman, who after this meeting Gen. Babcock ever afterwards called his "Sylph," was Louise Hawkins, familiarly called Lu. She was born in St. Louis, but her father dying, leaving her mother in very poor circumstances, the family moved to a small town on the Illinois Central Railroad, in Southern Illinois. When Lu. was fourteen years of age she fell in love with a young fellow who accomplished her ruin, which being discovered by her mother, Lu. left home and went to St. Louis, where she found employment with Wm. Barr & Co., as a seamstress. Her extraordinary beauty would not permit her to long remain in such a menial position, and from a seamstress, clothed in the garbs of humble circumstances, she soon developed into a lady of leisure, clad in the purple of fine linen and decked with jewels rare and beautiful. She is still a resident of St. Louis, and though unmarried, yet her every want is promptly administered to by a wealthy gentleman of the city in whose elegant residence near Grand Avenue, she is queen.

This is the origin of the signature attached to some of Babcock's and Joyce's confidential telegrams, and the explanation here given will explode many conjectures made by astute correspondents.

Shortly after my return to St. Louis, in December 1874, I told Col. Joyce that it would be well to make another small contribution to the President and Gen. Babcock. To do this we procured a box of the finest cigars we could find and enclosed in the box with the cigars a $1,000 bill, which we sent by express addressed to Gen. Babcock. In due time, Col. Joyce received a letter from Babcock acknowledging receipt of the cigars with enclosure, to which was added a few lines to the effect that " we," referring to Grant and himself, " enjoyed the excellent flavor of those cigars."

CHAPTER V.

On the 26th of January, 1875, Mr. Bristow, who had circulated suspicions that the Government was being defrauded out of the revenue on whiskey manufactured in several large cities in the country, decided to inaugurate an investigation by ordering a change of supervisors, so that frauds would undoubtedly appear, because of the lack of understanding between the distillers and the new officials; or, if there were any honest supervisors, they would readily detect the manner in which the frauds were being perpetrated. Let me remark, however, that every one engaged in the illicit whiskey frauds, knew that Bristow's investigation meant something; that he was exceedingly anxious to ferret out the guilty parties and bring them to punishment; hence, every act of his was watched with painful interest, and we were compelled to use the full influence of the President to keep Bristow from enforcing orders which would be certain to expose the Ring and every member of it.

When this order for a change of supervisors was issued (to take effect Feb, 15th), by which I should have been transferred to Philadelphia, I realized the necessity of having it countermanded at once, to accomplish which, I sent the following dispatch:

St. Louis, Feb. 3d, 1875.

Hon. J. W. Douglass, Internal Revenue Office, Washington:

Don't like the order; it will damage the Government and injure the administration. Will explain when I see you.

John McDonald.

On the day after I transmitted this telegram, I sent Col. Joyce to Washington to influence the countermanding of the order, but before his departure I was gratified by the receipt of the following telegram:

Washington, Feb. 4th, 1875.

Gen. Jno. McDonald, St. Louis:

The order transferring you to Philadelphia is suspended until further orders.

(Signed)   J. W. Douglass, Commissioner.

Immediately after receiving this, the following dispatch was repeated to me over the wires, which showed me at once the cause for the unexpected telegram from the Commissioner:

Executive Mansion, Washington, Feb. 4th, 1875.

J. W. Douglass, Internal Revenue Office.

Sir:—The President directs me to say that he desires that the circular order, transferring Supervisors of Internal Revenue, be suspended, by telegraph, until further orders.

(Signed)   Levi P. Luckey.

(Note.—Luckey was Assistant Secretary to the President.)

Upon receipt of this Col. Joyce, before departing, sent the following dispatch:

St. Louis, Feb. 4th, 1875.

To Gen. O. E. Babcock, Washington :

We have official information that the enemy weakens. Push things.

(Signed)   Sylph.

Col. Joyce then left for Washington for the purpose of seeing the President, and our friends there, with relation to the order.   The President suspended the order that we might have the necessary time to straighten our crooked affairs, but concluded, at that time, to permit the transfer order to go into effect when we should inform him that affairs would permit it without exposure.   But we had all things in such excellent working condition in St. Louis that I was anxious to avoid a change.   It was with this understanding Col. Joyce started for Washington and, while en-route, the train on which he was a passenger met with some delays, creating some anxiety, which was explained by the following dispatch:

Gen. Jno. McDonald, St. Louis :

Six hours late.   Watch Tweed's crowd.   Work wires with B.

(Signed)   Carney.

Tweed's crowd referred to Bristow's actions, and working the wires with B, meant for me to keep myself posted by wire through Babcock.

After his arrival in Washington, Col. Joyce went direct to the President and to Gen. Babcock, and to them explained the situation and the views I entertained, as here indicated.   After receiving their assurances that all our wishes should be respected, even at the expense of Bristow's serious displeasure, Col. Joyce sent me the following dispatch:

WASHINGTON, Feb. 6th, 1875.

GEN. JNO. McDONALD, St. Louis:

Order busted forever. D. and Company mad. Hold things level.

(Signed) CARNEY.

The signature of "Carney," was used here with an understanding. Col. Joyce was frequently called "Carney" by his intimate friends, who had given him the name on account of a song he very frequently sang, entitled "Mrs. Carney."

D. and Co., used in the despatch, referred to Douglass and Bristow. The anomalous position occupied by Mr. Douglass, as a member and enemy of the Ring, will be explained hereafter.

Col. Joyce remained in Washington a few days in order to discover the drift of Bristow's contemplated action; but being assured that nothing further would be done, he wrote me the following letter:

EBBITT HOUSE, WASHINGTON, D. C., Feb'y 8th, 1875.

DEAR GENERAL:

I have seen and talked to Douglass and Rogers, and, while they are all smiles to my face, there is surely an undercurrent of vengeance that is unexplainable to me. I can assure you that the late order transferring Supervisors was gotten up and promulgated for the main purpose of striking the St. Louis district. The President ordered the order revoked, and you can bet that the Commissioner (Douglass) and Secretary (Bristow) owe no love to you or Munn (the Supervisor at Chicago).

I am not, at this late day, going to put myself in the hands of Rogers or Douglass. They now speak of transferring Hedrick, (who is here), into your district, and if that fails, which it will, they will possibly send Fulton, Sewell, or Brooks and Hogue into our district.

The Commissioner has poisoned the Secretary (Bristow) and they have both tried to poison Grant, but he wont drive in their wagon worth a d—n. It is a h—l of a lick on Douglass to revoke the order.

I was up at Gen. Babcock's last night and had a long chat. He has seen Bristow and the Secretary talks fair, but we can not trust those who are not with us.

Hold things level for the present. The storm may blow over entirely. Anyhow we have to beat it. Watch the St. Louis crowd. Yours,

JOHN.

His anxiety to have me watch the St. Louis crowd meant to see to it that there was no illicit whiskey made until the effort at an investigation had entirely subsided.

The next dispatch was received in the afternoon two days later, and was as follows:

WASHINGTON, Feb'y 10th, 1875.

Gen. JOHN McDONALD, St. Louis:

Start home to-night. Things look lovely. Watch and wait.

(Signed) JOHN.

Some time in February, I think, in 1875, Hogue, the revenue agent, made another trip to St. Louis, and after making some investigations, found considerable crookedness; to suppress the report which he threatened to make, the distillers hastily contributed to him the sum of $10,000. This visit was made without the knowledge or authority of any of the Washington officials, but was conceived for the sole purpose of blackmail. In the testimony of Alfred Bevis, a distiller, given in the trial of W. O.

Avery, he stated that the money was given Hogue chiefly "because he was a good fellow," but the purpose is too transparent.

Notwithstanding the favorable turn affairs had taken at Washington, yet there was a feeling of great dread, because I was sure that Bristow was determined to push his investigation by some adroit means.

In the early part of March I ascertained that Geo. W. Fishback, formerly proprietor of the *Missouri Democrat*, was in Washington, and my suspicions were aroused that his visit was in the capacity of an informer. My reasons for entertaining such an idea were based upon a circumstance which transpired some time previously, to which I must direct the reader's attention. It was pretty generally known in St. Louis that just prior to the absorption of the *Democrat* by the *Globe*, the proprietors of the former were often in sore straits for the necessary money to continue the publication of the paper. In one of these impecunious moments Mr. Fishback came to my room at the Planters House, and, after a little preliminary conversation, introduced the object of his visit. He explained to me the financial embarrassment from which his paper suffered and urged me to loan him the sum of $5,000 for ninety days, in consideration of which he proffered me the support of the *Democrat*. In his pleadings he remarked that he could not see why I should refuse him the use of a few thousand dollars of the Government's money.

My reply to him was that I was not a bonded officer; that I did not handle a dollar of the Government's money as my duties were entirely supervisory. Finding all other resources failing him, he finally submitted to me an editorial article highly commendatory of my official acts as Supervisor, and exalting my influence as a Republican, and told me that if I would let him have the money he would print the article in the editorial columns of the *Democrat* on the following day. But to all his entreaties I turned him a deaf ear, not regarding the influence of his paper as at all consequential. From that time Mr. Fishback became an active and insiduous enemy of mine, and through intimate social relations he held with one of the distillers, he obtained some information concerning the conduct of the Ring.

With this explanation my anxiety to learn the object of his visit to Washington at this particular time is obvious. I therefore wrote to Gen. Babcock, telling him of my fears and asking him to casually meet Fishback and learn what he was doing. In reply to this enquiry I received the following despatch:

WASHINGTON, March 12, 1875.

To GEN. JOHN McDONALD.

Letter received. Have seen the gentleman and he seems very friendly. He is here looking after the improvement of the rivers. (Signed) O. E. BABCOCK.

For a short while I was satisfied, but when I begun considering the information Fishback was in possession of I felt certain that the distiller from whom he had learned so much had not neglected to tell him also that Babcock was a member of the Ring. Then the fact dawned upon me that Fishback's appearance of friendship and his assertion that he was looking after river improvements was only used to deceive Babcock as to his real purposes. My suspicions were then resting upon important facts as was afterwards proven. Mr. Fishback became a strong supporter of Bristow and gave him all the information in his possession, besides which, he suggested to the Secretary a means for verifying his statements, by appointing a man who had been a commercial reporter of the *Democrat*, as special agent, to examine the receipts and shipments of grain and whiskey reported at St. Louis for the past several years.

We had been running the distilleries crooked from the time Col. Joyce returned from Washington until some time in March, when the pacific condition of our affairs was suddenly interrupted by the appearance of revenue agent Yaryan, whose ostensible purpose was the investigation of railroad back taxes. But he was suspected and the distilleries shut down at once, while Yaryan, to carry his deception further, left St. Louis for Richmond, Ind., but returned after an absence of only a few days. During Yaryan's absence Holmes, a clerk in the Fraud Division of the Internal Revenue Bureau, came to St. Louis, explaining his visit as connected with the Knights Templar business. But his story was not believed and a sharp watch was kept upon his movements, and I soon learned that he was here as an aid to Yaryan to make an investigation.

Following is a letter I received while absent from St. Louis on on a short visit to my home in Wisconsin:

St. Louis, Mo., June 27, 1875.

Dear General:

Major Grimes has a very important letter for you; he does not like to trust it to the mails. What shall he do with it? I think it can be safely sent to your address. Please answer.

Truly yours,

A. Gunther.

I have inserted this letter here merely as additional proof of the secret correspondence between Babcock and myself. Maj. Gunther was a revenue agent under me and was acquainted with the facts concerning my relation with Babcock.

CHAPTER VI.

The visit of Yaryan in March and April, 1875, was
the first effective step taken to lay bare the frauds of
the Whiskey Ring. Yaryan had already (during his
first visit to St. Louis, in company with Brasher and
Gavitt,) discovered enough fraud to have exposed
the illicit combination, but it is perhaps doubtful
whether he could have secured a conviction of any
of the members save, posibly, two or three distillers,
upon the evidence he had then collected. But the
circle in which the organization was now uneasily
operating grew constantly smaller.

B

On the 17th of April I received a dispatch from
Commissioner Douglass ordering me to confer with
Supervisor Parker, of the adjoining district, with
reference to the seizure of some whiskey in Colorado.

In obedience to this order I sent Colonel Joyce
to Kansas City where Parker had reported, and the
result of his investigations is given in the following
letter:

St. Joseph, Mo., April 20th, 1875.

Dear General:

I spent yesterday at Kansas City conferring with Collector Parker, Gauger Hedrick and Revenue Agent Brown, in
regard to spirits seized in Colorado. Collector Parker has
seized some 250 packages in all, coming from Leavenworth,
St. Joseph, Kansas City and St. Louis; the most of it for
lack of brands. But the worst thing he says he has, is
some 14 barrels that came from the rectifying house of B. A.
Feinaman, in Kansas City, that are duplicated, that is, the
serial numbers of the tax paid stamps, as coming from Shin's
distillery, appear indented on the bung-staves and heads of
the rectified packages sent out by old Feinaman. This looks
serious for Feinaman, and possibly Shin, and how it can be explained away I cannot well see.

*   *   *   *   *   *   *   *   *   *   *

It seems that your district is now made the but-end of all
the investigations going on.

The war has begun and there is no telling where it will end.
You must consult with our friends in Washington.

*   *   *   *   *   *   *   *   *   *   *

I will go back to St. Louis to-morrow.

Yours,

John A. Joyce

Before receiving this letter, however, my serious
alarms were excited that some treachery was being
practiced, and to discover the source I determined

to go to Washington and confer with the President.
Accordingly, on the evening of the 19th, I left St.
Louis for the Capital. Upon my arrival there, on
the morning of the 21st, I found that the President,
Gen. Babcock and Secretary Belknap, were in
Boston attending the Jubilee. I stopped at the
Arlington House, where I met Senator Dorsey of
Arkansas, and to him I told my story of the manner
in which Secretary Bristow was interfering with my
affairs. The Senator advised me to join him in a
determined effort to influence the President to dismiss Bristow, a suggestion which, if I had acted
upon, would have undoubtedly prevented any exposure of the Ring; but, without disclosing to him the
methods I had intended to pursue, I left him and
called at the Treasury Department, where I formally
met Secretary Bristow, addressing him with only a
single inquiry, viz: "Did you send Mr. Holmes
into my district?" His reply was: "If my memory serves me right, I did. I left him without conversing any further, and went over to the Internal
Revenue Bureau where I met Commissioner Douglass, and with him I held an interview in which I
sought to learn who was responsible for the appearance of revenue agents in my district. Taking a
seat beside his desk I asked him what Holmes and
Yaryan were doing in my district without my being
first informed of their coming?

He replied: " Why, they are not in your district;
Mr. Holmes is now in the department."

I informed him of his mistake, but to be convinced, he sent a messenger to Holmes' room, and
there learned that he had been granted a leave of

absence for a few days by Secretary Bristow. This confused the Commissioner, especially after I told him that the Secretary had informed me, only a few moments before, that he had sent Holmes into my district.

The Commissioner arose in a somewhat excited manner, and remarked that he would see the Secretary and learn why he had not been consulted in this matter. He went over to see Secretary Bristow, while I awaited his return. He was absent about half an hour, and when he came back I saw a marked change in his appearence. He seemed loth to announce the result of his visit to the Secretary, and when I enquired of him what had passed between them, he said: "Well, General, the fact is, I cannot tell you just now; but will explain everything before you leave Washington. But I can assure you that no damage to you will result from the investigation." I then left the commissioner, and spent the remainder of the day at the Washington Club House, playing billiards, and talking to officials.

On the following morning, as I entered the dining hall of the Arlington House, I was somewhat surprised to see there some St. Louis friends and Senator Dorsey, whom I greeted, and then I noticed Secretary Bristow seated at a table across the room, and when he caught my gaze, he motioned to me to come over to his table. When I approached him, he insisted upon me taking a seat at his table, which I did, when the following conversation occurred:

Said he: "How are you getting on with revenue matters in your district?"

I replied that I was collecting all the revenue—and this was true at that time, for all the distilleries were running straight then.

He pressed the query further, by adding: "How long have you been collecting all the revenue in your district?"

I answered: Ever since the arrival of the officers you last sent into my district; but, said I, I presume you get daily reports from those agents (referring to Yaryan and Holmes), now at St. Louis, and know fully as much as I do.

"Yes," he replied, "I get reports from out there, and have collected considerable evidence."

I enquired of him the nature of his evidence, but he responded by saying: "Well, I can't exactly tell you that, but I have got a barrel of it (at the same time spreading his arms, and bringing his fingers together in a gesture, showing it was so large round), but as yet it implicates only the distillers and dealers."

Then I enquired if he was after the officers, too.

"Oh, no," he replied, "I am only trying to collect the revenue. I have been aware of the fact, that for a great while, the revenue has not been collected;" and added: "What portion of the revenue has been collected in your section of the country?"

I answered that in my opinion, about two-thirds.

He then asked me if I didn't think it could all be collected.

I told him it might be under certain circumstances; he then desired to know what circumstances were essential.

Ex-Sec'y Bristow.

I answered him by saying that the first thing necessary would be an entire change of officers, and an increase of officers as the labor was too great for the number then employed.

He further consulted my opinion respecting my belief in the ability of the same number of officers to collect the revenue, provided the officers were honest.

To this I made answer that if the officers would renounce politics and could secure honest subordinates it might be possible, but, I added, as the service is now organized I think it extremely doubtful if you can increase the collections.

Then he enquired why I had come to such a conclusion, explaining the cause for addressing me such inquiries by saying he was seeking information that would assist him in applying such methods as would result in a thorough collection of the revenue.

My reply was, that the subordinate officers generally had been permitted to grant the distillers and rectiffers privileges which the law did not warrant in order that money might be raised, ostensibly, for political purposes; that by the operation of this vice the local officers had become, in a measure, subordinated to the distillers' and rectifiers' interests to the great detriment of the public service, and that the same influence permeated the entire service from the outlet to the fountain head. I concluded my answer by telling him that I would confess my inability to correct all these evils, which would involve a thorough reformation, and that if he had concluded to inaugurate a system which would strike all the troubles and taints of the service, then I should tender my resignation.

His next enquiry was: "Have you come to Washington with the intention of resigning?"

I replied that I had not, but said I, I have canvassed the situation in my own mind since my arrival here and concluded to have a talk with the President and Gen. Babcock, and, if they do not change my mind I shall resign, as I do not wish to fight a buzz-saw in this matter.

He asked me what I meant by the use of such an expression.

My answer was, that he was my superior officer and had authority to send men into my district to make investigations whenever he should choose, and that I could not retain my self-respect and permit that to be done, without their coming with instructions to report to me; that I was a friend of the President and of Gen. Babcock and that whatever I had done in my district was in good faith.

He assured me that he was not fighting the President's friends but was only seeking to collect the revenue.

I told him that all the officers in my district were the President's friends and that if he persisted in secretly sending revenue agents out there to make investigations it would be certain to precipitate a fight between the President and the Treasury department.

He replied to this by saying that he had not anticipated such a result, but said he: "If I should make a change of officers, or declare my policy to enforce the law in the spirit and letter, do you believe they they would tender their resignations as you propose to do?"

I expressed my belief in the affirmative.

He then asked me to ascertain the feeling of the officers with regard to the idea he had expressed, and, upon my return to St. Louis, to report to him. He assured me that he intended to collect the revenue at all hazards, and said it would be much more gratifying to him to have the officers resign than to be compelled to remove them.

He was anxious to learn if the Government officers at St. Louis could be relied upon to prosecute parties guilty of violations of the revenue laws.

I replied that they could, but I doubted the expediency of the Government bringing suits against the distillers and rectifiers for two reasons, which I explained as follows: These men, said I, have been led to believe that the money they have paid upon the whiskey they have illicitly manufactured was used for political purposes, and that their operations have been sanctioned, not only by the district officers, but also by that power which recognizes no superior; that prosecutions would result in closing the distilleries and thereby entirely close that source of revenue. The second reason I assigned was its inexpediency because of the injury it would entail upon the Republican party by arraying against it the most efficient workers within the ranks.

He told me that, while he was anxious to preserve and secure the further success of the Republican party, that he made his duties as an officer of the nation paramount to his allegiance to party, and that, regardless of political results, he would collect the revenue.

I admired the sentiments of the Secretary, as I told him, but I also expressed to him my grave doubts of his ability to withstand a fight which his contemplated actions invited, and assured him that his first efforts would arouse a political spirit like an avenging Nemesis, and that his opposition would come from a higher power than perhaps he had considered, and, united with that, would be the consolidated influence of office-holders and politicians. I did not forget to add in this connection, that I had already been approached by a prominent Senator, who requested my aid in uniting in an appeal to the President, to be signed by a number of prominent officials, asking for his (Bristow's) removal. But, I added, it is not my wish to inaugurate a breach between yourself and the President, so I refused.

This last answer of mine somewhat confused him for, after a pause, which indicated a gathering of ideas, he asked me if I had seen the President since my arrival in Washington.

I replied that I had not, but that I was waiting his return from Boston, and was anxious to see him.

Then, with some anxiety pictured in his face, he inquired if I intended talking with the President upon this matter in the same direct and pointed manner I had spoken with him (the Secretary).

Said I: General, I shall talk to the President not only as plainly as I have talked with you but I shall be much less reserved in my conversation with him.

He then asked me if, after my intended interview with the President, I would return to him and report the substance and result of the conversation.

My reply was that I would repeat to him so much of the interview as would be agreeable to the President, but that, as the matter would be canvassed between us in a confidential manner, I could not betray any trusts.

The Secretary remarked that he was aware that I occupied a more intimate and influential relation with the President than any other person in the West.

This closed our conversation, which had lasted about two hours. When I went out into the hotel office, I learned that the President and Gen. Babcock had returned from Boston; so I went directly to the White House, where I was fortunate, upon entering the Executive room, to find the President alone. I drew a chair up near him, and after passing a very few words of general remark, I proceeded directly to disclose the object of my visit.

I first explained to him that my district was being visited by revenue agents without my knowledge; that there was a veil of secrecy over the actions of the Secretary in matters wherein I was deeply interested, and in which I should be consulted, and that this secrecy also prevented the Commissioner of Internal Revenue from giving me instructions, so that there was a rapidly widening breach in the revenue service; that if the policy outlined by Secretary Bristow should be pursued, it would result in the destruction of the Republican party.

To this the President replied that he had talked with the Secretary concerning the collection of information by revenue agents, but that his idea was that the evidence thus gathered should not be used against the revenue officers, but only against the distillers and business men; that he had thought such action even a wise party act.

To this I replied, by assuring him that the officers were too intimately associated with the distillers and rectifiers to escape an exposed connection should prosecutions be begun; that these men had been the largest contributors to the campaign fund when the collections were applied to that purpose, but that for a long time past the money thus raised had gone into the pockets of individuals, as he well knew. In addition to this, I reminded him that if the prosecutions were based upon conclusive evidence, that the distillers and rectifiers would not alone suffer, but that the officers and *every one having guilty knowledge*, would be liable to the same punishment. I told him further, that these agents, in getting this evidence, would be certain, almost, to leak some of their information, which would run directly into the newspapers.

To this the President responded, that the papers were so full of scandals that, unless the proof were furnished, their reports would hardly be credited by the public. He told me that when the agents made their investigations, their reports could easily be controlled in the Department, and that they should be.

I argued with him that the safest plan would be to recall the agents, because, said I, if they get this evidence, it is certain, sooner or later, to obtain publicity. I also gave him my impressions concerning the intentions of Secretary Bristow, which were, that if unrestrained, the investigations would be most searching, and with a mountain of searing evidence, it could not be hidden from the public. I further told him that the Secretary had already assured me he had "a barrel" of information, sufficient to convict a large number of the distillers and rectifiers.

The President then said: "What disposition, in your judgment, should be made of this evidence?"

My reply was, that it ought to be shoved into a red-hot stove.

Said he: "Well, I hardly think it would be policy to burn it up;" but, said he, "don't you think it would be a good plan to have it all sealed up securely and placed in a vault where no one could get at it?"

I answered, that would subserve present necessities, but that it would be resurrected sometime, when there was a change of officers.

He then told me that he would prevent a further accumulation of the evidence, by having the agents re-called, and that he would confer with the Secretary as to the most desirable means for preventing any of the evidence from becoming public.

I responded by saying: "Well, General, if you have an understanding with the Secretary, you can control things."

He acknowledged that he had no understanding with the Secretary, but that, at all events, the evidence would be controlled.

I remarked: You and the Secretary ought to work together.

His response was: "Yes, we ought to; but if we don't, one of us will have to quit, and it will not be me."

I said: No, I don't presume it will be you, as your time is fixed by the public, and the Secretary's tenure depends upon individual pleasure.

He then asked me what effect Bristow's action would have in other districts, and upon the party.

I told him that, as he understood everything that had been going on in my district, it was only necessary for me to assure him that the same condition of affairs existed throughout the entire country and in every district; that if the matter were allowed to reach the public it could no more be stopped than the waves of the ocean before the wind; that it would expose the internal operations of the Republican party, the sources from whence its life was derived, and that the party would collapse like a balloon rent by lightning.

He manifested much anxiety, and was, indeed, sorely agitated. His response to my opinion was: "Well, it *must* be stopped."

Our conversation then drifted on to Bristow, in the course of which I repeated to the President everything that had occurred between the Secretary and myself at the breakfast table. I gave him my earnest opinion that Mr. Bristow had inaugurated a scheme for thoroughly exposing us, and that unless he was checked with much show of determination, such would be the result. I further told the President that the Secretary had requested me to call at his office upon my return from the White House and repeat to him the substance of the conference with the Executive, which I qualifiedly promised to do.

The President expressed his anxiety to have me do this, and to tell the Secretary to carefully guard the evidence he had, against the possibility of publicity until he (Grant) could confer with him (Bristow) as to its disposition.

I replied to him that I would go over and see the Secretary and report in the evening or following morning. I then arose to go, and, as I did so, made the remark that I had a package of money for Gen. Babcock, which I intended then to deliver.

"Yes," he replied, "Bab (as he almost always called Gen. Babcock), is in his office."

I walked into the private secretary's room but found it full of visitors, so that I did not speak to Gen. Babcock for a few moments. When I caught his attention I greeted him, and in a sotto-voice, informed him that I had a package for him.

He told me that, as he had just returned from Boston and was very busy, he could not talk with me then, but asked me to dine with him at 5 p. m.; that his family was out of the city and that he would be alone.

I then left the White House and started to the Treasury Department, but, on the plateau, between the White House and the Treasury, I met Secretary Bristow on his way to see the President. We stopped and entered into a conversation, in which I informed him that I had just left the President, having been engaged with him ever since leaving the breakfast table.

He asked me if I had talked freely with the President.

I told him that I had, and thereupon repeated to him nearly everything the President had told me, including his desire to have the evidence referred to carefully guarded until the President should confer with him. I did not forget to tell Mr. Bristow that I had told the President the best disposition to make of the evidence was to shove it into a red-hot stove, but that the President thought a better plan would be to seal it up securely and place it where there was no possibility of any one seeing it.

Mr. Bristow smiled, and remarked, that he had not secured the evidence for such a purpose, and then asked me to go over to his office and wait his return, as he desired to talk further with me.

I asked him if he would speak to the President about the matter before leaving the White House.

He replied that if opportunity was afforded he would.

I went over to the Secretary's office and waited there nearly an hour before Mr. Bristow returned. When he came in we held a general conversation in which we went over the same subject as in the morning and my conference with the President. I then asked him if he had consulted with the President with regard to the disposition of the evidence. He replied, that the subject had been mentioned. I then asked him if the President had suggested to him the destruction of the evidence, or sealing it up to prevent its publicity or use.

His reply was that the matter was talked about but no conclusion had been reached.

I enquired of him if he and the President had disagreed.

He said that the President's views were not exactly like his own, but thought they would be in accord in the course of a few days.

I became convinced that the Secretary was not talking to me without reserve, and that he was keeping his own decisions from me, so I begun making inquiries to ascertain what he proposed to do in my district; whether he intended making seizures, etc.

He told me that he thought he would seize the property of the distillers and rectifiers, against whom he had evicence.

I suggested to him a more advisable course in submitting a proposition that would compromise the trouble. I told him that I thought these men would pay up all the back taxes and settle with the government, which would prevent them from being broken up.

He told me that he had not thought of this, but that he should consult the best interest of the Government before taking any final action.

We here dropped the subject, but he requested me to call upon him frequently while in the city that we might talk further upon the matter. After assuring him that I would, we parted.

From the Secretary's office I called on Commissioner Douglass with whom I had some conversation, in the course of which I told him that, after considering the indignities of Mr. Bristow, I had concluded to resign.

He said he did not blame me for having such an intention and assured me that he had a strong inclination to do the same thing.

I did not remain long with the Commissioner, and went over to the Washington Club House, where I played billiards and talked with friends until 5 o'clock, p. m., when I went to Gen. Babcock's residence. I found Gen. Babcock and Gen. Horace Porter at the house, together, but in order to meet me privately Gen. B. invited me to go up stairs with him to see a newly fitted up room, and a bullfinch which he had recently purchased. (This bullfinch Gen. Babcock afterwards gave my wife, and from this circumstance he very frequently signed his confidential letters to me as " B. Finch " and " Bull Finch," as will be seen hereafter in his printed correspondence.)

When we were alone he offered me a chair and we sat down and had a lengthy conversation. But before we had talked long I drew a package containing $5,000. from my side pocket and gave it to him. This money had been collected by Col. Joyce before his departure for Kansas City and given to me for delivery to Gen. Babcock, as I was then expecting to visit Washington. He thanked me for the money, saying at the same time " well, it isn't much, but it is very acceptable at this time."

At this juncture the door bell rung and the servant came up stairs to tell the General that there was a gentleman at the door who wished to see him. He went down stairs, but after an absence of a few minutes he returned with a piece of paper in his hand, which he handed me with the remark,

C

"there, now, General, you see how our money goes." I looked at the paper and saw that it was a receipt for $500, signed by Krounce, the Washington correspondent of the New York *Times*. He then explained to me that the money was paid for the appearance of an article in the *Times* in relation to some change of officers in Boston, which this article was intended to prepare an excuse for

I told him that he ought not to grumble if he got value received.

He replied that he was not grumbling, but that the demands for money were so numerous that at times he was sorely puzzled to raise necessary funds.

We then conversed upon the subject matter I had discussed with Secretary Bristow and the President. I repeated to him my intention to resign and get out of the service.

He advised me to do so, saying at the same time, that if I would leave St. Louis and go to New York, that we could arrange schemes there to make a great deal more money than we had derived from the Whiskey Ring; that I would be worth a great deal more to them in New York, (meaning himself and the President) than I was in the West.

We talked perhaps half an hour when he took me into the front room and showed me the bull-finch, which sang until I was perfectly enraptured with it. He then told me that he had purchased the bird for my wife.

We went down stairs, and shortly afterwards dinner was announced. While dining, Secretary Belknap came in and, on invitation, sat down with us.

After dinner, Belknap and Porter left, and Gen. Babcock and I went into the billiard room and played billiards, and continued our conversation on the contemplated action of Secretary Bristow, until nearly midnight. He told me that there was going to be a change of Cabinet officers before the next campaign; that Spinner and Williams had resigned and Delano would go next. He also informed me that an effort was being made to dismiss Belknap, but he said that scheme would not work. He talked considerably about me going to New York, but did not say what special position he wanted me to occupy.

On the following day I breakfasted late, after which, I called to see Gen. Babcock. When I entered his room he handed me the following dispatch:

ST. LOUIS, April 23rd, 1875.

To O. E. BABCOCK, Washington.

Tell Mac to see Parker of Colorado, and telegraph to commissioner to crush out St. Louis enemies.

(Signed,) "GRIT."

This telegram was from Col. Joyce and its meaning was for me to form a combination and influence the President to dismiss Secretary Bristow and have the revenue agents recalled from St. Louis.

I told Gen. Babcock, after reading the telegram, that I was not going into any fight, but would resign.

He then again asked if I would not go to New York.

I told him that for a time I preferred to go home and take a rest, but would let him know after a season.

I left Gen. Babcock and went into the Executive room, where I met the President, with whom I had some further conversation on the Bristow investigation.

I asked him if he had conferred with the Secretary on the matter of advisable disposition of the evidence collected?

He replied that he had talked some to the Secretary about it, but not enough to settle the matter. He said that he was not yet fully convinced of Mr. Bristow's intentions, though said he, "the Secretary seems to be a little arbitrary, but there shall be no trouble."

Said I: General, you don't mean for me to infer that the Secretary is manifesting an open hostility to you?

"Oh no, no," replied the President: "Not that, but he merely shows a decided wish to have his own way, which will not be permitted; unless he changes present apparent inclinations."

Well, I remarked: I should like to get an idea of what I may expect, so as to be prepared for any policy."

The President spoke up quickly, saying: "If any new phase develops important for you to know, I will write you at once."

I interposed an immediate objection, telling him that he must not think of writing, as my correspondence was liable any time to fall into the hands of detectives, reminding him that already two or three important letters addressed to me, had been intercepted and stolen.

After a few moments further conversation, I told

the President that I had made up my mind, after considering the matter fully, to tender my resignation.

His reply was: "Oh, no, don't do that, I assure you that no trouble growing out of this matter will affect you, and besides, I don't know who could fill your position out there, taking care of the newspapers, etc."

I replied to him that I would again consult with the Secretary and Commissioner, after which I would let him know definitely what I proposed to do.

I then called on Secretary Bristow and had another lengthy interview with him, in the course of which, I repeated to him the President's language just used to me, and further stated that unless I could be of some special service to the Government in settling the difficulties in the West, that I should resign.

The Secretary told me that he did not know of any special service I could render, unless it would be by a conference with the other officers in my district respecting their resignations.

I told him that I would confer with them, and that I felt certain they would all tender their resignations.

I then called on Commissioner Douglass, to whom I announced my determination to resign.

He expressed his regrets, saying that our official relations had been very pleasant, but that he thought I had adopted the proper course; that the Secretary had taken matters so exclusively into his own hands, that he thought he (Douglass) would resign in a few days, also.

From the Commissioner's office I returned to the hotel, when I found the following dispatch from Col. Joyce:

St. Louis, April 23rd, 1875.

To Gen. McDonald, Washington:

Don't leave Washington until everything is absolutely settled.

(Signed,) "John."

To this I sent the following reply:

Washington, April 23d, 1875.

Jno. A. Joyce, St. Louis,

I leave for St. Louis to-night.

(Signed,) Jno. McDonald.

After sending this dispatch I went to the Club house where I drafted my resignation, and then went directly to the White House. I showed the draft to Gen. Babcock, and he had a copy of it made by one of his clerks.

Following is a copy:

Washington, D. C., April 23d, 1875.

To His Excellency, the President:

Dear Sir.—I have the honor, for personal reasons, to herewith tender you my resignation of the position of Supervisor of Internal Revenue, which I have held for nearly six years, the resignation to take effect at your pleasure.

In submitting my resignation, I desire to express to you my heartfelt gratitude for the many kindnesses received at your hands during an acquaintance of over twenty years, during much of which time it has been my good fortune to have served under you in the civil and military service.

I am unable to express on paper the depth of my appreciation of those kindnesses, but will ask your attention to my *future* loyalty, both to you *personally* and to our government. for a full expression of all I owe to both.

I am, Mr. President, your obedient servant,

John McDonald.

Gen. Babcock, after reading the letter, compli-
mented it and said that he did not believe the President would accept it, but hoped that he would so
that I could go to New York.

I took the letter over to the Secretary and showed
it to him.

He pronounced it a fine letter, and said that while
he had hardly expected me to take such a step yet
he thought it a proper one.

I sat and conversed with him quite a time, repeat-
ing much that had previously passed between us.
I told him that my impression was he was getting
into deep water, but that I proposed to step aside
and let him sail his own boat. Another remark I
made was in declaring that while I was in politics
I always made everything subservient to party, and
that all my efforts had been centralized in making
the Republican party a success.

His reply was that that was an element in
the party which was doing it a great injury;
that an honest collection of the revenue and a
thorough discharge of official duties would do
much more towards perpetuating the party than
a distribution of money obtained by corrupt prac-
tices.

Yes, said I, my ideas are so different from those
of others in the party that it is better for me to get
out; that I would tender my resignation and return
to St. Louis that night.

He asked me if I could not arrange to stay over
until Monday; that he was going to New York
that evening, but would be back Saturday night
and he would like to talk further with me; that

he might obtain from me some further suggestions which would aid him in perfecting the revenue service.

I replied that I had already telegraphed that I
would leave Washington that night, and it would be
impossible for me to remain there any longer; but
that I would endeavor to see him again before he
started away.

I left the Secretary and again went to the Club
House where I remained until about four o'clock,
when I returned to the White House. As I entered
the front door I met the President and Mrs. Grant
coming out to take a ride, the team which I had
given the President being in waiting for them.

I addressed the President telling him that I had
my resignation with me which I wished to give him.

He replied, "well, I am just going out riding;
can't you come in to-morrow?"

I told him that I intended leaving Washington
that night and that I would like for him to receive
my resignation then.

"Well," said he, "if that is so, why, you can
hand it to me."

I gave him the letter and he stepped aside to read
it. Mrs. Grant and I then entered into a short
conversation in which she assured me that the team
I had given the President had afforded them more
pleasure than anything they had ever possessed;
that the President had purchased a great many
horses but he had never before been able to get a
team that suited them. She thanked me repeatedly
for the gift and declared that nothing could have
pleased them so much.

When the President had examined the letter a few moments he turned to me and with a significant smile on his face he remarked, as he placed it in the inside pocket of his coat; "I'll take care of this," leaving the inference that he would not accept my resignation unless it became necessary, a circumstance he did not anticipate.

When the President and his wife drove off, I went up stairs to see Gen. Babcock; I waited until he finished some writing, and then, at his invitation, I accompanied him to his residence, and took dinner with him. After dining, we played billiards until nearly train time, when I returned to the Arlington House where I met Secretary Bristow, as he was getting into a cab to go to the depot. He asked me to write to him upon my return to St. Louis, but the time was too limited for us to have any special conversation. Soon afterwards I took the train for St. Louis, since which time I have never seen Mr. Bristow.

AN OPEN LETTER TO EX-SECRETARY B. H. BRISTOW.

DEAR SIR: When I made up my mind to expose the great Whiskey frauds which culminated so disastrously to many in 1875, I determined to deal with facts in an impartial and fearless manner. You know enough of my nature to know that I am no sycophant, and that nothing could induce me to lower my head to any man. It has been necessary for me to use your name in this history of the official corruption whose conception occurred in the mash tub; but I have sought to secure neither your praise nor your enmity, relying entirely upon my own manhood and the vindication of my own conscience. As officers of the Government we occupied diverse

relations, and the devotion to your trusts has resulted in my
bitter humiliation and loss of fortune. But animosity assumes
no character in this drama; it is a play in which the parts are
all taken by men whose records is the piece for their acting.

When you met me in Washington City, in April, 1875, you
were anxious to see me, but no more so than I was to consult
with you. There was a Damocletian sword suspended over
some one's head, but who was beneath its gleaming point we
knew not. I felt secure in my position, but you felt justified
in yours, and my spirit of boldness was born of assurances
which, perhaps, you had anticipated. I have not changed my
attitude and make it apparent here, because you would not
recognize me in any other garb now, when I came to you for
the purpose of reviving the memories of that fight, in which
many suffered for their guilt, whilst other covered their grosser
sins with ermine of official power; while you, even as a plaintiff, was compelled to see your escutcheon stained by the
hands of your superior, in order to destroy your purpose to
grapple Fraud at the fountain head.

You, of all others, best know the spirit which sealed my
lips, and know how I realized that, in the silence of my voice,
I could hear the sentence of my punishment. Then how well
you can appreciate that the cry of those who were clothed
with a stronger power, though whose guilt made them mortals
none the less, has drowned the weak utterances of myself,
calling the Nation to look upon the crimes of those who commissioned me. Are there none to believe McDonald because
he went to prison, in order that his superior in crime and
power might not be forced to a cell of infamy, by which the
very face of America's Republic would be seared with the
tears of disgrace? It may be so, for it has been so before;
therefore I call upon you, in the name of that fragmentary portion of the people whose conception of crime is that it may be
perpetrated by the greatest of men, and especially in response
to that patriotic demand, that the guilt of every man, however
high in power, who shared the benefits of the illicit whiskey

frauds, be made public, and over your signature speak whether I have reported you aright. Not alone this, but I here declare that after your conversation with the President and myself, on the 22d day of April, 1875, you became convinced that the President was cognizant of the revenue frauds being perpetrated in my district, and that subsequent facts confirmed your opinion that President Grant was a silent member of the Whiskey Ring; that he used his influence to prevent disclosures, and to defeat the prosecutions of members of that ring; that in all his acts, he impeded your efforts to convict Babcock, Avery, McKee, Joyce and myself; that he endeavored to have you suppress and destroy evidence, and in all matters connected with a prosecution of the whiskey cases in 1875 he was your enemy, because of your efforts to secure convictions.

Have I perverted your language to secure a more favorable showing for myself?   Did I try to prejudice you against President Grant by reporting to you language as emanating from the President which subsequent interviews convinced you he did not use; and, lastly, have you ever discovered that anything I ever did, was intended to deceive you as to President Grant's wishes or intentions?

By replying with frankness to this letter, unsparing of the feelings of all concerned, with no other purpose than to tell the whole truth, you will confer an absolute blessing upon the American people, and will receive the especial gratitude of

Yours Truly,

JOHN MCDONALD.

Immediately upon my return from Washington I held a conference with all the U. S. Revenue officers in St. Louis with relation to their resignations. Col. Joyce tendered his resignation about the 27th, and Collector Maguire adopted the same course in a day or two after. I went directly to Wm. McKee, who was still publishing the *Globe*, on Third near Pine street, and explained the situation to

him thoroughly.   He manifested the greatest
alarm, and begged me to see him daily and report
the actions of the Government.   I was then in
almost daily correspondence with Gen. Babcock,
and upon receipt of his letters, I would take them
down to the *Globe* office, where I usually found
Mr. McKee and Collector Maguire, and together
we would read them.

The draw-strings of the Government kept squeez-
the Ring tighter, and we began seriously to reflect
upon the probability of our own punishment.   In
my correspondence with Gen. Babcock I did not
neglect to acquaint him with our fears, and ask
his interposition to prevent a collapse that would
entail disaster.

Following is one of Gen. Babcock's letters to
me in reply to expressions of my anxiety conveyed
in my correspondence with him: [A fac-simile of
which is given herewith.]

DEAR FRIEND:

Keep steady on.   Do not lose your grit.   Some of the gaugers and distillers want to squeal, and have, by such action,
defeated the *plans* in a measure.   *They will not be allowed to
turn informers and then go free themselves.*   Who ever goes to
your city will be instructed to make no such promises.   When
the attention of the public is called to Milwaukee, Chicago,
Evansville, Cincinnati, as it will in a very short time, no special attention will be called to your city.

You want to help any one that goes to your city, and trust
to the reliability of the friend whom you telegraphed.   Sorry
your officials have to leave the service.   Steer your ship in the
tempest, any one can do it in the calm.

Yours truly,

May 7th, 1875.   HORACE HOUGHTON.

Dear Friend

Keep steady on — Do not lose your gait. Some of the gaugers and distillers want to squeal — and have by such action defeated the clause in a measure, they will not be allowed to turn informers and then go for themselves. Who ever goes to your city will be instructed to make no such promises — When the attention of the public is called to Milwaukee — Chicago — Louisville — Cincinnati as it will in every short time — no special attention will be called to your City.

You want to help any one that goes to your city and trust to the reliability of the friends to whom you telegraphed — very few officials have to leave the service — Steer your ship in the tempest any one can do it in the calm.

Yours truly

Horace Houghton

May 7th 15.

Personal.

Gen John McDonald

Politeness of
Maj Grimer

This letter came to me through Major E. B. Grimes, the Quartermaster. On the envelope (which is bordered with black), in one corner is the word "Personal," and in the lower left-hand corner "Politeness of Major Grimes."

On the same day I received the following letter through the mail: [A fac-similie of which is also given.]

OFFICE PUBLIC BUILDINGS AND GROUNDS.

WASHINGTON, D. C., May 7th, 1875.

DEAR GENERAL:

Your letter at hand. I shall send the photographs in a day or two, and will try to get Gen. Belknap's. Sorry your assistants have resigned; it must keep you quite busy.

I have delivered your message. Hope the bird was a good traveller. Your friend is doing the best he can. You can, I believe, rely upon him.

The new commissioner takes his place on the 15th, and change generally will take place at that date, though your services will be needed till the first of June. All well here but busy. Regards to Mrs. McD., Joyce and wife, and other friends.   Yours truly,

O. E. BABCOCK.

Gen. J. A. McDONALD,
      St. Louis, Mo.

An explanation of this first letter is as follows: I wrote Gen. Babcock telling him, as I had told Secretary Bristow, that the best plan for a settlement of the troubles then culminating, would be to accept a compromise from the distillers and rectifiers; but I wrote him if these men were pressed by the Secretary that an explosion would be certain to follow. The General informs me in this letter that some of the gaugers, with the hope of securing

Cor. Penn. Ave & 21st St.

Washington D.C. May 9th 1875

Dear General

Your letter at hand — I shall send the photograph in a day or two. And will try to get Gen Belknap. Sorry your assistant has resigned it must keep your quite busy

I have delivered your message. Hope the bw. was a good traveler Your friend is doing the best he can you can I believe rely upon him. The new Commissioner takes his place on the 15th. and change generally will take place at that date. though your services will be needed till the first of June — All well here but busy Regards to Mr. McD. Joyce and wife and other friends

I am truly

O E Babcock

Genl A. McDonald
St Louis Mo

immunity, have shown a disposition to become informers, thereby preventing the Secretary from entertaining a proposition to compromise.

To intimidate the distillers and subordinate revenue officers, **Gen.** Babcock wants me to assure them that they will not be allowed to go free by becoming informers. (There were only two persons who could give these men such assurance, viz. Grant and Bristow, and as Babcock was the President's private secretary, he could speak for him, but not for Bristow.) He further states that if the distillers, etc., can be prevented from volunteering evidence, that after the attention of the public is called to other cities, where the Secretary was then developing fraud, that then, he intimates, I might get out of the service without any charges being made against me or the administration.

Before I left Washington, as I should have previously stated, we considered the advisability of conducting our correspondence over fictitious names, as we anticipated an interference through the surveillance of detectives. He therefore arranged to send me all his confidential letters through Major Grimes. To prevent exposure, should his letters be misplaced, he informed me of his intended use of the names of **Houghton,** Brown and B. Finch, or Bull Finch (an idea suggested by the bird he gave my wife).

The letter of same date as the one just explained, and mailed me from Washington, should be understood as follows: The photographs referred to, is a response to a request I had made of him to secure for me pictures of all the members of the Cabinet

and of the President. I had previously told him
that I was making a collection of my friends' photographs, with their autographs, which I intended
having arranged in a handsome cabinet. It may be
well to inform the reader, in this connection, that
after my indictment Gen. Babcock sent me an elegant, large sized picture of the President, with his
autograph, but to avoid a suspicion which might be
attached to such a circumstance, he placed the date
April 9th on the picture, to give the inference that
it was given to me before, instead of after my indictment.

The friend referred to meant President Grant,
who was then using his efforts to prevent Secretary
Bristow from pushing matters too far, and for a
considerable time he undoubtedly thought he could
dissuade the Secretary from carrying his investigations to that point where exposure would result.

The reference made to the new Commissioner was
relating to the removal of Mr. Douglass, who was
to be succeeded by Pratt on the 15th, as stated.

CHAPTER VII.

If a seeming but not real digression is pardonable
I will here explain the very peculiar and anomalous
attitudes of Commissioner Douglass: As has been

shown in an earlier part of this book, Douglass received his appointment almost directly through the
influence of Whiskey Ring members.   He had been
to many rehearsals where he had learned the part
he was to play in the interest of the Ring.   He
knew that President Grant and Gen. Babcock were
cognizant of the revenue frauds then being perpetrated, and having the consent of his superiors, as
well also as instructions from those who gave him
the position, he was a true friend of the Ring up to
the fall of 1874.   I will not do Mr. Douglass injustice as I have been and will be careful throughout
this expose not to say nor infer a single fault which
positive evidence does not substantiate; hence I
must admit the fact that he did not, to my knowledge, receive a single cent of the income derived
from the manufacture of illicit whiskey.   His only
crime consisted in such a desire to hold office that
he sacrificed or subordinated himself to the Ring's
interest in order to secure and retain his position.

In the fall of 1874 Mr. Douglass discovered that
Secretary Bristow had formed a determination to
inagurate a searching investigation of revenue matters in order to satisfy himself why the collections
had so materially fallen off.   When this course was
decided upon Mr. Douglass was not slow to find
that Mr. Bristow was not consulting him but was
taking matters in his own hands.   This scared the
Commissioner and to prepare for an exposure which
he felt was coming he changed his attitude and pro-
fessed, suddenly, an almost consuming desire to
ferret out every semblance of fraud.   The investigations proceeded, however, without any special

assistance of his, until Mr. Bristow was startled by proofs which showed conclusively that the Whiskey Ring had been in full operation for five years; not only this, but in searching through the pigeon-holes, in the Commissioner's office, the Secretary found a large number of reports from revenue agents who had been sent into my district, and had explained the frauds that were being perpetrated, and also the Woodward letters. This discovery decided the Secretary in his former opinion that the Commissioner had at least some guilty know-ledge of the revenue frauds, and a change was at once determined upon. This was about the last day of April, and without any consultations, the Secretary dismissed Mr. Douglass, the office to be declared vacant on the 15th of May, on which day Hon. D. D. Pratt succeeded to the position.

On the 10th day of May, Lucien Hawley and E. H. Chapman, armed with the proper authority from Washington, quietly dropped upon St. Louis, land-ing as it were in the midst of the distilleries and rectifying establishments, ten of which they seized without giving me any notice.

This act carried consternation with it, but I felt secure in my position and maintained a bold front, in evidence of which I here append the following correspondence. The moment I learned of the seizures I sent the following telegram:

ST. Louis, May 10, 1875.

To HON. J. W. DOUGLAS, Commissioner Internal Revenue, Washington :

I am informed by letter of this date from Collector Maguire, First District, Missouri, that nearly all of the distilleries and several rectifying houses of this city have been seized by Government officers, thereby relieving storekeepers and gaugers, and demanding their keys. The above being done without my knowledge, I ask for instructions in the premises.

JOHN McDONALD,
Supervisor Internal Revenue.

Following is the reply :

WASHINGTON, May 11, 1875.

To JOHN McDONALD, ESQ., Supervisor Internal Revenue, St. Louis :

Supervisor Hawley was assigned to special duty and has full instructions.   (Signed)   J. W. DOUGLASS.

In the afternoon of the day on which the seizures were made Mr. Hawley called on me at my office, and handed me his letter of authority and instructions, as follows:

TREASURY DEPARTMENT, May 7, 1875.

SIR :—Under authority conferred on the Secretary of the Treasury, by Section 3,159, Revised Statutes of the United States, you are hereby temporarily assigned to special duty in the State of Missouri.   I am, very respectfully,

B. H. BRISTOW, Secretary.

Mr. Hawley's personal letter informing me of his instructions is as follows:

LINDELL HOTEL, St. Louis, May 10, 1875.

JOHN McDONALD, ESQ., Supervisor Internal Revenue :

SIR :—I have the honor to hand you herewith copy of a letter of assignment, directed to me by the Hon. B. H. Bristow, Secretary of the Treasury, assigning me to special duty in the State of Missouri.

The duty to which I am assigned has reference to spirits, manufacture, sale, rectification, shipment, etc.

I am especially authorized to make seizures, as is also Mr. E. R. Chapman, of Washington, head of division, and we have made ten seizures, as follows: Rudolph Ulrici, Bingham Bros., John Busby, Bevis & Fraser, Lewis Teuscher, distillers; G. Bensberg, Bevis, Frazer & Co., F. C. Federer, J. L. Benecke, and Quinlin Bros. rectifiers.

While I remain in Missouri, my address will be Lindell Hotel, St. Louis.   Respectfully, LUCIEN HAWLEY,
Supervisor Internal Revenue.

To these letters I wrote the following reply:

OFFICE SUPERVISOR OF INTERNAL REVENUE, }
ST. LOUIS, May 11, 1875. }

SIR :—I have the honor this day to acknowledge receipt of your favor, dated yesterday, transmitting copy of letter from the honorable Secretary of the Treasury, assigning you to special duty in this state, and to say that any assistance myself or the officers of this District can render you in the furtherance of your duty, shall be done cheerfully.

During your stay in this city, I would be pleased to extend to you the courtesies of my office, where there will be a desk set a part for the exclusive use of yourself and Mr. Chapman.
Very Respectfully, JOHN McDONALD,
Supervisor Internal Revenue.
To LUCIEN HAWLEY, ESQ., Supervisor Internal Revenue, Lindell Hotel.

Almost immediately after mailing the above I sent another letter, as follows:

SUPERVISOR'S OFFICE, St. Louis, May 11, 1875.

SIR:—Please inform me if the distilleries, situated in the First District of Missouri, seized by your authority yesterday (the 10th inst.) were at the time of seizure operated according to law and regulations. Also, whether officers in charge of them were at their respective posts of duty.
Very Respectfully, JOHN McDONALD,
Supervisor Internal Revenue.
To LUCIEN HAWLEY, Supervisor Internal Revenue, Lindell Hotel.

To this latter note I received on the same day the following reply:

LINDELL HOTEL, May 11th, 1875.

SIR.—I have received your note of this date, making inquiries in reference to the distilleries which were seized yesterday, and the officers belonging to them.

Two of the distilleries only were running at the time; two others had spirits in the warehouse, and one was entirely vacated. Whether or not at the time of the seizure they were operating according to law cannot yet be determined until we make a more full examination, as in the haste with which we were compelled to visit the distilleries, we might fail to discover the irregularities, if they had existed at the time. The officers in charge were on duty, so far as I know, except at the distillery of Teuscher, at that place the storekeeper was absent at the time of seizure, and did not return for several hours, the distillery being in full operation until shut down by my orders.

Very respectfully,

LUCIEN HAWLEY, Supervisor.

JOHN McDONALD, ESQ., Supervisor Internal Revenue.

Reports of every character were flying fast, some of which reached the President, and a constant irritation was the result. The following letter from Gen. Babcock shows why it was disturbing the President and himself·

DEAR FRIEND;

Your enemies, to do you harm, report to the Secretary that you are on 'Change and accuse him of being in the interest of some Kentucky people, and boast that you can prove it, etc. I tell him I am sure it is not so and that your enemies start these stories.

A lot of gaugers and storekeepers want to peach and say they can prove that McDonald is in it, etc., etc. No such person has been allowed to make any such statement, as they want to be protected. Keep your head level and undertake nothing you cannot carry out for certain—and beware of skunks—who profess to be friends; they wish simply to deceive you and your sincere friend,

B. FINCH.

May 14th, p. m.

*Send under cover to Geo. D. Benjamin, 2,100 Pa., Avenue.

Notwithstanding the fact that I tendered my resignation to the President on the 23d of April, it was not until a month later that it was accepted. Gen. Bristow urged my dismissal, because he was then well informed of my connection with the Ring and was equally well convinced of the President's connivance if not indeed his direct complicity with all the whiskey frauds. But with the hope that I might be able to cover a major part of the most damaging evidence, I was continued in office until the 25th of May, as will be seen by the following acceptance of my resignation by Mr. Bristow:

TREASURY DEPARTMENT,

WASHINGTON, May 22d, 1875.

SIR.—By direction of the President, your resignation as Supervisor of Internal Revenue is hereby accepted, to take effect upon the qualification of your successor.

I am very Respectfully,

B. H. BRISTOW, Secretary.

MR. JOHN McDONALD, St. Louis, Mo.

The doubtful reader may desire to know why, if the President was my co-conspirator, he accepted my resignation at all, and also why he did not interpose his authority and suppress Mr. Bristow,

*NOTE.—This letter, bearing the signature suggested by the bull-finch Gen. Babcock sent as a present to my wife, as heretofore explained, is reproduced on the following page in fac-simile.

Dear Friend;

Your enemies, in my opinion to do you harm report to the Laity that you go on change and accuse him of being in the interest of some Ry people & boast that you can prove it &c &c. I tell him I am sure it is not so. and that your enemies start these stories — A lot of gougers or storekeepers want to search and try they can prove that McDavid is in it &c &c. No such person has been allowed to make any such statement as they want to be protected — Keep your head level — and undertake Nothing you cannot carry out for Certain — and beware of Skunks — who profess to be friends — they wish simply to deceive you & your sincere friend

May 14th = Cm —   B. Finch,

Send under cover to Geo D Benjamin . 2100 Pa Avenue,

when the Secretary's actions had assumed such a threatening attitude. Let me here explain: In my interview with the President in April, as reported, I gave him my opinion that if he permitted Secretary Bristow to continue his investigations, that no power could suppress the reports made by revenue agents; that this information would certainly leak out in some manner and that it would soon assume proportions for evil as irresistible as the waves of the ocean. The President did not so regard it, and his idea was that to make a specious showing of administion honesty would produce a favorable effect, and advance his political interests by procuring his re-nomination for the Presidency. This idea obscured the results from him which I could see was sure to follow, and relying upon his power to run his vessel within an inch of the most dangerous breakers without coming in contact with the reef, he considered the glory that would reward him and, like the indolent oarsman who rides at first in the easy swirl of the seductive maelstrom, he realized only when it was too late the roaring charabydis he had been drawn into. My predictions were fully proven but not until he had ridden too far upon the wave of popular approval, and to recede would have been to expose the hollowness of his purposes and pretentions. He could not dismiss Mr. Bristow, the author of the reform, and in order to continue the hypocracy which was drawing to him so much commendation the President was compelled to acquiesce, at least, in some of Mr. Bristow's demands; one of these demands was for my removal. When this came the

President, fully realizing the danger his rash measures had seduced him into, drew my resignation
from his side pocket, where it had lain for one
month, and permitted the Secretary to accept it.
His reliance, henceforth was in my silence, and his
natural good luck. Daily he advised with Gen.
Babcock, and through him he communicated his
wishes to me. And here I desire to call the attention of the reader to a fact which is very important,
and which may possibly be overlooked by some, viz:
That the President does all his official correspondence through his secretary. It is perhaps difficult
to define the lines of distinction between the communications of the secretary and the President in
matters of doubtful character, and the only means
we have of ascertaining, in the absence of the
President's signature, is by considering all the circumstances indicative of his sanction. I shall
therefore request the reader to accept this fact as a
reason why I have not included letters from the
President with those from Gen. Babcock, his private secretary.

My next letter from Gen. Babcock, of which a
fac-simile is also given, is as follows:

May 28th, 1875.

DEAR FRIEND:

Some one sends the enclosed to me. I have cut the name
out. I do not know of any subordinate in your city that I
can do anything for, as I have no particulars, and I am not
aware of the slightest thing that Mr. Hawley can find against
me. * * You may know this hand writing.

I received your favor some time since and am pleased with
what you say. The writer of the anonymous note evidently
thinks I sent the lightning dispatch. He is mightily mistaken.

Please send the anonymous note back to me under same address as your last personal note was sent.

I shall attend to your wishes to the best of my ability. Had there been nothing except in your city your proposed plans might have been carried out. We will talk that all up when we meet. Your sincere friend,

H. B. Brown.

The enclosed note referred to, reads as follows:

United States Internal Revenue.
Collector's Office, District Missouri,
May 26th, 1875.

Gen. O. E. Babcock (Cut out.):

If you don't protect the subordinate officers in St. Louis, who are now in trouble, lightning will strike in Washington. Hawley is after *you.*

(Signed.) A Friend Who Knows.

The explanation of the sentence contained in the letter, "I received your favor some time since, and am pleased with what you say," is an acknowledgement of a declaration I made in the letter, to which this is an answer, "that I would stand by him (Babcock) and the President until hell burnt down, and froze over, and I should then skate across and stand by them on the other side." I quote my language in full—although it is profane enough for a Cardinal of the twelfth century—in order that the reader may know the character of the correspondence between the President, Gen. Babcock, and myself.

The day previous to the seizures noted before, Mr. Newcomb, of the firm of Newcomb–Buchanan Distilling Co., of Louisville, was in Secretary Bristow's office, and, in the course of the conversation, the Secretary asserted his intention of seizing

May 28th 95

Dear Friend.

Some one sends the enclosed to me. I have cut the name out. I do not know of any subordinate in your city, that I can do anything for as I have no particulars: and I am even unaware of the slightest thing that Mr Hardley can find against me. some friendly acts of mine may be misconstrued. but I do not know of any— You may know this handwriting. I received your favors some time since—and am pleased with what you say— The writer of this anonymous note evidently thinks I sent the lightning dispatch—he is mightily mistaken— Please send this anonymous note back to same murder address as your lost personal note was sent = I shall attend to your wishes to the best of my ability— Had there been nothing except in your city—your proposed plans ought to have been carried out.— We will talk that all up when we meet—

Your sincere friend.

—H B Brown—

all the distilleries in the West on the following day. When Mr. Newcomb left the Treasury Department, he repeated the declaration of the Secretary to a Mr. Barnes, an employe of the Newcomb-Buchanan Co., who at once sent the news to Bollman & O'Hara, rectifiers in St. Louis, in a dispatch in which the phrase " Lightning will strike St. Louis on Monday," was used. It was to this telegram Gen. Babcock refers in the letter just quoted.

The anonymous letter of warning which he sent me to ascertain the author, I retained until the General possibly forgot to remind me again that he wanted it returned. I remember that upon receipt I showed the anonymous letter to a number of my friends, all of whom concluded, with myself, that it was in the handwriting of Joseph Fitzroy, who was the collector of the Ring, and knew of the President's and Gen. Babcock's connection with the conspiracy.

The signature, H. B. Brown, and his instructions for me to direct my answer to the same person as before, has already been explained. It will be observed that in all the letters he omits the place from whence they were written. This was only another precaution used to prevent detectives from discovering the writer, should the correspondence fall into their hands.

In the early part of June the Grand Jury, then in session in St. Louis, returned an indictment against me, and also against Joyce, Fitzroy, and Bevis, a distiller, charging us with " wilfully and maliciously destroying public records." On the day after this was found, I was arrested by U. S. Marshal New-

L

comb, and gave bail in the sum of $5,000. But this
step only increased the anxiety of the President and
Gen. Babcock, and on the 17th I wrote Gen. B.,
informing him of my indictment, but conveyed my
assurance that he and the President could only be
reached criminally through me, and whatever the
ordeal might be, I should go through it without betraying them in the slightest. I asked him to use
his influence to have Maj. Gunther retained in the
service. Following is his reply:

DEAR FRIEND:

Got yours of the 17th ; glad to hear all will be right : shall
do all in my power to retain your friend ; it will not be my
fault if I do not, as I will convince you when me meet. I
don't think Dyer your friend. I still believe there is some one
who is near you or the Colonel who betrays you ; *trust none.*
Where is the Colonel?

Regards to all. Keep cool. Will explain a good many
things when I see you.

Yours truly,

June 22d.   B. F. INCH.

It will be observed that in this letter, of which a
a fac-simile is herewith given, he uses the signature
" bull-finch," in yet another abbreviated style.

The first part of this letter is readily understood
as in answer to mine of the 17th, but the reference
to Dyer calls for a somewhat extended explanation: Col. D. P. Dyer was at this time the United
States District Attorney for the eastern district of
Missouri. The prosecution of all the whiskey
cases devolved upon him, and how effectively he
performed his duties, will be seen hereafter. Some
time ago, the reader will remember, I explained the
arrangements by which I received Gen. Babcock's

Dear friend –

Don, yours of 17= glad to hear
all will be right – shall do all in my
power to retain your friend – will not be
my fault – if I do not as I will convince you
when we meet – I don't think Dyre your
friend – I still believe there is some one
who is near you or the col who betrays you
trust no one – Where is the Col –
Regards to all – keep cool – will explain
a good many things when I see you

              Yours truly
              E F Such

June 22 –

Personal

       Genl John A McDonald
         Planters House
           St Louis
             Mo.

confidential letters through E. B. Grimes, the
quartermaster at St. Louis.   This man Grimes now
plays a somewhat important part in the concluding
acts of the whiskey drama.   When the Grand Jury
began returning true bills of indictment against
members of the ring, Gen. Babcock, being much
alarmed, wrote to Grimes, instructing him to wait
upon Col. Dyer in person and, to use the General's
expression, " sound him; " to ascertain, after grad-
ual approaches would permit such a proposition,
if the Colonel would not conduct the prosecution in
such a manner as to visit the President's friends
with special leniency.

Grimes performed the services required of him
and came up to see me directly after his interview
with Col. Dyer.   He was in excellent spirits, and
told me that the Colonel would be governed by his
instructions from Washington.   Mr. Grimes apprehended no trouble whatever, feeling sure that
everything could be hushed up or *nolle pross'd*, and
this was the purport of his letter to Gen. Babcock;
but the General was not satisfied, as he explains in
his letter to me of June 22d, and requested Grimes
to have another more pointed interview with Col.
Dyer.   I shall never forget the comical seriousness
pictured in Grimes' face when he called on me after
his "pointed " talk with the Colonel; it was an admirably proportioned combination of despair, incre-
dulity, and absolute wretchedness.   I could not
restrain my laughter, although the news was quite
discouraging enough to have spread over the whole
Whiskey Ring like an attack of cholera morbus.
His aspect was one of those compensating influ-

ences of nature in which some sweet is always mixed with the bitter. Grimes drew his chair up close to mine, and, although there was no one within ear-trumpet distance of us, he commenced in a low, slow, and serious monotone: "General, the jig is up." Then a long pause. "Col. Dyer is as determined as Bristow, and tells me emphatically that if the President is in the Ring he is going for him." Then another pause. "I don't know what to make of it." Another pause. "But I've done all I can with him." Another pause. "Well, if he persists in covering the entire White House with disgrace, my suggestion would be to have him dismissed." Then, with an air of virtuous scorn and a contempt for minor scruples, having eased his burden of information, told me that he should write to Gen. Babcock fully. And thus we parted.

Maj. Grimes never lost his solicitude for our interest, and whenever he received a letter from the White House he would search for me with special anxiety to deliver the communications as soon as possible. When he was unable to find me he would mail notes like the following, which I herewith copy verbatim, and do not therefore make myself amenable to the crime of extraordinary profanity which one of them contains:

DEPOT QUARTERMASTER'S OFFICE, }
ST. LOUIS, May 3d, 1875. }

DEAR GENERAL:

Come to my office at once. I have an important letter from Washington that must be delivered to you in person.

Yours truly,
GRIMES.

The following note from Grimes was enclosed in an envelope containing Babcock's letters, forwarded to me at Ripon, Wis.:

St. Louis, July 7th, 1875.

DEAR JOHN

I send you two letters. I would have sent them before, but things are not so safe as I would like.

Your friend,

WHO GETS LETTERS FOR YOU NOW AND THEN.

P. S.   Look out for breakers, by God!

[See fac-simile on opposite page.]

In this connection, while the name of Maj. E. B. Grimes and the part he acted in the whiskey drama is familiar, I desire to quote a part of his testimony given in the trial of the U. S. *vs.* O. E. Babcock, and then leave him for a time to play shuttle-cock with the reader, using his conscience as the ball.

CROSS-EXAMINATION BY MR. STORRS.—Q. State, if anything, what McDonald said upon receiving any one of these letters from you, with regard to Gen. Babcock's complicity with the Ring.

A. The only time I ever spoke to McDonald, I forget whether it was the first or the last letter I gave him — it was one or the other — I said: "McDonald, has Babcock anything to do with this thing?" He said: "Grimes, I don't believe he knows a bit more about it than you do, and," says he, "you don't know anything about it."

RE-DIRECT EXAMINATION.—Q. Did he say in that same conversation that he, himself, did not know anything about the Whiskey Ring?

A. Yes sir, he did.   [Laughter.]

The following letter will explain the anxious position General Babcock occupied; how he was haunted with the fear that either Col. Joyce or myself, taking umbrage at some of his indiscreet expressions, would, to save ourselves, place the

TWO MEMORANDUMS FROM
QUARTERMASTER GRIMES,
May 2, 1875.

Depot Quartermaster's Office,

St. Louis, Mo. (May 2ᵈ 1875

Dear General

Come to my office
at once I have
an important
letter from Washington
that I must deliver
to you in Person
yours truly
Simon

Oct 30/75 —
General I would
like to see you
at my room
after 8 oclock in
the morning
Simon

St Louis
July 7th 1875

Dear John I
send you two letters
I would have sent
them before But
things are not as safe
as I wold like.
Your Friend.
who gets letters for
you now and
then Look out
for brokers
Boy Grand

administration in a defensive attitude by telling what we knew. He was very solicitious of our good opinions, and all his letters and acts were to nerve us to keep our promises not to betray Grant or himself. This letter is written in policy phrases, and signed with his proper name, so that in event it should fall into other hands it might be easily construed in his favor. [I present, on the opposite page, a fac-simile also of this letter:]

(Confidential.)

LONG BRANCH, N. J., July 10, 1875.

DEAR MACK :—

I enclose you a newspaper article, which you have undoubtedly seen. I want to say that I have not seen the correspondent who wrote this in several weeks, and I have never made any statement that could be construed into this. I do not suppose it is necessary for me to write this, but I do it to assure you that I do not believe in joining in abuse of you and Joyce (who have always been kind to me) now that you are in trouble. When that matter is disposed of and you gentlemen are vindicated, as I believe you will be, if I have any complaints to make I will make them to you and not to newspaper correspondents. Unless I know something very different from what I know now, I shall have no complaints to make, for I am not aware that I have ever received anything but kindness at the hands of you or Joyce.

Please remember me to Mrs. McD., Joyce and Mrs. J., and believe me,   Very Truly Yours, O. E. BABCOCK.

To GEN. JNO. McDONALD.

P. S. I thought I had the newspaper article. It was from the Chicago *Tribune* and represented that you had abused the confidence of the Secretary of the President, with whom you had corresponded, &c. As I said before, I never said such a thing.   O. E. B.

P. S. I have seen Joyce's manly card in the paper. When are you coming East.   O. E. B.

GEN'L O. E. BABCOCK,

July 19th, 1875.

Confidential

Long Branch N.J.

Dear Mack   July 14th 75,

I enclose you a
newspaper article — which
you have undoubtedly seen —
I want to say that I have
not seen the conspirices who
wrote this in sixteen weeks — and
I have never made any statements
that could be construed into this.
I do not suppose it is necessary
for me to write this . but I do it to
assure you that I do not believe
in joining in abuse of you and
Joyce (who have always been
kind to me) now that you are
in trouble — When that matter is all.
disposed of — and you gentlemen
are vindicated — as I believe you
will be . if I have any complaint
to make I will make them to you

are not to newspaper correspondents
Unless I know something very
different from anything that I
know now I shall have no complaints
to make, for I am not aware that I
have ever received anything but kindness
at the hands of either you or Joyce —

Please remember me to Mrs McD —
Joyce and McD — and believe me

Very truly you
O E Babcock

To Gen J H McDonald —
Planton House
St Louis Mo —

P.S. I thought I have the newspaper article.
It was from the Chicago Tribune — and
represented that you had abused the
Confidence of the Leelys of the Bur
with whom you had corresponded
&c. as I said before I have never
said such a thing — you OEB

P.S. I have seen Joyces manly case in the paper
When one given counsine Lest OEB

In the next letter, from Babcock, however, even as a bull-finch, (B. F.) he pipes like a craven, with notes of no doubtful import. It records his agony of mind like a phonograph, and grinds out his anxious fears with more literal distinctness. It is not only himself who is complaining at the confessional, but linked hand in hand and heart in heart, he leads with him his *pater criminis*, President Grant, on whose brow the purple of authority seems bleached by con-tact with the gorgon of villainy. [A fac simile of this letter may be found on the opposite page:]

July 14.

DEAR FRIEND :

I am told that some valuable information, that was taken from a safe, was sent to Cincinnati to the care of one Maj. Blackburn, a lawyer of that city, and that it is believed it can be purchased from him if enough money is paid. The price for it is high, but it is believed it can be purchased if price enough is paid, and that they are trying to buy it.

Your friend, B. F.

Does the reader want me to explain this pano-rama of Grant and Babcock's infamy; shift the scenes until all the black lines are plainly discern-ible? Well, while my pen is to it and the people grown more morbid by looking upon the great fes-tering body of corruption which I have here exposed to their view, I'll show them more. "This valuable information" Gen. Babcock re-fers to, was stolen out of the safe of the U. S. District State Attorney's office at St. Louis, or at least I have been so informed. It consisted of evi-dence fully establishing my guilt and pointing to President Grant and Gen. Babcock as accessories.

Dear General   July — 14th

I am told that some valuable
information that was taken from a safe
was sent to Cincinnati - to the care
of one Maj Blackburn a lawyer of
that City - and that it is believed it
can be purchased from him - if enough
money is paid - the price for it is
high - but it is believed that it can be
purchased - if price enough is paid - and
that they are trying to buy it.

            Your friend
               S F.

Personal

Gen. John McDonald
    St Louis
      Mo

"They are trying to buy it," means that the President, together with himself and others in the ring, were then negotiating with Blackburn for the evidence, and they desire me to contribute a part of the necessary money.

I did not regard the information spoken of as specially damaging, because I knew. that if the government officers here really meant to convict me that there was so much evidence against us all that, like a river, it could not be exhausted by dipping up the water while the source remained. I replied to him in this manner, and the matter was not referred to again in our correspondence.

In the latter part of July, I left St. Louis and went up to my farm in Wisconsin, near Ripon, but was not allowed to remain there long as all the members of the Ring were now in deep distress, and they looked to me for assistance, sending me a dozen letters every day imploring me to return. Before leaving St. Louis for Wisconsin, I employed Judge Chester H. Krum to defend me from the charges preferred in the indictment already alluded to, and as he will figure largely from now until the close of this exposure, I will here introduce him to the reader.

When Missouri was added to my district in 1870, Chester H. Krum was U. S. Attorney for that District, and I think he was one of President Grant's earliest appointees. After McKee, Ford and myself had completed our combination with the President to turn out crooked whiskey and devote the unpaid tax to cumulating a campaign fund, I spoke to Ford and asked him if Krum could be depended upon to ignore the operations of the Ring. Mr. Ford replied that he had advised with Mr. Krum upon the matter and that no trouble need be apprehended from that source. Subsequently I talked with Mr. Krum concerning the illicit whiskey, then being manufactured, but I never went into details with him, only enough to satisfy me that he knew what was going on.

In the fall of 1872, Mr. Krum, having become impressed with the idea that he could not continue in the office of U. S. district attorney without inviting trouble by being drawn into complications which he felt certain would arise, concluded to resign and become a candidate for Circuit Judge at the ensuing election. Directly after his nomination by the Republican party of St. Louis he came to me for financial assistance. I gave him $600, and as I handed it to him he remarked: "Is this some of the Whiskey Ring money?" My reply was: Most assuredly; do you think me foolish enough to give you money out of my own salary? "Then," said he, "if I need any more I will know where to get it." As he did not ask me for funds again, and was elected, the presumption is he needed very little outside assistance. Although he was elected for a term of six years he resigned almost as soon as I was indicted in order to defend me, and knowing who was connected with the Ring his idea was, as he expressed to me, that he could make more money in appearing as attorney for those who might become involved. He no doubt expected to see the President and Gen. Babcock appear as defendants before the Grand Jury, then in session, should conclude its labors. In fact he said: "All you fellows will be brought into court before this thing ends," meaning that McKee, Maguire, Babcock and the President, etc., would all need his assistance.

With this knowledge the reader can have a better understanding of events as they are disclosed and comprehend the Judge's relation to members of the Ring. The following letter from him addressed to me while I was in Ripon, will serve as a comprehensive introduction of Judge Krum as a conspicuous character in this melo-drama. [This letter is produced in fac-simile on the opposite page.]

Krum & Madill,
ATTORNEYS AT LAW,
307 Olive Street.

(Private.)   St. Louis, Aug. 10, 1875.
Dear General :

I think that matters are about ripe for our interview with U. S. G. Avery leaves to-night and is going to Long Branch. A friend of his here will write strongly as to matters before the Grand Jury. Newcomb will be within reach, I think, by the latter part of this week. If you think it advisable for me to go on, telegraph me : "Broke my leg this morning, cannot come," and I will meet you at the Palmer House in Chicago. I shall register as Henry B. Gordon. Don't make any arrangements about my going on unless it will do some good, and get all of your facts in shape.   Yours, etc.,

C. H. K.

This letter has reference to the active efforts that were then being made to secure the removal of Secretary Bristow. Avery, whom the Judge mentions as having had a friend to write a strong letter with reference to the actions of the Grand Jury, is Wm. O. Avery, one of our Washington friends whom

LETTER FROM

CHESTER H. KRUM,

August 10, 1875.

KRUM & MADILL.

ATTORNEYS AT LAW

807 OLIVE STREET,

St. Louis, Aug 10 1875

Dear Genl:

I think, that matters are about ripe for an interview with U.S.G. Avery leaves to-night and informs to Long Branch. A friend of his here, will write strongly as to matters before the Grand Jury. Newcomb will be within

lunch. I think, by
the allie print of this
week. If you think it
adviseable for me to
go on, telegraph me
"Broke my leg this
morning, cannot come",
and I will meet
you at the Palmer
House in Chicago.
I shall register as
Henry B. Gordon. Don't
make any arrangements
about my coming on
unless it will do some good

schedule of your facts in shape. Yours

CHK

Bristow had shoved out of his office only to have
him fall into the hands of a Grand Jury that indicted him for complicity with the Whiskey Ring
frauds. There was a partial understanding between
the other members of the Ring in St. Louis and
myself to first ascertain if the President could control the government appointees, the Secretary, district attorney, etc., and if he could not, then to
make a demand for their dismisal and the appointment of a new set of officers all round. This letter
manifests the alarm of the St. Louis parties, who
concluded to send Judge Krum to Washington,
after consultation with me, for the purpose of delivering to the President their desire.

C. A. Newcomb was at this time U. S. Marshal,
and while he had never been a member of the Ring,
it was thought he had a knowledge of its existence,
and Judge Krum thought he could count on the
Marshal giving them some assistance by delaying
service of papers. He wrote me this letter for the
purpose of securing my sanction to his going to
Washington to press the President for a dismisal of
Bristow and Col. Dyer. The President had been
communicated with daily and was well advised as
to every step taken by the Grand Jury and the
officers in St. Louis.

When this letter came to me I had decided upon
another course entirely, and at once wrote him
that I did not now consider it advisable for him to
visit Washington. After considering my position
I could not see why I should exhibit any anxiety.
I knew that Grant and Babcock were, in a measure,
in my power, because they were my superiors and

equally guilty with myself. So my conclusion was to let the White House end of the line take care of itself and to offer no further obstacle to Bristow's foray.

My determination brought forth abundant fruit, by alarming the President and his chevalier scribe, who, being unable to account for my *nonchalance*, and quite at sea as to my intentions, learning of my return to St. Louis they took the train and arrived in the city on the 24th of September.

The visit of the President and Gen. Babcock was made under circumstances that would disguise their real purposes from the public, and in order to fully develop this fact I will be somewhat circumspect even at the risk of becoming tedious. Arrangements were made for an annual meeting of the Grand Army of the Potomac to be held at Des Moines, Iowa, in the latter part of September. The President desired to attend this annual reunion and he could use this fact as an excuse for coming to St. Louis. He was accompanied on the trip by Col. R. S. Stephens, at that time General Manager of the Missouri, Kansas & Texas railroad, but who is at present a resident of Attica, Wyoming County, New York. Col. Stephens has given me liberty to use his name in this connection, and to state that he knew that the President and Gen. Babcock visited St. Louis expressly to see and consult me on what I wished done regarding my indictment.

My first notification of their arrival was through Maj. Grimes who came to me at the Planter's House, where I was stopping, and taking me by the arm said, " There is a gentleman over the way who wishes to see you; will you go over with me now ? "

M

I crossed the street with Maj. Grimes and followed
him up stairs to a room over John Bonnett's restaurant. Upon entering the room I found Gen.
Babcock, who cordially greeted me and then informed me that he had ordered a dinner and wine
expressly for me. I saw that a very sumptuous re-
past had been provided for two and on his invitation I took a seat at the table. Maj. Grimes did
not dine with us for, as I learned from the General,
matters had been arranged for a strictly private
conversation between us.

He began the interview by saying: "The old
man (meaning Grant) and I have come out here to
see what you want done. This thing has gone far
enough and must stop right here. We have taken
rooms at the Lindell, and at four o'clock this afternoon I want you to see the President privately and
tell him exactly what you want." I did not make
any reply at once so as to permit him to make a full
statement. He said there had already been scandal
enough, and he declared that the trouble would not
be allowed to continue if "we" (the expression he
used) "have to dismiss every man in the Government service." He told me that he had ordered
the dinner there so as to have an opportunity to
have a full talk with me, adding that, as he had
always attended to the details and interests of the
Washington end of the Ring, he wanted to hear
what I had to say before having a meeting with the
President. He further remarked that the old man
(Grant) was too easy, and that he wanted me to say
to him that it was time to take the bull by the
horns (*sic*) and stop the investigations and prevent

a prosecution of any of the members. He gave it
as his opinion that, inasmuch as Bristow, Wilson,
Dyer, Henderson, etc., were appointees of the President, that they could be restrained by the President's wishes, especially if the matter assumed the
position of " quit or go;" that a prosecution of the
President's friends was a serious reflection upon the
President, which could in no event be tolerated.
He talked in this manner for nearly half an hour,
and when he paused to hear my suggestions, I
replied, in substance, that I had to disagree with
him in all his propositions. Said I, judging, as you
do, from Washington, it is impossible for you to
comprehend with what irresistible force the charges
and demand for a complete investivation of fraud
in connection with the illicit whiskey combination,
is being made. The time was when this trouble
might have been averted, and I told the President
when in Washington that if he did not muzzle or
dismiss Bristow and call in all the revenue agents,
that a wave of exposure would certainly engulf us
all. No, said I, it is worse than folly to speak of
suppressing facts possessing such importance and
pregnant with such terrible possibilities, those
which, in part, have already reached the public and
placed everybody in a fever heat of anxiety to hear
it all. I added: The President's indiscretion did
not stop in ignoring my suggestions, but extended
to the appointment of D. P. Dyer as district attorney, who was a special friend of Mr. Bristow's, and
who had, in fact, shown some antagonism to Grant;
following this, Gen. Jno. B. Henderson was appointed in July, to aid Dyer, and these two men,

said I, are determined to push everyone to the wall who has the least guilty knowledge of the whiskey frauds. I assured him, however, that the prosecutions could not extend to the President or himself except through Col. Joyce or myself, and that he might depend upon me to carry the secrets I had like facts hidden under the mold of centuries. I advised him to return with the President, to Washington, and to take no part in averting prosecutions, which might be construed against them, and to leave the St. Louis boys take care of themselves.

Somewhat surprised, he asked: "Why, General, what do you mean by that; don't you want us to do anything out here for you?"

I replied: The fact is, the papers have so worked up this matter that any action which you might take, to prevent a complete exposure of the Ring, would be only to invite your own ruin; that they had already asserted that the President knew of the existence of the Whiskey Ring, and any interference from him now would confirm the truth of the charge with the public.

He then enquired my opinion of the ultimate results if matters were allowed to go on.

I frankly told him that the result would be the conviction of Col. Joyce and myself.

He threw up his arms and, manifesting much horror at my prediction, exclaimed: "My God! we will never permit that; why we will dismiss everyone who is in enmity with us, and thus we can at least prevent the further progress of these measures until Grant's term of office expires."

I told him that, upon a more mature reflection, I thought he would adopt my ideas as the better. I said: It is possible that before our cases come to trial Bristow, Wilson, Dyer, or Henderson will be guilty of some indiscretion or impolitic act which would furnish the President with a plausible pretext for ordering their dismissal. He assured me that a very small excuse would be sufficient, and that he thought before things went much further that a cause would be found to get rid of them.

I also told him that, under the circumstances, and especially considering my indictment, that it would be very indiscreet for the President to receive me at his rooms; but that I would call at the Lindell and see the President publicly, and as chance afforded, would ascertain from him whether he approved of my determination. I informed him of the fact that there were detectives watching the President himself, and that my footsteps were continually dogged by them. Said I, you need not be surprised to see an account of our meeting and interview here published in the morning papers.

He replied that he had no fears of seeing any notice of this meeting, because, said he, "Maj. Grimes arranged this place of interview, and we came here together in a closed carriage."

(It was subsequently shown that the President was under the surveillance of detectives, who reported all his acts and movements to Secretary Bristow. It was owing to my refusal to hold a private interview with him that he escaped being disgraced by such a circumstance).

Our conversation then drifted from the prospective trials to other private matters connected with our mutual interests. He asked if Maj. Grimes had read to me all the letters he (Babcock) had written to him, as instructed.

I informed him that Maj. Grimes had read me a great many of his (Babcock's) letters, and that after reading, Grimes invariably burned them.

I have since thought that the General was laboring under the hallucination that I had treated his correspondence as Grimes did; if so, I can imagine his surprise when this book finds its way into his possession.

We talked of my visit to Washington in April, and in referring to the manner in which my suggestions had been regarded, he said that the President had frequently told him how sorry he was he had not heeded them. He further told me that Secretary Bristow had sought the sanction of the President to dismiss me instead of accepting my resignation, but that Grant had positively forbidden the Secretary to do this, and that he would only consent to an acceptance of my resignation after a month had been consumed in the most persistent and pursuasive argument.

Our conversation lasted for more than two hours, during which we ate a very hearty dinner and consumed two bottles of wine. When we parted I repeated to him my determination not to see the President privately, but, I remarked, you may speak to him and ascertain how he receives my policy of action, and report to me at my room in the Planters House this evening.

True to our appointment, Gen. Babcock called on me, and related with much ecstacy how the President was delighted with my considerate ideas, and credited me with a wisdom that was so gratifying that it inspired him with the hope that my *finesse* would yet bring them out of their distressing dilemma. He spent perhaps an hour with me, during which we reviewed all the phases of our troubles, and traded opinions until we thoroughly understood each others wishes. I told him that I would seek the occasion to meet the President in the rotunda of the Lindell Hotel directly after supper on the following evening, so as to give our meeting a casual or accidental appearance, which would prevent comment.

I saw no more of the General until the next day about eleven o'clock, when he called at my room, and again renewed the conversation we had on the previous day. He asked me what had induced me to adopt the course I had.

I thought the question somewhat strange, after he had conveyed the congratulations and pleasure of the President, but I made reply to him that it was to protect my superiors from disgrace if they would keep faith with me.

He then enquired if I had fully considered the ordeal I should have to submit to in bearing the opprobrium of a conviction.

Said I: That is just the part of the funeral I have considered; I have already been abused to the limit of newspaper possibility, and there is nothing to it now but standing up in court and passing through a few changes, and at most hear the turn of the bolt on my liberty.

At the mention of the "bolt," the General interrupted me by saying: "Oh! it will not come to that; they will never turn a key on you, because the old man (Grant) tells me that if they convict you, he will pardon you the moment the verdict is announced. Don't have any fears about that, but I can't believe this arbitrary action will ever be necessary."

I told him that I expected the President to pardon me at once, in case of my conviction, and that it was because of this and the friendly obligations I owed him that I proposed to stand and take the full brunt of the law, in order that my fidelity might be proven.

He next asked me if I were not under a heavy expense, and upon receiving an affirmative reply he assured me that all my expenses including loss of time, lawyers fees, etc., should be refunded, and not only that, but after the trouble had been settled and Grant was re-elected, that my nerve and devotion would have passed the crucible of test and that I could have any office in the gift of the President, by the mere asking. This allusion to the election of Grant a third time led us into a discussion of the effect the whiskey trials would have upon the President's chances, which lasted for some time. Before leaving he said that the President, while approving of my course thoroughly, yet he was very desirous of meeting me privately so that he might have a lengthy conversation, and assure me of his high regard and warm attachment. I asked him to inform the President that I would call at the Lindell

Hotel between seven and eight o'clock that afternoon, and would be in the parlor corridor so as to
meet him publicly.

Nothing further passed between us at this interview, but about four o'clock Gen. Babcock called
at my room for the third time, and told me he had
arranged with the President to meet me in the
manner I desired, at half-past seven o'clock; that
at that hour the President would be promenading
in the corridor so the meeting would appear as accidental.

At the hour appointed Col. Joyce and I went to
the Lindell but when we entered the corridor
we found that the President and his party were
still at supper. We waited for them not above five
minutes, when the company, consisting of the
President and his wife, Sec'y Borie and wife, Fred
Grant and wife and Gen. Babcock, came out of the
main dining room and walked towards the parlor.
Col. Joyce first met the President and while they
were conversing I spoke to Mrs. Grant with whom
I chatted for a few moments. At the conclusion of
his interview with Col. Joyce the President came
up to me, while Mrs. Grant walked into the parlor.
I asked him if Gen. Babcock had informed him
fully as to the course I had adopted for shielding
him from exposure. He replied: " Yes, and I want
to assure you that all Gen. Babcock promised will
be fulfilled to the letter, and we will make the circumstances for your protection even more favorable
than you can suppose."

We talked of Bristow, Solicitor Bluford Wilson,
Dyer and Henderson, and he spoke with much

feeling at the course they were pursuing, saying, that he was convinced that they were at enmity with him and their removal had become a necessity which was prevented only by policy. He took the occasion to admit that if he had acted upon my suggestions in April every appearance of trouble would have been averted, but that matters were still in his power and he could relieve me of any burdens the prosecution could impose upon me.

Our conversation lasted only a few minutes for I told the President that a lengthy interview would excite comment, so he bade me a very reluctant adieu, assuring with his last words that under any and all circumstances I should be protected as I had pledged myself to protect him. On the 27th, the day preceding the departure of the President and his party for Des Moines, Ia., Justice Miller, then sitting for this district, rendered his opinion upon the demurrer to the indictments of Col. Joyce, Al. Bevis, Jos. Fitzroy and myself, which concluded as follows: "Without delaying further, I will say that both Judge Treat and myself are of the opinion that the indictment is essentially bad, and the demurrer must be sustained."

Notwithstanding this decision we were placed under bonds to appear before the next Grand Jury. Gen. Babcock congratulated me upon this first victory and expressed the opinion that it would cripple the prosecution, but I assured him that this decision afforded little balm, for our enemies were determined and would push us to the wall, and that this would prove an unimportant obstacle.

In the latter part of the June term other indictments had been found against us charging conspiracy, which fact I neglected to state in the earlier and proper part of this narrative, so that when the demurrer to the indictment charging us with a willful destruction of public records, was sustained, we were at once re-arrested upon a bench warrant and placed under bonds in the sum of $11,000, to answer to two indictments charging us with conspiracy and one charging us with destruction of public records. Col. Joyce was also indicted during the September term by the Grand Jury, sitting in the western district, and his case was transferred to Jefferson City where he was afterwards tried. It was rumored that an indictment had also been returned against me at Jefferson City, and to satisfy myself of its truth, in company with Col. Joyce I went up to the capital where I learned that the report was false. Col. Joyce, however, gave bond before Judge Krekel, and we returned to St. Louis. On the 6th of October Col. Joyce went to Washington to procure copies of official papers on file at the department which we wanted to use in the trial of our cases, and on the evening of the 8th I proceeded to my home in Wisconsin. On the 11th Col. Joyce arrived at my home on his return from Washington and remained with me until the 15th, when we both returned to St. Louis, while Col. Joyce, on the 18th continued on to Jefferson City where his case had been called for trial. On the next day, in company with Judge Krum, and Ex-Gov. Thomas C. Fletcher, Joyce's attorneys, I proceeded to Jefferson City, having been subpœned as a witness for Col. Joyce, whose trial begun on the 20th. On the 23d the trial was concluded and a verdict of guilty was returned against him "for failure to report official investigations." The Colonel was remanded to the charge of the U. S. Marshal who did not, however, place him in jail until several days after.

On the morning of the 24th I again returned to St. Louis, where I remained for some time arranging with my attorney the theory of my defence, but making occasional trips to Jefferson City in the meantime.

On the 2d day of November, while in attendance at court, awaiting and expecting my arraignment, Col. Dyer and Gen. Henderson consulted with me as to the propriety of my pleading guilty and be-becoming a witness for the Government. They promised me immunity from punishment if I would adopt such a course, but I positively refused, knowing that their object was to secure the conviction of the President and Gen. Babcock through my testimony.

On Monday, the 15th, my case was called, and the court denying my application for a continuance, I was placed on trial, which continued until the following Monday, when a verdict of guilty was returned. During the progress of this trial, as well, also, as during every day after the Presidential party left St. Louis, for Des Moines, I received one or more letters from Gen. Babcock through Maj. Grimes, in which the most flattering language complimenting my fidelity, and the elaborate promises of the interference of the President when I should ask it, was conveyed. I was exhorted to stand fast and true, supported by a firm reliance in the strong and unfailing friendship of the President and himself.

On the third day of my trial, while I was descending the steps of the post-office, Gen. Henderson stopped me, and with most impressive and pursuasive language, he urged me to plead guilty. He assured me of the certainty of my conviction, and that to avoid punishment, I ought to avail myself of this last opportunity. He told me that I was involving the Government in a large expense by forcing continued trials, and that he knew I was in possession of evidence which would assist the Government in convicting all the guilty parties. He repeated, that if I would enter a plea of guilty, my punishment would be only nominal, and besides it would subserve important purposes for the Government. But to all his entreaties I was obstinate, and persistently refused, replying to him that I would accept all consequences. When he turned away from me, he said: "Well, some day you will discover how great was your error."

On the evening of my conviction, which occurred about seven o'clock, I was remanded to jail, my bond having been fixed at $50,000, and the lateness of the hour precluded me from obtaining sureties. I was accompanied to jail by Judge Krum, my attorney, who advised me to give bail on the following day and then call for the President's intervention by asking for immediate pardon. My friends, without exception, pleaded with me to demand my pardon. Maj. Grimes received a letter from Gen. Babcock on the day of my conviction, in which he told Grimes to assure me that the President would pardon me immediately upon my request.

But I refused the proffer of a pardon, and if this fact were allowed to remain unexplained there is scarcely one of the thousands who will read this book that would give the slightest credence to the statement. My reasons were, nevertheless, of the most plausible character: At the particular time of which I am writing the most damaging charges were being made against the President and Gen. Babcock, and I knew that the Grand Jury was then investigating allegations against the latter, and the public was daily expecting his indictment. My position, serious as it was, did not make me forget what I conceived to be my duty. I had avowed my determination to protect the President and Gen. Babcock even at the sacrifice of my own feelings and humiliation. I realized that if the President granted me a pardon in the face of public opinion, which was very excited, that it would clearly establish the fact of my intimate affiliation with both Grant and Babcock, and the impeachment of one and conviction of the other would be a foregone conclusion. I entertained the hope that the Grand Jury would not indict Babcock and if it did that the daily information furnished the President by E. W. Fox, a member of the jury, who had forsworn himself in order to protect Babcock, would enable Attorney General Pierrepont to devise means by which to annul its effects. There was, in fact, much to inspire me with the belief that the excitement of the hour would be succeeded by a calm which would permit the President to pardon me without drawing public execration upon himself.   Understanding the peculiar attitute of my position I am sure the reader will be charitable and just enough to admit the force of my reasons.

My personal discomforts, while in confinement, were not so great as those unacquainted with the circumstances would suppose.   I was visited daily by nearly all my friends, who provided admissible luxuries and, by the cheering assurances of their continued regard, and respect for the defiance I had manifested, mitigated my punishment until I was little else than a king in his well embarricated castle.

Among the daily callers at my citadel was E. W. Fox, at one time collector of the port at St. Louis, and, I believe, the inventor of wooden insoles in army shoes which, during the war, furnished such a blessed margin of profit to army contractors.   Fox was always a jolly fellow, having one of those full-faced, burgomaster forms which indicated a contentedness of disposition when filled up with some effervescent spirit mixed with the substantials.   His visits were very pleasant because he was a member of the Grand Jury which was then in session, and he never failed to tell me every day just how the investigation against Babcock was proceeding.   He was our mutual friend and was rewarded for it, as Grant had promised, in this manner: The people of St. Louis knew Fox too well to accept him as a goverment officer, so the only thing that remained was to appoint his son as consul to Brunswick, Germany, at a salary of $2,500 in gold per year. This son was only nineteen years of age at the time of his appointment, while the regulations require all consuls to be at least twenty one years of age, but then he was large enough and the President couldn't afford to regard requirements when his own and Babcock's interests were risked against such stakes. Fox, however, did more than I have already mentioned, and I must not be so unmindful of my duty to the public as to omit the full measure of his services. Before the adjournment of the Grand Jury he succeeded in securing the adoption of a letter completely exonerating the President from any complicity or knowledge of the whiskey ring; but it was impossible for him to prevent Babcock's indictment so he could only do the next best thing: notify the President by telegraph the moment the indictment was found.

Following is the Grand Jury letter:

U. S. Grand Jury Room, }
St. Louis, December 9, 1875. }

To U. S. Grant, President of the United States, Washington, D. C.

The undersigned, late United States Grand Jurors for the Eastern District of Missouri, in the discharge of their sworn duty, have found it imperative upon them to present to the U. S. Court of said district the names of many officials and other persons, as being connected with a conspiracy to defraud the internal revenue of the United States.

As citizens of our common country, sincerely desiring to uphold the hands of our chief Executive in securing an honest collection of the public revenues, we cannot refrain from thus testifying to our estimation of the moral support which we have leaned upon, as imparted in your notable instructions to the Secretary of the Treasury: "Let no guilty man escape."

With this, all good citizens can contribute their share in aiding the government and in sustaining your administration in its endeavor to conduct it with purity and fidelity.

We, individually and collectively, tender to you our highest considerations of esteem and confidence, and an assurance of our appreciation of the wisdom, patriotism and independence displayed in directing the measures necessary for detecting and correcting the gigantic frauds which have so lately preyed upon the public revenues.

We have the honor to be, with great respect, your fellow citizens:

R. D. Brewington, Marion Co
John Riggin, St. Louis Co.
Theon Barnum, St. Louis Co.
John T. Lloyd, Lewis Co.
Jas. D. Overton, Marion Co.
Henry Griffin, St. Louis Co.
Wm. K. Haynes, Marion Co.
Geo. R. Rathburn, Jefferson Co.
J. W. Cody, Scotland Co.
J. M. Shepard, Marion Co.
Thos. Meyers, Scotland Co.
John M. Settle, Lewis Co.
Wm. H. Herron, Adair Co.
E. W. Fox, St. Louis Co.
Wm. C. Ebert, Scotland Co.
S. F. Hinckley, Jefferson Co.
G. H. Barker, Scotland Co.
Jared Barde, Marion Co.
A. H. Linder, Adair Co.

On the day this letter was adopted, Fox came to my department of the municipality and, with joy beaming from his little grey eyes, he said: " Now General, what do you think of that; haint that policy and diplomacy; wasn't that one of the brightest ideas of the century, etc.?" I agreed with him that it was a master stroke; in fact, he filled me to such an extent with the importance of

N

his accomplishment, that I yielded to his solicitation and assurances of pecuniary distress, and loaned him the sum of $200, the memory alone of which remains as a memento of his insinuating address and magnanimous disposition. With this money Fox posted to Washington and secured his boy a consulship, and when he returned to me again he was so happy that I fairly envied his poverty, because his happiness seemed to consist chiefly in obtaining small loans on long time, which no man, except in like circumstances, could do.

On the 4th of November, the Grand Jury returned indictments against Wm. McKee, proprietor of the *Globe-Democrat*, and Constantine Maguire, revenue collector, charging them with conspiracy to defraud the Government.

On the 13th of the same month, Col. Joyce was sentenced by Judge Krekel to a term of three and one-half years' imprisonment in the penitentiary and to pay a fine of $2,000. Before the sentence was passed, when asked by the court if he had anything to say, Col. Joyce arose with becoming dignity and with an appearance the very personification of scorn and contempt, he delivered the following address, which I quote here to give the reader an idea of the oratorical gift possessed by the Colonel, and the caustic sarcasm of his tongue:

COL. JOYCE'S ORATION BEFORE SENTENCE.

Before this Honorable Court passes sentence, I beg leave to state that my conviction was secured by perjured testimony of self-convicted thieves. Feineman, the rectifier; Brongesser, the gauger, and Rendleman, the storekeeper, all lineal descendants of those ancient scoundrels who crucified Christ, came upon the witness stand and paraded their own infamy by acknowledging that they had stolen whiskey from the government, through a term of years, at the rate of from one dollar to fifty cents per barrel. The pencil of Gustave Dore could not do justice to these three wandering Israelites, who seemed ever on the lookout to steal small things when big ones were conveniently at hand. Feineman and Fagan are identical characters, and should be imortalized in living infamy. I dismiss these pillars of fraud and perjury, consigning them to the devouring fury of a rotten conscience.

I was indicted for failing to report in writing certain alleged knowledge and information of certain fraudulent transactions of petrified perjurers. The jury found me guilty on the counts, but as a matter of fact, the conclusion was as false as the evidence. I agree that it had the appearance to the jury of failure of duty. We know, however, that things are not always what they seem. I simply declare upon my honor as a man, and my allegiance as an American citizen, here in the presence of this Honorable Court, to the whole world, and facing my God, that I am absolutely innocent of the charges trumped up against me by pretended friends and viper enemies. It has not been shown in evidence, or even intimated by anybody, that I ever received a single cent in any fraud on the revenue. Then where is the motive that induced me to withold the information? I did make a report in writing to Supervisor McDonald and Commissioner Douglass. The report, it is alleged, was not in full. Neither was the information in my possession full or complete, as the facts were out of my district. The District Attorney of the United States, in his concluding speech, introduced my copy book, showing the transmittal letter to Supervisor McDonald as something fraudulent. My lawyers or myself had no opportunity to explain the letter in evidence, which could have been done to the utmost satisfaction of everybody connected.

Your Honor, from the beginning of the case to the end, extended to me the kindest consideration and fairest rulings. For this, I thank you in the name of the people and in the name of justice. I stand here to-day, strong and bold, in conscious innocence, and my heart is actuated by that noble impulse that nerved Winkleried when he opened the breach for the liberty of his country, or by that lofty courage that inspired Sir Walter Raleigh at the block. Like Raleigh, I may have puffed smoke through the window at the execution of some official Essex, but I never yet trampled upon the royal robes of the Virgin Queen. For myself, I have no fear of any punishment on earth ; yet, in behalf of my past good character, this is the first suspicion of guilt that ever darkened my life, and in consideration of the support I owe my wife and children, I ask that magnanimity at this bar of justice that would be reasonably claimed by yourself under like circumstances. A few short years will sepulcher the living of to-day with the dead of yesterday, and the celestial sunlight of to-morrow will bring us all to the bar of Omnipotence, where the judge, jury, lawyer and client, will meet upon the level of eternity and part upon the square of final judgment. Then all hearts shall be laid bare, and truth will rise in splendid triumph.

The blood of innocence flows free and unruffled through the life-channels of this frame, and the artificial lusters that surround the victims of crime find no lodgment in my heart. When I look back to the field of battle, when I fought and bled for my country in the hour of terrible trial, I wondered whether patriotism was but a name, and the gratitude of nations but a mockery and a sham to lure the brave to destruction. My simple sin is that of omission, and for it I suffer the deepest humiliation, while the glorious services and recollections of the past are buried in the grave of forgetfulness. Is this just ? This epidemical era of reform has risen like the rush of a mighty flood, and sped on towards the gulf of punishment. The good and the bad suffer alike. The stream is full of driftwood and dead timber, while many young oaks and tall sycamores on the banks are loosened from their firm foundation and dashed into the river of destruction. But the rain falls lightly on the mountains, the sun shines warmly on the plains, and the floods even now are settling into its former bed, where the crystal water shall again reflect the green foliage of the oak and sycamore, and the gentle breezes and birds of Spring shall make merry music in the cathedral aisles of a generous nation. The prison walls that hemmed in Gallileo, Columbus, Tasso and Napoleon, did not measure the minds of the men. It is true their bodies suffered some torture, but the proud spirit that was in their hearts leaped the bounds of clay and soared away into the illimitable regions of science, poetry and war, making them monarchs of the hour and masters of eternity.

Humble as I am in the walks of life, my soul is inspired by their illustrious example, and it shall be my future endeavor to show the world that, although I may suffer for a time the penalty of perjured testimony, yet like a mountain crag, I shall breast the pelting storm, and lift my head clear and bold to the coming sunshine of truth and redemption. I have done.

CHAPTER VIII.

Avery's Trial and Conviction—Henderson Charged with Attacking the President—The Power of His Address to the Jury—What he Said—The President Advised of Henderson's Fearless Denunciation of Thieves, and Peremptorily dismisses him—The Correspondence—Krum Becomes the Medium through which Babcock and I Correspond—Pierrepont's Circular Letter to Suppress Testimony—Krum's Letter—Congress Rebukes Grant Through Pierrepont—Report of the Judiciary Committee on the pierrepont Letter—Trial and Conviction of Wm. McKee—Krum, as Babcock's Attorney, Writes a Note Requesting Information Respecting a Damaging Letter from His Client—Gen. Babcock Buys the Letter from Hardaway—Babcock Placed on Trial—Everest's Testimony—Babcock Buys a Witness from the Post Office—How Magill Perjured Himself—Babcock Admits that he Paid Magill to Give False Testimony—Krum Writes Me for Permission to see the Babcock Letters—The Interview in My Cell—The President's Deposition—Comments on the Deposition—How Grant Perjured Himself—Porter, Babcock's Counsel, Attacks Me—Babcock writes a Letter Begging Me Not to Hold Him Accountable—Why I Could Not be Forced to Testify—The Jury Acquit Babcock—$10,000 Presented to Him at the Conclusion of his Trial—Babcock Calls on Me at My Cell—Begs Me for His Letters—Liberal Offer of Money—Promises to Pardon Me—Babcock's Brother Tries to Buy the Letters From My Old Chief Clerk—Upon Refusal to Treat Theatens Him With Personal Injury—Expressions of Belief in Babcock's Guilt by Jurymen—Why He Was Acquitted.

On the 24th of November, the case of Wm. O. Avery (who is now well known to the reader) was called, and both sides being ready the trial proceeded, Judge Chester H. Krum entering an appearance as counsel for the defendant.

Avery's conviction was not secured until the 3d of December, after a bitter fight in which the most exciting scenes occurred.   Gen. Jno. B. Henderson, formerly a United States Senator from Missouri, and Maj. Lucien Eaton, at that time Register in Bankruptcy at St. Louis, in an early period of the prosecution, had been engaged by the government to assist the District Attorney to prosecute members of the Whiskey Ring against whom indictments had been found.   During the trial of Avery, Gen. Henderson took a more than prominent part—he assumed a most aggressive attitude, as the circumstances warranted and, proceeding upon the President's instructions to "let no guilty man escape," he intended that if the power lay within him to make the court write "guilt" over the head of every member of that conspiracy.   In the closing argument (December 3d), Gen. Henderson made, confessedly, one of the most powerful appeals ever heard at the bar.   It not only carried conviction, but aroused an enthusiasm among the audience, which was so completely captivated by his forensic eloquence, that it was almost impossible for the officers of the court to restrain the vociferous demonstrations.   In that masterly argument he used the following language, relating to the order changing Supervisors, and the orders recalling revenue agents sent into my district to make investigations:

"What right had Babcock to go to Douglass to induce him to withdraw his agents?   Douglass was placed in his position to see that the revenue laws of the government were properly enforced. What business, then, had Douglass with him? When an official goes into office, he should be free and independent of all influences except that of law, and if he recognizes any other master, then this government is tumbling down. What right had the President to interfere with Commissioner Douglass in the proper discharge of his duties, or with the Secretary of the Treasury? None, and Douglass showed a lamentable weakness of character when he listened to Babcock's dictates. He should either have insisted that his orders, as they existed, be carried out, or should have resigned his office. Now, why did Douglass bend the supple hinges of his knee and permit any interference by the President? This was Douglass' own business, and he stood responsible for it under his official oath. He was bound to listen to no dictation from the President, Babcock, or any other officer, and it was his duty to see that that order was carried out or resign. Would that we had officials who possessed more of that sterner stuff of which the office holders of olden times were made. Why do they not leave their office when they cannot remain there honorably? Is it to be that because a man holds an office at the hands of another, he is to be a bonded slave?"

W. D. W. Barnard, a cousin of President Grant's, was in the court-room during the delivery of this speech, and regarding the language as a serious reflection upon the President, he sent a dispatch to Washington that night giving the offensive remarks in full.

It should be remembered that this speech was made at a time when the Grand Jury was investigating charges preferred against Gen. Babcock, and hence they had a double significance. The President and his coterie of barnacles felt outraged, nay—frightened at this boldness, and as they had long been seeking an occasion to get rid of Gen. Hender-

Gen. John B. Henderson.

son, they accepted this as their opportunity. The following telegrams will be understood in this connection:

WASHINGTON, Dec, 9th, 1875.

To HON. D. P. DYER, U. S. Att'y, St. Louis:

Evidence has reached here that in the trial of Avery, Mr. Henderson took advantage of his position as special counsel of the government, to assail the President, who was not on trial. His efforts in that line will be no longer paid by this department. You will give a copy of this dispatch to Gen. Henderson.

(Signed) EDWARDS PIERREPONT, Attorney General.

To this Col. Dyer sent the following answer:

ST. LOUIS, Dec. 9th, 1875.

HON. EDWARDS PIERREPONT, Attorney General, Washington:

The information which you say you have, that Mr. Henderson, in the trial of Avery, assailed the President is entirely unfounded. Shall I inform him that he is discharged as special counsel of the government in the revenue cases in this district?

(Signed) D. P. DYER, District Attorney.

The following telegram was sent at the same time by Gen. Henderson:

ST. LOUIS, Dec. 9th, 1875.

HON. EDWARDS PIERREPONT, Attorney General United States, Washington:

I have seen your last dispatch to Col. Dyer. My speech in the Avery case was extemporaneous. Maj. Eaton mailed you on Tuesday, a sworn copy from the stenographer of so much as he thought related to the President. I did not see it, *but I stand by the speech as made. I said nothing beyond what my sworn duty required, and for that I have no apology to make.*

(Signed) J. B. HENDERSON.

On the following day Col. Dyer received the appended dispatch:

WASHINGTON, December 10th, 1875.
HON. D P. DYER, U. S. Att'y, St. Louis :

The sworn report of Mr. Henderson's speech, forwarded by Mr. Eaton, and referred to by both you and Mr. Henderson in your dispatches of yesterday as a correct report, was read in full cabinet to-day. It was regarded by every member as an outrage upon professional propriety thus to reflect, without shadow of reason, upon the President, by whom his employment by this Department was sanctioned, in order that no impediment might be placed in the way of bringing to speedy punishment, every defrauder of the revenue at St. Louis. You will advise Gen. Henderson of his discharge from further service, and secure in his place the aid of the most able and efficient counsel you can find, without regard to his politics.

(Signed)   EDWARDS PIERREPONT, Attorney General.

This abitrary act called upon the President the well merited censure of the Republican and Democratic press alike.   It was the first indefensible step taken to prevent an honest and thorough prosecution of all the Whisky Ring members, and the suspicions which before attached to the President now assumed the nature of well founded charges.

The removal of Gen. Henderson from a position as assistant to the district attorney, in which he had distinguished himself by an energy and efficiency that struck terror to the heart of every member of the illicit whisky conspiracy, was not alone the last and desperate resort of an alarmed and implicated administration—it was a virtual confession of its own guilt.   The President was betrayed by his personal fears into an act that stamped him with ineffaceable suspicion.   It was the result, again brought home to the administration, of disregarding my advice not to commit an indiscretion which would excite the already fevered pulse of the public.

On the 9th of December the Grand Jury concluded its lengthy sesssion by returning an indictment against Gen. Orville E. Babcock. The excitement over this announcement was almost equal to that exhibited by the northern people when they received the news of the capture of Richmond in 1865. It was a stroke of lightning, as it were, and everyone thought they saw the hand of justice hovering over the heads of those who were fortified by the influence which attaches to the Executive.

I cannot here undertake to describe my own feelings but every reader cannot help reflecting upon the position I occupied. I was as Jove himself with the thunderbolts of conviction in my hands, and though the gratings of a prison were between me and my liberty, yet how easily could I have uttered a breath which would have toppled the very foundations of the White House. To me it was not a suspicion—it was the sternness of solid fact, but I realized that my own safety and liberty, with a satisfied conscience of my loyalty to Grant and Babcock, was in their exoneration or acquittal.

I could not yet demand my pardon from my friend—the President—because he had been borne out so far in the ocean where nothing but the breakers of destruction surrounded him. The finger of odium pointed at him until his eyes were like Macbeth's, seeing the ghosts of his many crimes. Still I waited with patience, and lips sealed with secrecy. Letters of encouragement and promise came daily to me, fresh with the impress of the pardoning power, and my determination was braced by the resolutions I had framed out of my own sacrifice and anguish.

On the 13th of December Col. James O. Broadhead was appointed special counsel to take the place of Gen. Henderson, and as the holidays were near at hand nothing was done of public importance except an active preparation for the trials which were to be called early in the new year.

After my incarceration I received no letters from Gen. Babcock nor any information through Maj. Grimes, but Judge Krum, especially after his retention as counsel for Babcock (Nov. 17th), kept me thoroughly posted, and was the telephone through which the General and I talked almost daily.

In the early part of January Judge Krum, at my solicitation, went to Washington in order to put into use my plans for protecting Babcock and the President. I told him that the first consideration was the suppression of the evidence of the minor members of the ring, who were then disposed to become witnesses for the government on account of the promises made to protect them from punishment. I further told him that Joyce had loaned Frazer a letter from Gen. Babcock, some time before the disclosures were made, in order that it might in turn be shown to the other distillers, so as to convince them that the White House was fully cognizant of the frauds (Frazer afterwards made oath to this fact). I knew that many subordinate officers had the strongest circumstantial evidence of Babcock's guilty knowledge, and if they could escape punishment by telling what they knew that Babcock would certainly be convicted.

On or about the 12th of January, Judge Krum returned from Washington, and informed me that he had brought the attention of the President and Gen. Babcock to the importance of adopting my suggestions and, at the President's request, he had drafted a letter of instructions for the Attorney General to send to every District Attorney who was engaged in the whiskey prosecutions. He said that the matter would certainly be attended to and, as he predicted, the circular-letter did appear, but not until some time in February. It read as follows:

DEPARTMENT OF JUSTICE, ⎫
WASHINGTON, Jan. 26th, 1876. ⎬

HON. ————————, United States District Attorney:

SIR:—My attention has been called to a number of newspapers, stating that there would be no further prosecutions against any guilty persons who confessed their crimes in St. Louis, Chicago, and Milwaukee. I cannot believe this to be true; but, as the assertion has been made that so many guilty persons are to remain unpunished, I have forwarded a letter to each of those cities to inform each District Attorney of the fact.

I know that many rumors find credence in these times of excitement, and trust that your sound judgment will prevent any wrong, and anything that will look like favoring or protecting men who have defrauded the Government. It is the repeatedly expressed wish of the President that no guilty man should escape. I am not aware that any of the officials charged with the execution of the laws contemplated to favor or protect any of the accused, and even the appearance of such favorable treatment should be carefully avoided. I write this as a matter of caution, for I am determined to have these prosecutions so conducted that, when they are over, the honest judgment of the honest men of the country—which generally never fails to hit the right—will be: "That no one has been maliciously prosecuted, that no one has escaped through favoritisms or partiality, and that no guilty person, who has either been convicted or *confessed* his guilt, was left unpunished.

EDWARDS PIERREPONT, Attorney General.

After reading the letter in print Judge Krum assured me that it was the same he had written and left with the President.

Before the expiration of January I received the following letter from Judge Krum, which will be found upon the next page in fac-simile:

JANUARY 29th, 1876.

DEAR BOY:

I have no time to call and merely drop this line. *We* are all right. I have the most positive assurance that *the* matter of which we have talked so often will be accomplished *dead sure*. And, moreover and best of all, as to *enemies* "let no guilty man escape" means just what the words imply.

The goose does hang *altitudilum*.   (Signed) C. H. K.

(The italicised words are his own.)

The full meaning of this letter cannot be gathered except when the following facts are ascertained: All the evidence submitted to the Grand Jury, upon which Babcock was indicted, had been forwarded to the President by E. W. Fox, and when Judge Krum went to Washington in January, he met Emory Storrs, of Chicago, who had also been retained as Babcock's leading counsel. They, therefore, examined all the Grand Jury evidence and considered it insufficient, and if they could prevent the introduction of new testimony, Babcock's acquittal would be certain.

On the day Judge Krum wrote me this letter he received a communication from Babcock, in which

CHESTER H. KRUM,

January 29th.

Jany 29.

Dear Boy:

I have no time to call, and merely drop this line.

We are all eighth.

I have the most positive assurance that the matter of which we have talked so often, will be accomplished dead sure.

And, moreover, & best of all, as to Revenue, Let no bill, than an Escobe

means just what
the words import.
The goose does have
altitudilum.
_____

No man
allowed to
appeal

C H R.

assurance was given that the circular letter would
be issued by the Attorney General. To this fact is
due his manifestations of delight and the assuring
manner in which he wrote me. "The matter
of which we have talked so often" was our
well considered plans to procure the acquittal
of Babcock, upon the result of which I was to
be immediately pardoned, and Bristow, Dyer,
and other objectionable officers to be dismissed.
He used the word "enemies" to designate those
who were anxious to become informers in order to
avoid punishment; so, having been informed by
Babcock that the circular letter order would be
issued, the Judge gleefully writes me that no guilty
man should escape, so that no fears need be entertained of Babcock's guilt being proven by those
who knew all the facts.

When the Pierrepont letter made its appearance
everyone who had manifested the slightest interest
in the prosecution of the Ring members was fairly
horrified at this most extraordinary attempt at a
direct interference with the policy adopted by the
district attorneys. It was such a flagrant outrage
that Congress was compelled to take some cogni-
zance of the act, which was done by the following
resolution, introduced by Representative Lord, of
New York, on the 25th of February:

Resolved, That the Attorney General be requested to inform
the House by what authority and for what purpose he recently
gave instructions to his subordinates alleged to be in contravention of a long established rule relating to testimony of
accomplices in criminal actions.

To this resolution **the Attorney General made the** following reply:

DEPARTMENT OF JUSTICE,
WASHINGTON, Feb. 26th, 1876.

To THE HONORABLE HOUSE OF REPRESENTATIVES:

I am in receipt of the following resolution of the House of Representatives of February 25th, [then follows **a** copy of the resolution] to which, in reply, I have the honor to suggest that the resolution must have been introduced under a misaprehen-sion. No instructions have been given by the Attorney Gen-**eral to** his subordinates, in contravention of any rule relating to testimony of accomplices in criminal actions, and no in-structions that had any such purpose could be fairly **attribu-**ted. The only specific instructions which have been given **on** the subject are those of certain districts where whiskey frauds are being prosecuted, and these are merely in confirmation and approval of the arrangements made to use the testimony of accomplices. As these arrangements and instructions re-**late to matters in progress, the** House will readily see the propriety of withholding **special** information thereto until the trials are **over.**

I have the honor to add that in no instance since I have been Attorney General has there been a proposition of any subordi-nate of mine relating to testimony of accomplices in criminal actions which has not met my prompt **and** cordial sanction.

I have the honor to remain, yours very obediently,

EDWARDS PIERREPONT, Attorney General.

This answer to the House resolution is one of the most remarkable documents ever prepared by an attorney; it first denies his contravention of estab-lished rules, and then confirms the charges, after which it contributes a caustic insult to the House.

In the following month, March, the Judiciary Committee of the House was instructed to examine the Pierrepont letter, together with his reply to the

House resolution, and to make report thereon.
The committee, on the 31st of March, brought in
their report, which, stripped of its formal and re-
dundant matter, reads as follows:

REPORT OF JUDICIARY COMMITTEE ON THE PIERREPONT LETTER.

The Attorney General, to prevent bargains with criminals
likely, as he says, to bring great scandal on the administration
of justice, and as a precaution against any such possible
wrong, wrote the letters, and asserts that cautious circumspec-
tion and judgment were required to see that criminals should
not successfully combine to shield themselves, by charging
their own crimes upon innocent men ; therefore, it became
necessary to notify his subordinates of his determination that
the prosecutions should be so conducted that when they were
over it should appear "that no guilty one who had been
proved guilty or confessed himself guilty, had been suffered
to escape punishment."

The question therefore arises whether the Attorney General,
in so instructing his subordinates, acted in contravention of
the long-established rule relating to the testimony of accomplices in criminal actions.

The testimony of accomplices has been used against their
associates from the early ages of our jurisprudence. The evidence of accomplices has at all times been admitted, either
from a principle of public policy, or from judicial necessity, or
from both. The general rule is, that a person who confesses
himself guilty is a competent witness against his partners
in guilt. (Barbour's Criminal Law, 424.) Archibald in his
criminal pleadings and evidence page 154, says: "An accomplice may give evidence against those jointly guilty
with him, but although in point of law they may be found
guilty on his testimony alone, yet in practice it is not usual
to convict on the testimony of an accomplice *   *   *
unless   *   *   *   *   confined in some material

part of the testimony of other creditable witnesses." The necessity of such a rule is apparent. In the cases to which the letter of the Attorney General relates, conspiracies are essential to their existence. When each conspirator knows that any one of the necessary accomplices may gain immunity by revealing the conspiracy, it leads him to hesitate, and after the conspirators have committed the crime for which they combine it is very difficult, if not impossible, until one or more of their number seeks the immunity given a witness, for the State to bring the conspirators to justice.

But the Attorney General answers that he only intended to prevent criminals from combining "to shield themselves, by charging their crimes upon innocent men." How does he know, particularly at this distant point, who are innocent men? Does he judge from their apparent respectability or high official position? Of the classes of apparently respectable citizens and high officials many have confessed their guilt and others have been proven guilty. Did not the high officials and apparently respectable citizens at first vigorously protest their innocence? Why did not the Attorney General, as did the Secretary of the Treasury, allow some discretion to his subordinates? Why did he say that no guilty man who confesses himself guilty shall be allowed to escape punishment, when by the necessary force of the language accomplices are included?

The report then quotes the rules of law in answer to the Attorney General's position, and says: But under the rule, laid down by the Attorney General, the legal adviser of the President, based upon allegations made to the President, these rules are of no avail. The subordinates of the Attorney General would be guilty of no perfidy unknown to an honorable profession should they permit accomplices to testify without informing them that they could expect no favor, although both the court and jury should be convinced that they spoke the truth. All experience has shown that without such expectations accomplices will not testify, and existing conspiracies to commit crimes may not only go on with impunity, but new conspiracies may be organized with comparative safety. It is alleged that the letters of the Attorney General had the effect of suppressing testimony in a recent important case. That the defendant in that case understood it would have that effect appears from the fact stated by the Attorney General that such defendant distrusting, perhaps the Attorney General, surreptitiously made it public.

The committee recommend the adoption of the following :

Resolved, That in the judgment of this House, the long established rule relating to the testimony of accomplices in criminal actions is necessary to prevent combinations for criminal purposes, and greatly aids in the disclosure of conspiracies to commit crime, and that the letter of the Attorney General to the District Attorneys of the United States residing in St. Louis, Milwaukee, and Chicago, dated the 25th day of January, A. D., 1876, stating the determination of the Attorney General that no person confessing himself guilty should escape punishment, is in contravention of such rule, and that the Attorney General should immediately revoke the instructions covered and implied by the announcement of such determination.

I will here take the liberty to quote an editorial from the Missouri *Republican*, of February 22d, which reflected the sentiments of both the press and public at the time so faithfully that no additional comment is necessary :

" The resolution introduced in the House yesterday, by Mr. Lord, of New York, (Republican) inquiring of the Attorney-General why a certain letter was written, calculated to interfere with the prosecution of the whiskey conspirators, goes straight to the point, and its prompt adoption is a cheerful indication of a healthy sentiment in the lower branch of Congress. Pierrepont is too shrewd a lawyer not to know that his instructions relative to the treatment of those members of the Ring who had pleaded guilty and testified against their partners in sin, were a direct bid for them to keep their mouths shut in the trial now pending in this city. No explanation will convince the public that these instructions were not delib_ erately prepared for the express purpose of throwing obstacles in the path of justice. They might have been withheld until all the trials were concluded and then forwarded to the proper officials for their guidance in the distribution of punishment. They were sent just the time when they would do Babcock the most good and the cause of the Government the most harm. That they were inspired by the President is only an aggrava- tion of the wrong, not an apology for it.

The simple truth of the matter is that the now famous Pierrepont letter is a part of the policy of the administration in regard to the whiskey Ring; a policy which, while saying, "Let no guilty man escape," wanted no guilty man to be con- victed, in whom the administration had a lively interest. It was an impudent and inexcusable interference with the dis- cretionery powers which district attorneys have always exercised, and without which every combination of thieves would be ' bigger than the Government.' So plain and palpa- ble was its object that nobody has ventured to defend it, except, perhaps, one or two ring organs, whose praise is more to be dreaded than a condemnation of honest people. There- fore, the House resolution is a deserved rebuke, not only to the Attorney-General, but to that unscrupulous Executive who never lacks tools to do his bidding. The country heartily endorses the inquiry and will wait patiently for the reply."

On the 20th of January, Wm. McKee was arraigned for trial. His attorneys were Hon. Dan. Voorhes, Hon. W. H. Hatch, Judge Henry C. Clover, Judge Bayless W. Hanna, and Judges John M. and Chester H. Krum. The Government was represented by U. S. District Attorney, D. P. Dyer, Maj. Lucien Eaton, W. H. Bliss, and Col. James O. Broadhead. Every step in the case was bitterly contested, and in St. Louis, where the defendant had occupied a high position for more than thirty years, the excitement was very great. The evidence was so overwhelming, however, that on the morning of February 1st a verdict of guilty was returned. On the same day Col. Constantine Maguire, having not the slightest hope for an acquittal, entered a plea of guilty. Both the defendants were allowed considerable time to procure pardon, but their efforts were of no avail. McKee made great exertions to obtain testimony upon which to base his application for a new trial. They remained at liberty under bonds until the court passed sentence, sometime in the latter part of April.

On the morning of February 6th, I received the following note from Judge Krum, who was expecting daily to hear the name of his client, Gen. Babcock, called for trial:

February 6th, 1876.

DEAR FRIEND:

I hear that some one has a letter from B. (Babcock) to you, which was written about the time of Joyce's trip to California, and which relates to his trip. This information comes from a party who says he can get the letter. He has shown a copy to B., (Babcock) or what he says is a copy.

What is there in this story? Answer by bearer and on the square.   CHESTER H. KRUM.

I wrote the Judge a short reply, in which I disclaimed any knowledge of the letter, which had never reached me.

On the same night Judge Krum paid me a visit and explained the matter fully: he said a copy of the letter had been handed to Babcock by Chat Hardaway, who was a discharged gauger, and that Babcock, recognizing the letter, sent for the original for which he paid Hardaway a large price.

There were three Hardaway brothers, one of whom, Chat, had been a gauger, and Henry a store-keeper, both of whom had been dismissed from the service several months before. The other brother, Joshua, was a letter carrier. The first two had been placed in the revenue service by Con. Megrue, and were, of course, members of the ring until their discharge. Judge Krum very properly advanced the theory that at the requests of Chat and Henry Hardaway, Joshua had watched the delivery, and knowing Gen. Babcock's hand writing, he had filched this letter in question from the mail. At all events the letter never reached me, and it is also a fact that the original letter was purchased by Gen. Babcock from Chat Hardaway, to whom he paid a large sum of money, the amount of which I do not now remember. This transaction occurred on the evening of the 6th, being the day following Gen. Babcock's arrival in St. Louis.

On February 8th, Gen. Babcock was placed on trial, charged with conspiracy to defraud the Government, there being five counts in the indictment. His counsel consisted of Hon. Emory A. Storrs, of Chicago; Judge John K. Porter, of New York; Ex-Attorney General Geo. H. Williams, and Judges John M. and Chester H. Krum. The prosecution was represented by the same attorneys as those in the McKee case. The jury was composed of the following gentlemen:

R. N. Blackwood, of Lewis Co.
Matt Woodruff, Clark Co.
W. E. Wilson, Lewis Co.
Ezra Johnson, Lewis Co.
B. F. Snyder, Knox Co.
J. M. Keathley, St. Charles Co.
W. Blakeley, Adair Co.
D. W. Taintor, Gasconade Co.
E. B. F. May, Franklin Co.
W. S. Jewett, Jefferson Co.
W. T. Jackson, Marion Co.
Harvey Sessons, Lewis Co.

This trial was one of the most remarkable and in many respects the most noteworthy of any ever held in America. Not that there were any intricate problems of jurisprudence involved, but because it arrayed the people directly against the Executive. It was essentially a fight between justice and the cormorants of power and mighty influence, and alas, that it must be said, justice was defeated.

The court-room was densely packed with interested people during every day of the trial, while the streets in the vicinity of the United States Courts were literally crowded with anxious persons eager to catch every floating rumor appertaining to the distinguished defendant. I cannot here undertake to give even a synopsis of that great judicial inquiry, but there is one particular part of the testimony which it is important I should quote, as it presents a photographic picture, as it were, of the desperation of the defendant and his friends. Those who have read my full statement are familiar with the case against Gen. Babcock, which embraces many facts, however, not in possession of the prosecution at the time of the trial.

It will be remembered by many who have read reports of this trial in the daily and weekly press, that Abijah M. Everest, revenue gauger, who had also performed the duties of Collector for the Ring, suddenly disappeared from St. Louis, when disclosures were first made. He remained in Europe for several months, and until he learned that the government was visiting informers with special leniency. A short correspondence with his friends here, convinced him that the most advisable course to pursue would be to return, plead guilty and become a witness for the government. This course he adopted, reaching St. Louis barely in time to give his testimony in the Babcock cause before the prosecution closed.

Among many other important matters he testified to were the following, which I have copied from the official report:

Question—How long did you continue to act as collector for the Ring? Will ask you before that, how did you become collector for the Ring? What arrangement was made by which you assumed the duties?

Answer—Col. Joyce asked me if I would. He said Fitzroy was sick and was going away, and he would like me to take his place.

Ques.—What time was that?

Ans.—In August, 1874.

Ques.—How long did you continue to collect for the Ring?

Ans.—Until the seizures in 1875.

* * * * *. * * * * *

Ques.—I will get you to state whether, in 1875, or at any time before April, you were present in the office of the Supervisor, and had a conversation with Joyce at any time other than the day you met them each week?

Ans.—I remember in 1875 I was.

Mr. Krum—When?

Ques. by Mr. Dyer—State when and where you had a corversation with him with reference to the matter.

Ans.—It was in the Supervisor's office, in 1875.

Mr. Krum—When?

Ans.—February or March—along, I think, in the latter part of February.

Ques. by Mr. Dyer—Well?

Ans.—He asked me about—

Mr. Storrs—One moment.

Mr. Dyer—This is an act, or accompanying an act—

Mr. Storrs—I would like to have the witness receive the same admonition from your Honor that he has already received.

Ques. by the court—Was this conversation in connection with any act that Joyce requested you to perform?

Ans.—Yes sir.

Ques.—Did you perform that act?

Ans.—I did.

The Court—Go on.

Witness—He gave me a package of one thousand dollars and told me to go to the Sub-Treasurer's office and have it changed into two five hundred dollar bills.

Ques.—State what the denomination of the bills you carried to the sub-treasury were?

Ans.—I did not notice particularly and therefore cannot answer.

Ques.—Well, what did you do at the sub-treasury?

Ans.—I passed the package to the teller, and he gave me two five hundred dollar bills in return.

Ques.—Then what did you do?

Ans.—I went back to the office and gave them to Col. Joyce.

Ques.—Who was in the office at the time?

Ans.—Nobody.

Ques.—After you gave him the bills, what did he do with them?

Ans.—He separated the bills and looked at both of them, and he picked up two envelopes laying on his desk, and put them in the envelopes.

Question by the Court.—Into separate envelopes?

Ans.—Yes, sir.

Question by Mr. Dyer.—Go on and state now, in your own way, what he did, and what you did?

Ans.—I gave him the money and he took up the envelopes, both of them, and put one bill in one envelope and I presume the other in another.

Mr. Storrs.—Hold on ; we don't want a particle of presumption.

The Court.—State what you know.

Witness.—He picked up both envelopes, examined the bills, took one five hundred dollar bill, put that in an envelope, and transferred it to the rear of the other one. He then pulled out a letter, and placed the other five hundred dollar bill 'in the other envelope.

Ques.—Then what did he do?

Ans.—He then sealed the envelopes, and he talked a little while, and he gave me the envelopes to put in the post-office.

Ques.—When he gave you them, what did he say to you?

Ans.—He asked me if I wouldn't put them in the box, across the street from his office, which I did.

Ques.—In the United States mail box?

Ans.—Yes, sir.

Ques.—State whereabouts the box was situated, as regards the office, where the letter was delivered to you?

Ans.—The box was situated on the south-west corner of Fifth and Pine.

Ques.—State what you did with the letters Joyce handed you?

Ans:—I put them in the ——

Mr. Krum.—We object to that ——

Judge Dillon.—What he did with the letters?

Mr. Krum.—Well, go on.

Mr. Dyer.—State what you did with the letters?

Ans.—I put them in the box as he directed.

Ques.—I will get you to state to the jury whether you observed the directions?

*   *   *   *   *   *   *   *   *   *   *   *   *

Ques.—Where was Joyce at the time you deposited the letters in the letter box?

Ans.—He was watching me from the window.

Ques.—At the time you deposited the letters, did you observe him at the time?

Ans.—I saluted him, and he saluted me.

Ques.—You put the letters in?

Ans.—I was facing him when I put them in.

Ques—After the letters came in your hands, and before they were deposited in the box by you, did you examine and see the name and direction on the envelopes?

Ans.—Yes, sir.

Ques.—Will you state to the jury how the letters were directed and to whom they were directed?

Ans.—There was one of them directed to W. O. Avery, Washington, D. C., and one to Gen. O. E. Babcock, Washington, D. C.

Ques.—Anything else on the envelopes?

Ans.—There was a post-mark, and each one of them had "Personal" on the left hand corner.

This testimony created a most profound sensation. Everest had always stood high in St. Louis until his social star paled before his confessions of implication with the Whiskey Ring. But the fact of him pleading guilty threw no discredit upon his statements, and when he told the story of Joyce's remittance to Babcock, by mail, there was not a person in St. Louis, I dare say, who did not feel that Babcock's guilt had been positively fixed. But the defense was equal to the emergency; they had suborned witnesses before; had purchased testimony and crippled the efficiency of the courts, so they could not hesitate at this critical point to buy a man in whose mouth they could put a story and make him a machine for its repetition. Poor Jim Magill was selected for this purpose. He was at the time a letter-carrier, but he had seen much of the hardships of life enforced by pecuniary distress. He had been a straggler in the army, a street car driver and conductor, a policeman, clerk, and a man of all jobs. The promise of a rich reward was too tempting for the conscience of the poor fellow, so after attending a few rehearsals before Babcock, Storrs, and Krum, he committed his story, and, regarding his oath only as a voucher for the price of his manhood, he gave the following testimony:

Question.—Do you recollect the circumstances, Mr. Magill, any time in February or March, of delivering to Col. Joyce, from the letter box, two letters

Answer.—Yes, sir.

Ques.—You may state when that occurred, the circumstances under which it occurred, and everything which you now remember with reference to it.

Ans—In the latter part of February I was coming down Pine street——

Judge Dillon.—What year?

Mr. Storrs.—1875.

Witness. (continuing)—Near Fifth, and Mr. Joyce accosted me and told me that there were two letters in the box on the southwest corner of Fifth and Pine—he did not say, but pointed there—that he would like to get them back again.

Ques —What did you say to him?

Mr. Broadhead.—Is Mr. Joyce connected with it?

Judge Dillon, (to counsel for defense)—Was anything done?

Mr. Storrs.—We will follow it up by showing that the letters were delivered.

Judge Dillon.—Does your objection still hold, Col. Broadhead?

Mr. Broadhead.—No, sir.

Mr. Storrs, (to witness)—Go on.

Witness.—I asked him to describe the letters which he wanted back, which he did. He said one was directed to W. O. Avery, Washington, and marked "personal," and the other was addressed to O. E. Babcock, Washington, and marked " personal " on the corner.

* * * * * * * * *

Ques.—What was done after he made that request of you?

Ans.—I opened the box, although it was off my district.

Ques.—Then what did you do?

Ans.—I searched among the letters and found the letters he described, and he made some remark about the seal, or something of that kind, and I gave them to him.

Ques.—Did he give you any receipt for the letter?

Ans.—No, sir.

Ques.—Did you ask him for a receipt?

Ans.—I did. He made some remark—I can't exactly recollect what he said—and then I said: " Look here, Col. Joyce, I want a receipt for those letters, or, if not, put them back in the mail; I will wait and go along with it. He replied 'that's all right hunki dori, its only a blind, that is just the whole business.' "

Ques.—Is it customary to require a receipt.

Ans.—Yes, sir.

Ques.—Is it infrequent that letters are delivered back?

Ans.—Yes, sir.

CROSS-EXAMINATION BY COL. DYER.

Ques.—Did you ever at any other time open a box off your district other than that time?

Ans.—Yes.

Ques.—Who for?

Ans.—Once a week.

Ques.—Did you ever open a box off your beat and take a letter out for some one else, and if so, who ?

Ans.—Yes.

Ques.—Off your beat?

Ans.—Yes, sir ; I have done it on Main street.

Ques.—Who for ?

Ans —Well, I don't recollect —for business houses.

Ques.—Name the house, if you please.

Ans.—Well, I don't recollect.

Ques.—Give me the name of one letter ?

Ans.—I don't recollect.

Ques.—Give us the name of the party, if you took any letters out of the mail boxes at the instance of any one on Main street?

Ans.—I don't recollect, because the matter occurred so frequently that I did not retain it in my memory.

Ques.—Well, can you give the name of one house on Main street for which you took letters out of the box?

Ans.—No, sir.

Ques.—I ask you outside of your district. You say that you have taken letters outside of your beat for other persons ?

Ans.—I say that I collected all the routes once a week in the city of St. Louis, at the hour of 5, half-past 5, or a quarter after 5 ; that the merchants came to me and said they had dropped letters in ; the business card was on the envelope ; and I gave them to them without any further question. The postage, probably, would not have been paid.

Ques.—Name one merchant that you did that for?

Ans.—Well, I can't name one ; I may as well say the whole of them.

Ques.—Do you mean to say every man on Main street?

Ans.—Nothing of the sort ; but I do mean to say this : that parties would put letters in the letter-box and they might forget the enclosure or the stamp.

Ques.—I want to know the name of any gentleman it St. Louis for whom you took a letter out of the box?

Ans.—George W. Fishback

P

Ques.—When?

Ans.—I can't locate the time.

Ques.—Off your beat?

Ans.—No, sir; on my beat.

Ques.—Did you, at any time take letters out of the box?

Ans.—I told you I took them hundreds of times.

Ques.—Will you name a man?

Ans.—Well, I told you my recollection in the matter; the matter occurred so often that I did'nt consider it necessary to retain it in my recollection.

Ques.—Can you, by taxing your memory?

Ans.—No, sir. Mr. Dyer, I came here to tell the truth, the whole truth, and you can't make me tell any different.

Mr. Dyer.—That is all right; but I want to know exactly what parties you delivered letters to.

Witness.—Now, Mr. Dyer, I will tell you one thing: I collected the boxes from Washington Avenue to Spruce, and the river to Sixth street, and as you are not aware, I will tell you— we have got a certain thing to do with collections, and if parties come and want letters, I have got no time to fool about it.

Ques.—Will you then name one man for whom you took out a letter off your beat?

Ans.—Well, I could not positively.

Ques.—Can you name any man that you think you took a letter out of a box for off of your beat?

Ans.—Yes, sir.

Ques.—Well, who?

Ans.—Well, I wouldn't like to swear about the parties for whom I have taken letters out.

Ques.—Then you don't know, do you?

Ans.—I know that I have.

Ques.—Do you know the men for whom you have done it?

Ans.—Well, I don't know the men, but I have an idea of the firms; but I wouldn't state it positively.

Ques.—Then you were in the habit of taking receipts for those letters that you took out of the delivery box?

Ans.—Yes, sir, as a general rule.

Ques.—You carried receipts with you?

Ans.—Yes, sir, when on a business route ; I am on a residence route now.

Ques.—At the time you speak of, did you have receipts?

Ans.—I did for a fact.

Ques.—Joyce did not sign a receipt, you say?

Ans.—He got possession of the letters before I demanded a receipt.

Ques.—And then, after you demanded a receipt, he refused to give it, did he?

Ans.—He said it was hunky dori, or some such remark, and then I asked him if I would wait for the letters ; I thought perhaps he had forgotten to put something in the letter, or something of that kind ; he said "that is hunky dori," "that is only a blind," or something of that kind.

* * * * * * * * *

The facts connected with this testimony must be related here: On the night of Gen. Babcock's acquittal, February 24th, he called on me at my quarters at the jail, in company with Judge Krum. After being there a short time Gen. Babcock requested Judge Krum to step outside of the cell in order that he might have a private conversation with me. In the course of that interview he related to me his troubles and the expense he had been put to, etc., and many other things which I will relate hereafter, in its proper place. But among other things he told me that before leaving Washington to appear for trial he had learned of the arrival of Everest, and also of the facts that the Prosecuting Attorney had caused his return to America in order that he might relate in court the transmission by mail of the $500 remittance; that his counsel had decided to secure a man to give testimony of the nature submitted by Magill, but that it was not until after the trial was begun that they had selected Magill for the purpose. He then told me that he had been compelled to pay Hardaway a big price for the letter, already referred to, and that he had to reward Magill with a most extravagant sum; " but," he remarked, " the result has paid me well for the expenditure."

There are some peculiarities about Magill's testimony which render it extraordinary, when considering the fact that it was the creation of two of the most acute lawyers in the nation. In the first place Magill, though he was a letter carrier, had no more right to open a letter box outside of his district than any citizen not connected with the mail service; and in the second place if he had possessed the right it would have been a crime for him to have returned a letter from the mail box without taking a receipt therefor. But I will not cast a reflection of stupidity upon the reader by drawing attention to the self-evident falsity of the entire Magill testimony. No one believed a word of it at the time and no intelligent person believes a scintilla of it to-day. Col. Joyce states that the remittance was made just as Everest testified, and that he never dreamed of such a thing as having the money and letters returned to him.

During the progress of the Babcock trial Judge Krum paid me visits very frequently, and he begged me for some of Babcock's letters, especially those of a friendly nature which he might use in the trial as an evidence that the relations of myself and Babcock were purely social. I told him that I would look over my correspondence and would select some letters such as he wanted and let him take them provided they were returned to me at the termination of the trial. Following is one of his notes after eliciting this promise from me:

February 16th, 1876.

DEAR GENERAL :

If you can get *all* of the letters during the day, please do so and leave them in your *room*, so that I can look over them with you. The Government's case is all in.

My messenger will carry any message you want to any person to whom you need to send a message. He is one of the boys from the office, and is close mouthed and perfectly reliable. I will be in to see you to-night. All well and very hopeful.   C. H. K.

On the same evening, as per his engagement, Judge Krum came to my cell, and as I had sent for all my letters he at once expressed a wish to look through the correspondence at his leisure. I pertly told him that he could not examine the letters; that if he were not satisfied with those I chose to let him have that I should give him none. I selected from the letters I had with me from Babcock, those of the following date: March 4th, 1872; January 20th, 1874; January 30th, 1874; December 26th, 1874, and May 30th, 1875. I made a memoranda of these dates, and gave the letters to him only upon his solemn promise, as a gentleman, to return them to me at the conclusion of the Babcock trial. These letters were never returned to me, and subsequent to the trial he told me that the letters, on the following day after he received them, were given into the possession of a party of gentlemen in

Babcock's room at the Lindell hotel, consisting of Gen. Babcock, Mr. Storrs, Williams, and Babcock's brother, and that Storrs and the Babcocks, after remarking that they could make no use of the letters, threw them into the grate where they were speedily burned.

On the ninth day of the Babcock trial the President's deposition was introduced in court and read, as follows:

PRESIDENT GRANT'S DEPOSITION.

Be it remembered that, on the 12th day of February, in the year of our Lord 1876, I did call and cause to personally appear before me, at the Executive Mansion, in the City of Washington, D. C., between the hours of 10 o'clock a. m. and 6 o'clock p. m., n Saturday, U. S. Grant, to testify, and the truth to say on the part and on behalf of the defendant, in a certain case now pending in the Circuit Court of the United States, for the Eastern District of Missouri, viz: The United States vs. Orville E. Babcock. Agreeably to the stipulation hereunto annexed, and the said U. S. Grant, being about the age of fifty-three years, and first sworn to testify the whole truth, and nothing but the truth, in the matter of controversy aforesaid, I did carefully examine the said U. S. Grant, and he did thereupon testify as follows, viz:

Examined by W. A. Cook, Esq., as counsel for the defendant.

Question.—How long have you known Gen. Babcock, and how intimately?

Answer.—I have known him since 1863, having first met him during the Vicksburg campaign, that year; since March, 1864, I have known him intimately.

Ques.—Please state the various capacities in which he has been employed, and what positions he has held since 1863?

Ans.—From about March, 1864, to the 4th of March, 1869, he was an aid-de-camp on my military staff; since that time he has been acting as my private secretary. He has also, for several years past, been Superintendent of Public Buildings and Grounds.

Ques.—As your private secretary, please state what were his general duties?

Ans.—They were to carry to Congress all communications of the President, and to have charge of, and supervision of all correspondence, particularly that of an official character. In his capacity of private secretary he received my mails, opened my letters, and referred them to the appropriate departments, submitting to me all such as required any investigation or answer from myself.

Ques.—His relations with you were very confidential?

Ans.—Very.

Ques.—Do you know whether, during the time Gen. Babcock has been your private secretary, he has had frequent applications from persons throughout the country to lay their special matters before you, or before the various departments?

Ans.—That was a very frequent occurrence, indeed ; it happened almost daily.

Ques.—In what manner, so far as you have observed, with reference to the public interest, has Gen. Babcock discharged his duties as your private secretary?

Ans.—I have always regarded him as a most efficient and faithful officer.

Ques.—Are you acquainted with the general reputation of Gen. Babcock in the city where he now lives, and in the place where he has lived, among his acquaintances and associates, and in the army and elsewhere for honesty and integrity?

Ans.—I am acquainted with his reputation in the army and in this city.

Ques.—Please state what that general reputation is, and has been?

Ans.—If an intimate association of twelve years with a man gives one an opportunity of judging what others think of him, I have certainly had not only an excellent opportunity of knowing his character myself, but of hearing the general reputation he sustains.

Ques.—From these opportunities, what has been his reputation?

Ans.—Good.

Ques.—Were you acquainted with C. W. Ford, of St. Louis, in his lifetime, and what, if any, position did he hold at the time of his death?

Ans.—I was intimately acquainted with C. W. Ford ; first in the State of New York, when I was a lieutenant in the army, and he a young lawyer, residing in the same town where I was stationed ; and, subsequently, from 1854 to 1860, when we were both living in St. Louis county. He was, from 1854 until his death, connected with the United States Express Company in St. Louis, and from 1869, though I am not sure of the date, he was collector of Internal Revenue for the first district of Missouri, which position he held when he died.

Ques.—State, please, what, if any, applications were made at the time of his decease, as to the appointment of his successor?

Ans.—It is impossible for me to remember all the applications that were made for the place. I do recollect, however, that Gen. Babcock brought me a dispatch adressed to him by John A. Joyce, in which the latter particularly applied for the position.

Ques.—What other, if any, applications were made as to the appointment of a successor? But, first, let me enquire if you have the dispatch to which you have just made reference?

Ans.—I do not know.

Ques.—Do you know where it is?

Ans.—I do not, but presume it could be found ; I think it very likely it is in possession of Gen. Babcock's counsel or of the district attorney.

Ques.—Were there any requests or communications with regard to Mr. Ford's successor from his sureties?

Ans.—When Gen. Babcock exhibited to me the dispatch from Mr. Joyce, I said to him that, as Mr. Ford had died away from home, and very suddenly, I would, in the selection of a successor be, to a great extent, guided by the recommendation and wishes of his bondmen. I thought they would at least be entitled to be heard respecting the person to be selected, as upon them would devolve the settlement of the affairs of the office.

Ques.—What did you decide to do with reference to the appointment, and to whom, if any, did you decide to leave the nomination of Mr. Ford's successor?

Ans.—That information is embraced in the answer just given.

Ques.—Whom did the bondsmen actually recommend?

Ans.—Constantine Maguire.

Ques.—And on their recommendation exclusively he received the appointment?

Ans.—I could not say exclusively, because he was well recommended, and was satisfactory to the bondsmen of Mr. Ford.

Ques.—Did Gen. Babcock ever, in any way, directly or indirectly, urge or request, or seek to influence the appointment of Mr. Maguire, or did he ever exchange words with you upon the subject which indicated that he desired the appointment?

Ans.—I do not think he ever did, nor do I believe that he was aware of the existence of Constantine Maguire prior to his recommendation as the successor of Mr. Ford.

Ques.—Did you inform Gen. Babcock that you intended to leave the appointment of Mr. Ford's successor to his bondsmen; did you request him to notify the parties?

Ans.—I do not remember.

Ques.—Are the telegrams now shown you the ones received by you in relation to the appointment of Mr. Maguire?

Counsel for prosecution objected to this question, but it was overruled.

The following are copies of the dispatches and letters referred to.

Exhibit 1.

TREASURY DEPARTMENT, OFFICE OF INTERNAL REVENUE.
WASHINGTON, Jan. 4th, 1876.

DEAR SIR :

Enclosed herewith I send you the papers which you ask for in your note of the 3d inst., viz: Telegrams from Henry T. Blow, from McKee, Wm. H. Benton, and John M. Krum, recommending the appointment of Constantine Maguire as Collector of Internal Revenue of the First District of Missouri, *vice* C. W. Ford, deceased, referred to this department by the President October 28th, 1873.

Very respectfully,

D. D. PRATT, Commissioner.

LEVI P. LUCKEY, Secretary to the President.

EXECUTIVE MANSION, Washington.

Exhibit 2.

ST. LOUIS, Oct. 27th, 1873.

To HIS EXCELLENCY, U. S. GRANT, Washington:

If you received telegram from us please answer.

JOHN M. KRUM.
WM. H. BENTON.
WM. McKEE.

Exhibit 3.

ST. LOUIS, Oct. 25th, 1873.

To HIS EXCELLENCY, U. S. GRANT, Washington.

Please see our dispatch of this day to Delano and tell us, as securities of our friend, C. W. Ford, if we can protect ourselves from any wrong action of his deputies.

WM. H. BENTON.
JOHN M. KRUM.
WM. McKEE.

Exhibit 4.

ST. LOUIS, Oct. 27th, 1873.

To PRESIDENT U. S. GRANT, Washington:

As your personal and political friends, we urgently request

the appointment of Constantine Maguire as successor to our friend, the late C. W. Ford.

Wм. H. BENTON.
Wм. McKEE.
JOHN M. KRUM.

EXHIBIT 5.

ST. LOUIS, Oct. 27th, 1873.

To PRESIDENT U. S. GRANT, Washington:

It would be gratifying to your friends and the Republicans of our city, if Constantine Maguire could be appointed Collector of Revenue of the District. He is on Mr. Ford's bond, has the confidence of Mr. Ford's friends, and is really an honest, straightforward man, as well as capable.

HENRY T BLOW.

(Testimony continued.)

Ans.—I have no doubt these are the dispatches, or copies of the despatches, I received. If they are not, dispatches similar in tenor were received.

Ques.—Connected with these telegrams is a letter dated January 4, 1876, from D. D. Pratt, Commissioner. Will you be kind enough to explain how that letter was received by you, and what connection it has with these telegrams?

Ans.—The communication to which you refer, from the former Commissioner of Internal Revenue, is in answer to a request made in my name to be furnished with the telegrams recommending Mr. Maguire for the office of collector.

Ques.—Did Gen. Babcock, so far as you know, ever seek in any way to influence your action with reference to any changes, made or proposed to be made against Joyce or McDonald, or either of them?

Ans.—I do not remember of his ever speaking to me on the subject; he took no lively interest in the matter, or I should have recollected it.

Ques.—Did Gen. Babcock, so far as you know, ever seek in any way to influence your action in reference to any investigation in the alleged whiskey frauds in St. Louis or elsewhere?

Ans.—He did not. I will state, at this point, that I do not

remember one instance when he talked with me on the subject
of these investigations, excepting since his indictment. It was
then simply to say to me that he had asked Mr. Douglass why
it was his department treated all their officials as though they
were dishonest persons who required to be watched by spies;
why he could not make inspections similar to those which prevailed in the army, selecting for the purpose men of character,
who could enter the distilleries, examine the books, and make
reports which cou'd be relied upon as correct. Gen. Babcock
simply told me that he said this to Mr. Douglass.

Ques.—Do you remember the circumstance of John McDonald being in the city of Washington on the 7th day of February, 1874?

Ans.—I do not remember the particular date; I remember
the time in question.

Ques.—Did you ride with him on or about that date or
occasion, and was anything whatever said by him to you with
reference to the investigation of alleged frauds in his district?

Ans.—I picked him up on the sidewalk as I was taking a
drive. I invited him to go with me. I have no recollection of
any word or words, or any matter touching his official business.

Ques.—If I understand correctly, Gen. Babcock's conception
was, that in making the investigations, it would be wiser to
have it done by men of superior character than by men of
inferior or suspicious character?

Ans.—Yes, sir.

Ques.—Did Gen. Babcock, at or about that time, say anything to you with reference to such investigation, and, to your
knowledge, did he undertake to prevent them?

Ans.—I have no recollection of his saying anything about
that; certainly he did not intercede with me to prevent them.

Ques.—Do you recollect the circumstances attending the
promulgation of an order transferring the various Supervisors
from their own to other districts?

Ans.—I do.

Ques.—State fully with whom the idea upon which the order

was based originated, and the particular reasons which induced you to direct it to be so.

Ans.—Sometimes when Mr. Richardson was Secretary, I think at all events, before Secretary Bristow became the head of the Department, Mr. Douglass, in talking with me, expressed the idea that it would be a good plan occasionally to shift the various Supervisors from one district to another. I expressed myself favorably towards it, but it was not done then; nor was it thought of any more by me, until it became evident that the Treasury was being defrauded of a portion of the revenue that it should receive from the distillation of spirits in the West. Secretary Bristow, at that time, called on me and made a general statement of his suspicions, when I suggested to him this idea. On that suggestion, the order making these transfers of Supervisors was made. At that time, I did not understand that there was any suspicion at all of the officials, but that each official had his own way of transacting his business. These distillers having so much pecuniary interest in deceiving the officials, learn their ways and know how to avoid them. My idea was, that by putting in new Supervisors, acquainted with their duties, over them, they would run across and detect their crooked ways. This was the view I had, and explains the reason why I suggested the change.

Ques.—Can you state whether Mr. Douglass, at that time Commissioner of Internal Revenue, was aware of the fact that you suggested or made the order?

Ans.—I do not know that he knew anything about it.

Ques.—After the order had been finally issued, were any efforts made to induce you to order its revocation or suspension?

Ans.—Yes, sir, most strenuous efforts.

Ques.—Were such efforts made by prominent public men? Did you resist the pressure that was made upon you for the revocation or suspension of the order, and will you please state why you were induced to do so and by whom?

Ans.—I resisted all efforts to have the order revoked, until I became convinced that it should be revoked or suspended in the interests of detecting frauds that had already been committed. In my conversation with Supervisor Tutton, he said to me that if the object of that order was to detect frauds that had already been committed, he thought it would not be accomplished. He remarked that this order was to go into effect on the 15th of February. This conversation occurred late in January. He alleged that it would give the distillers who had been defrauding the Treasury, three weeks notice to get their houses in order, and be prepared to receive the new Supervisor; that he, himself, would probably go into a district where frauds had been committed, and he would find everything in good order, and he would be compelled to so report; that the order would probably result in stopping the frauds at least for a time, but would not lead to the detection of those that had already been committed. He said that if the order was revoked, it would be regarded as a triumph for those who had been defrauding the Treasury. It would throw them off their guard, and he could send special agents of the Treasury to the suspected distillers—send good men, such a one as he mentioned, Mr. Brooks. They could go out and would not be known to the distillers, and before they could be aware of it, the latter's frauds could be detected ; the proofs would be complete, the distilleries could be seized, and their owners prosecuted. I felt so conscious that his argument was sound, and that it was in the interest of the detection and punishment of fraud, that this order should be suspended, and I then told him that I would suspend it immediately, and I did so without any further consultation with anyone. My recollection is, that I wrote the direction for the suspension of the order on a card, in pencil, before leaving my office that afternoon, and that the order was issued and sent to the Treasury by one of my secretaries.

Ques.—Did General Babcock ever in any way, directly or indirectly, seek to influence your action in reference to that order?

Ans.—I do not remember his ever speaking to me about it or exhibiting any interest in the matter.

Ques.—From anything he ever said or did, do you know whether he desired that the order should be revoked or suspended?

Ans.—That question I think, has been fully answered.

Ques.—Has Gen. Babcock, so far as you know, or any one for him, undertaken to prevent an investigation of his alleged connection with what is known as the Whiskey Ring at St. Louis or elsewhere?

Ans.—To my knowledge, he has not.

Ques.—Has General Babcock, so far as you know, ever used any effort with yourself or any one else, to prevent the finding of indictments against any person suspected of complicity with the Whiskey Ring at St. Louis or elsewhere?

Ans.—He has not.

Ques.—Since the finding of the St. Louis indicments against these persons has General Babcock, so far as you know, ever exhibited any desire to interfere with or prevent a trial, or exhibited any interest or wish in that direction?

Ans.—He has not to my knowledge.

Ques.—Have you ever seen anything in the conduct of General Babcock, or has he ever said anything to you, which indicated to your mind that he was in any way interested in or connected with the Whiskey Ring at St. Louis or elsewhere?

Ans.—Never.

Ques.—In what manner, as regards the public interest, and as evincing his fidelity and integrity, has he performed his duties as your Private Secretary?

Ans.—Always to my entire satisfaction.

Ques.—Have you in any form observed or learned of anything in connection with Gen. Babcock's conduct which has tended to diminish your confidence in his ability and integrity?

Ans.—I have always had great confidence in his integrity and efficiency.

CROSS EXAMINATION BY MR. EATON. Ques.—General, of course you do not suppose, do you, that while General Babcock has been your private secretary, and in intimate and confidential relations with you, any one would voluntarily come to you with statements injurious to his reputation?

Ans.—I do not know any such thing.

Ques.—Perhaps you are aware, General, that the Whiskey Ring have persistently tried to fix the origin of that Ring in the necessity for funds to carry on political campaigns. Did you ever have any information from Gen. Babcock, or any one else, in any manner, directly or indirectly, that any funds for political purposes were being raised by any improper methods?

Ans.—I never did; I have seen since these trials intimations of that sort in the newspapers, but never before.

Ques.—Then let me ask you if the prosecuting officers have not been entirely correct in repelling all insinuations that you ever had tolerated any such means for raising funds?

Ans.—I was not aware that they had attempted to repel any insinuations.

Ques.—Speaking of C. W. Ford, I presume, General, that your confidence in him continued up to the time of his death?

Ans.—I never had a suspicion that anything was wrong.

Ques.—Did you regard his knowledge of men and affairs in St. Louis as trustworthy?

Ans.—I had as much confidence in him, in that way, as any person I knew in St. Louis.

Ques.—When did you cease to reside in St. Louis, General?

Ans.—In May, 1860.

Ques.—From 1860 down to the time of Mr. Ford's death, Mr. Ford's residence was also in St. Louis?

Ans.—Yes, sir.

Ques.—Did you have private correspondence with Mr. Ford during the time that he was Collector?

Ans.—I did.

Ques.—Did you preserve that correspondence?

Ans.—No, I never kept a copy of a letter that I sent to him in my life.

Ques.—Did you preserve letters that you received from him?

Ans.—No, sir, I did not preserve those. We corresponded regularly, because I had such confidence in him that I left him to conduct my own affairs there. And I had to be constantly sending him money. I would send checks to him of $500, $1,000 and $1,200 at a time, and he would pay out the money and account to me for it. My confidence in him was such that I did that without even saving my letters.

Ques.—Do you remember a letter of Mr. Ford's to yourself, dated May 30, 1870, in which he spoke of McDonald as a bad egg, and as saying too, that he was a disgrace to the administration?

The Witness.—Was that before or after McDonald's appointment?

Mr. Eaton.—I think that it was shortly after McDonald's appointment, very early in that year, if I recollect.

Ans.—I have no recollection of such a letter; I have an indistinct recollection that when McDonald was first recommended for the position, he (Ford) told me either in a letter or in a conversation that McDonald would not do; my recollection was that finally he united with others in recommending McDonald; I have a general knowledge that about the time McDonald was being pressed for the appointment Ford thought that it was not a suitable appointment. But my recollection is that he afterwards acquiesced in it, and possibly either joined in the recommendation which was written, and which will be found on file in the Treasury Department, or else he told me in a conversation.

Ques.—Do you remember whether John A. Joyce was recommended to you as Ford's successor by General Babcock?

Ans.—He was not.

Ques.—Was anything said to you by Gen. Babcock, between the time of the death of Ford and the appointment of Constantine Maguire, touching Joyce's fitness for the place?

Ans.—Gen. Babcock presented me a dispatch that he had received from Joyce, saying that he was an applicant, or making application for it. I do not remember the words of it;

Q

the substance of it was that he wanted to be Ford's successor.
My reply to him was, that I should be guided largely in selecting the successor of Mr. Ford by the recommendation of his
bondsmen ; he having died suddenly, unexpectedly and away
from home, I thought they were entitled to be, at least, consulted as to the successor who would settle up his accounts.

Ques.—Did you advise Gen. Babcock to telegraph to Joyce
to get the bondsmen of Ford to recommend Joyce for Collector?

Ans.—I made the statement in substance that I made in
answer to a former question. Whether I told him to so telegraph or not it would be impossible for me to say. That
might be regarded as at least authority to so telegraph.

Ques.—Did you see any telegram of that character from
Babcock to Joyce at any time ?

Ans.—I do not remember to have seen any.

Ques.—Did Gen. Babcock at any time show you a dispatch
from Joyce in these words :

"St. Louis, Oct. 28th, 1873.

See dispatch to President. We mean it. Mum.

Joyce."

Ans.—I do not think that my memory goes back to that
time. Since these prosecutions were commenced I have seen
that.

Ques.—I am not asking you in regard to that time?

Ans.—I do not call it to memory.

Ques.—Did you receive a protest against the appointment
of Constantine Maguire, signed by James E. Yeatman, Robt.
Campbell and others?

Ans.—I do not remember such a letter. If such a one was
received, it is, no doubt, on file in the Treasury Department.
Such a protest may have been received.

Ques.—Your purpose in leaving the nomination of Mr.
Ford's successor to his bondsmen was because they were liable, on his bonds, for the administration of his office was it not?

Ans.—Yes, sir ; further than that, some of them were men
I knew very well, and had great confidence in.

Ques.—Speaking of Ford's objection to McDonald, were you aware that in the matter of education, McDonald, when he was appointed, was an ignorant man, and barely able to write his name?

Ans.—I was not aware that he was not an educated man, but he was a man that had seen a great deal of the world and of people; I would not call him ignorant exactly; he was illiterate.

Ques.—Did you receive a protest against Mr. McDonald's appointment signed by Carl Schurz, G. A. Finkelnburg, R. T. Van Horn and other men in Missouri?

Ans.—I do not remember. It is a matter of record if it was received. I do not know that it would have had any particular weight with me if I had received it, his endorsement being good.

Ques.—Was not that objection based on the ground of his entire unfitness for the place?

Ans.—I do not remember; if it was received, it is no doubt a matter of record, and can be obtained.

Ques.—Did you ever see the paper now shown you; if so, state in whose handwriting it is?

Ans.—As to handwriting, I do not pretend to be an expert. I have had a good many letters from Mr. Ford; that looks like his signature; I do not remember to have seen that before; I do not think I ever did.

Ques.—Do you know the other signatures to the paper?

Ans.—No; I know all the parties, but I don't know all their signatures.

The paper alluded to in the question was as follows:

February 16, 1870.

Hon. C. Delano, Washington, D. C.:

If the contemplated change of Supervisor in this District is not fixed, I would suggest that the character of the new appointee should be investigated here and at Memphis.

Chester H. Krum, Att'y U. S. etc.
C. W. Ford, Collector.
C. A. Newcomb, U. S. Marshal.

Ques.—Did you see, at or about the time of its date, the affidavit now shown you, made by James Marr, taken from the files of the Treasury Department?

Ans.—If I ever did see the paper it has dropped entirely from my memory, and I think it would be impossible that such a document as that could be read by me and I not remember it.

Ques.—Do you remember at this distance of time on whose recommendation Joyce was appointed?

Ans.—My recollection is that when McDonald was appointed Supervisor he asked the Commissioner of Internal Revenue to give him an assistant from his office—some man that was acquainted with the duties. I think that there was no acquaintance existing at all between Joyce and McDonald at that time —that is my recollection. I never had heard of Joyce myself and did not know of the existence of such a man, until he was appointed on the recommendation, as I understand, of the then Commissioner, who thought him to be the most capable man in his office.

Ques.—Will you please state whether General Babcock showed you, on or about the time of its date, a dispatch in these words :

ST. LOUIS, February 3, 1875.

GEN. O. E. BABCOCK, Executive Mansion, Washington, D. C.

We have official information that the enemy weakens. Push things.   (Signed) SYLPH.

Ans.—I do not remember ever seeing that dispatch until since these prosecutions have commenced.

Ques.—Did you know that General Babcock was at that time in correspondence with Joyce about the transfer of Supervisors?

Ans.—I knew that he received frequent letters from Joyce, for I saw a number of them myself, and those that I did see were generally what he was doing in the way of writing editorials, which he would say in his letters he had written and asked how he liked the tone of them, and so on. I recollect of him saying in one letter that some papers in the State of Missouri

and perhaps in Arkansas—at different points, at all events—
were willing to publish as editorials, matter that he would
write for them.

Ques.—Do you remember that General Babcock, prior to
May, 1875, talked with you about the propriety of sending
detectives into the several districts to detect frauds?

Ans.—I do not; I remember of his telling me at one time
of what he had proposed to Mr. Douglass, but the date of it
I do not remember, and that was not a suggestion to me; it
was merely telling me what he had suggested to Mr. Douglass,
and this is the same that I before stated.

Ques.—Did you have any conversation with General Babcock,
prior to May, 1875, in reference to a letter written by J. J.
Brooks to Deputy Commissioner Rogers?

Ans.—I do not remember dates, but I remember of his
showing me a letter that had been handed to him from somebody in Philadelphia to Mr. Rogers, and he said that it
appeared to his judgment to be simply blackmailing, and I
think that was the occasion when he told me what he said to
Mr. Douglass; that is as I remember it now.

Ques.—Do remember where that conversation was?

Ans.—I do not; my recollection is that he had shown the
letter to Mr. Douglass before he did to me, and that was the
occasion when he told me of this suggestion.

Ques.—Did Gen. Babcock, about the time of its date, show
you a dispatch in these words:

St. Louis, Oct. 25, 1874.

Gen. O. E. Babcock, Executive Mansion, Washington, D. C.

Have you talked with D.? Are things all right?

(Signed) J—."

Ans.—I do not remember anything about it.

Ques.—Did Gen. Babcock, at or about the time of its date,
show you a dispatch in the following words.

St. Louis, Dec. 3, 1874.

Gen. O. E. Babcock, Executive Mansion, Washington, D. C.

Has Secretary or Commissioner ordered anybody here?

(Signed) J—."

Ans.—I do not remember particularly; I know that, as a general rule, where the dispatches required an answer, that he would get from me the answer he ought to send.

Ques—.You have no recollection of that?

Ans.—I have no particular recollection of the wording of the dispatch.

Ques.—Did General Babcock, on or about 13th of December, 1874, show you a dispatch from himself to John McDonald, in the following words :

WASHINGTON, December 13, 1874.

GENERAL JNO. McDONALD, St. Louis:

I succeeded.   They will not go.   I will write you.

(Signed)   " SYLPH."

Ans.—I have no recollection of it at the time. I did not remember about these dispatches at all, until since the conspiracy trials have commenced. I have heard General Babcock's explanation of most, or all of them since that. Many of these dispatches may have been shown to me at the time, and explained, but I do not remember it.

Ques.—Did you know at the time, that during the fall of 1875, subsequent to your visit to St. Louis, that General Babcock corresponded with Jno. McDonald after the latter was indicted, and sent his letters to McDonald, under cover, to Major E. B. Grimes?

Ans.—No ; I was not aware of it at the time.

Ques.—Did you know at the time that General Babcock sent cipher dispatches to Maj. Luckey at St. Louis over his own and fictitious signatures, on the 17th and 18th of last November ?

Ans.—I do not remember as to particular dates, but we have an Executive Mansion cipher, so that whenever myself and secretaries are separated dispatches may be sent without being read by operators ; we have always had such a cipher. I have no particular knowledge, but I know in a general way that they were corresponding while Mr. Luckey was there, during the Avery trial.

Ques.—Did you see the dispatches before they were sent ?

Ans.—I do not think I saw the dispatches.

Ques.—Have you any objection to stating the meaning, in that cipher of two words only, the words "Hamlet" and "Baggage."

Ans.—I never keep the cipher and I never wrote a cipher dispatch. I never travel without having a secretary with me.

Ques.—Do you know what those words mean ?

Ans.—I do not know. When I want to send a dispatch in ciphers, I give it to one of my secretaries in the ordinary form, and he transmits it.

Ques.—On or about December 5, 1873, did Gen. Babcock show you a dispatch from Joyce to himself in these words : "Is there any hitch in sending Maguire's name to the Senate, (Signed) "Joyce ? "

Ans.—I cannot remember particularly—I think, however, that Gen. Babcock did ask me if there was any reason why Maguire's name should not be sent. I have an indistinct recollection of his having asked me the question.

Ques.—You have said that you resisted the pressure brought to bear on you by prominent public men in regard to the suspension or revocation of the order transferring Supervisors. If you have no objection, will you please state the names of those prominent men who brought that pressure to bear on you ?

Ans.—There were many persons, and I think I could give the names of several Senators, and probably other members of Congress, but probably I should have to refer to the papers that are on file. I know that the pressure was continued from the Supervisors and their friends.

Ques.—Can you, from memory, name any Senators or Representatives ?

Ans.—I could name two or three, but I do not believe that it is necessary.

Mr. Eaton—I will not press it.

Ques.—Did Gen. Babcock at the time tell you he had endeavored to influence Commissioner Douglass to revoke that order.

Ans.—No.

Ques.—Since you say that Gen. Babcock **has not** manifested to you any desire to interfere or prevent **the trial of the** indictment against himself and others, will **you** be so good as to state whether any of his friends, for him, have at **any time** since these indictments were found endeavored to prevent **the trial** of the indictments against him or any other indicted parties, if so, please state who have made such efforts?

Ans.—They have not with me.

Ques.—Did Gen. **Babcock show you** a telegram from District Attorney Dyer, saying that the next conspiracy case would be tried on December 15th, 1875?

Ans.—He did; I do not remember about the date particularly.

Ques.—Now, I suppose, Mr. President, that the substance of your testimony is what we all know to be true, that if there **has been** any misconduct **on the part of Gen. Babcock** it has not **come** to your knowledge?

Ans.—Yes sir that is true.

Ques.—Do you know, of course you do know, whether Mr. Douglass suggested to Secretary Bristow the same thing about the transfer of Supervisors what you say he originally suggested to you?

Ans.—I do not know anything about it except from the Secretary himself.

Ques.—Do you recollect that Supervisor Fulton was ordered from Philadelphia to St. Louis, under the order for transfers?

Ans.—That is my recollection, that he was ordered to St. Louis.

Ques.—You say that Gen. Babcock has made no effort with you to avoid trial, but you do not know of your own knowledge, of course, whether he has made any efforts with others?

Ans.—No, I do not.

RE-DIRECT EXAMINATION BY MR. COOK. **Ques.**—(Handing witness a copy of a telegram), I wish you would state what you know in relation to that?

Ans.—This dispatch seems to be dated Washington, October 27, 1873. To Wm. H. Benton, Wm. McKee and Jno. M. Krum, your request in regard to Collectorship will be complied with.

(Signed)   U. S. GRANT.

Those gentlemen are a part of the bondsmen of Ford, and they had recommended Constantine Maguire for Ford's place as Collector.

Ques.—The original of that, I believe is in your handwriting?

Ans.—Yes; I wrote that myself—I saw the original this morning.

In taking the deposition of the President I desire to call the attention of the reader to the fact that the President of the United States could not be compelled to testify, as all processes of U. S. Courts are in his name; or, in other words, a subpœna by the marshal is a mandatory order of the United States, directing the marshal to bring into Court a certain witness. On Feb. 9th it was agreed between the counsel for Babcock and the Government that the deposition of the President should be taken orally, and in accordance with this stipulation Maj. Eaton was selected to represent the prosecution, and left for Washington on the evening of the 10th, for that purpose; and on the 12th day of February the President, Secretary Bristow, Attorney-General Pierrepont, Maj. Eaton, of St. Louis, W. A. Cook, of Washington, Attorney for Babcock, and Chief Justice Waite, acting as Notary, with two short hand reporters, met in the Executive Chamber of the President; it must be understood that the distinguished witness could not be coerced and that Maj. Eaton could not, even if he had had a disposition so to do, examine the President the same as a witness in a police court.

It is apparent all through the deposition that
whenever Maj. Eaton pressed the President he
either did not remember or gave the Major to understand that he (the President) did not think it
necessary. Secretary Bristow, although earnest and
determined in his prosecution of Babcock, felt a del-
icacy in placing the President of the United States
in a position where he would appear in the eyes of
the nation as a co-defendant in the case. All parties concerned understood and appreciated the del-
icate position they were placed in and that forty
millions of people were looking at them through the
medium of an independent press. All understood
that the object of the President's deposition was to
inform the court and the jury and through them
each individual member of every home throughout
the entire country the President's unbounded confidence in Gen. Babcock's integrity. It will be
seen that the President acted in a very independent
manner during the whole time of his cross-examination, knowing as he did that even if Bristow and his
counsel insisted on his answering all questions,
they could not compel him by legal process and that
if he could not get his recommendation of Babcock
before the jury by a deposition, he could do it by
an interview with a newspaper correspondent, as
the jury were permitted to read the daily papers
during the entire trial. All through his examination the President evaded answering anything that
would have a tendency to injure Babcock; in a
word, Gen. Grant desired to inform the jury that
he did not believe Babcock was guilty, or that he
was in any way connected with the Ring; and while

he was familiar with all the evidence against Babcock, the explanations of his private secretary in relation to all the telegrams and letters, which appeared to connect him with the operations of the Ring as the recipient of a portion of its unlawful proceeds, were such as to satisfy him that he was innocent and that his confidence in his integrity and efficiency remained unshaken, and that it was unnecessary to state the explanations. Grant knew at the time of these declarations that he had never received any explanations from Babcock, that could satisfy any man that he, Babcock, was not connected with the conspiracy. He was well aware of the fact that Babcock was not only in full fellowship but that he represented himself as well. As I have detailed in another part of this book, in my conversation with Secretary Bristow, Grant was entirely familiar with the operations of the Ring, and in the foregoing deposition he testified to nothing but known falsehoods, by withholding the truth. As it has always been a matter of curiosity among the people of this country to learn who were among the prominent men who approached the President for the purpose of having him revoke the order transferring Supervisors. I will here state that among others were Senators Clayton and Dorsey of Arkansas, Morton of Indiana, and Logan of Illinois. I wrote to several of these Senators, and to Babcock, that I would bring all the political power to bear I could in order to give the President an excuse for issuing such an unusual order.

With relation to that portion of the deposition in which the President declares that Babcock never

even spoke to him concerning the revocation of
the order changing supervisors, I can best make
answer by calling the attention of the reader to
Babcock's letters and telegrams, and then allow the
public to decide whether or not Grant perjured
himself.

While the reader may think these are little details
it must be borne in mind that the whole evidence
of the President did not amount to anything outside of his statement that his confidence in Babcock, notwithstanding all that had been brought to
light during and previous to his trial, remained unshaken.   So far as his testimony relates to me personally I brand the same as a tissue of falsehood
from the beginning to the end.

All the evidence in the Babcock case was submitted on the 17th, and on the following day the defense
filed a motion with the court, asking for instructions
to the jury to acquit.   This motion was argued for
two days, which consumed the remainder of the
week.   On the following Monday Judge Dillon,
before whom the case was tried, rendered his decision, refusing to so instruct the jury.   On the 22d
Judge Porter delivered his address for the defendant, which occupied one entire day.   During his
speech he took occasion to excoriate me by directing all the shafts of approbium and contempt at my
character.   Gen. Babcock became alarmed for the
result of the bitterness of his counsel towards me.
He was afraid I would gather the suspicion that the
abusive epithets were used with his knowledge and
sanction, and that it would excite my anger to such
an extent that I would become a tell-tale even at

that late day, and thereby bring disgrace upon him and the President. This I could easily have done, as I had not yet been sentenced and had never given testimony. The prosecution sought to induce me to testify, but I steadfastly refused, shielding myself behind the rule that I could not be compelled to criminate myself; but I also refused to go into court as a witness, and as the punishment for not answering could only be a commitment, I was already in jail, and therefore the penalty would have no effect; I accordingly exercised my option and refused to appear as a witness.

In order to avert the possible consequences of Judge Porter's caustic personalties, Gen. Babcock wrote the following note which Judge Krum sent direct to me, instead of a note conveying Babcock's wishes. (A fac-simile of the note will be found on the following page.)

(CONFIDENTIAL.)

LINDELL HOTEL, 3.30 p. m., Feb'y. 22d.

DEAR JUDGE:

You can see Gen. McD., or if you cannot see him write and tell him how sorry I am that Judge P. attacked him so bitterly. I spoke to him the last thing before I left the hotel, and asked him not to attack Mack. I cautioned him also in the morning, but you know what a bitter fellow he is in a speech, and I suppose he forgot.

I know Mack will know it was not my wish, but I want him to know I took pains to request him not to do so, for I do not wish to add one single pang to his pain, for I know he would not to mine, and on the contrary would help him, as I know he would help me. Please see to this to-night, and oblige

Yours truly,

O. E. BABCOCK.

To Hon. CHESTER H. KRUM.

Confidential.

Lowville Hotel
500 Pm Tue 52?

Dear Judge,

As you see by M. D. —
or if you cannot see him, tell him
how sorry I am that Judge D. attacked him
so cruelly, I spoke to him the last thing before
I left the table — and asked him not to attack
Mack. I continued him also in the
morning — but you know what a bitter
fellow he is in a speech, and I suppose he
forgot. I know Mack will know it was not
my wish — but I want him to know I took pains
to request him not to do so — for I do not wish
to add one single pang to his pains for I know
himself, not to injure and on the contrary would
help him as I know he would help me.

Attend well to this tonight and oblige

yours truly
O. E. Babcock

Hon Chester H. Kimm

On the following day, the 23d, Judge Krum came to see me at my cell, and explained that he had reached home so late on the previous evening and was so tired that he could not visit me; that Gen. Babcock was very much worried over Judge Porter's remarks about me, and was anxious that a full explanation might reach me at once.

I replied that the speech had no effect so far as I was concerned, and, said I, suppose I had become angered, you don't think I could do Gen. Babcock any injury now?

"Well," responded the Judge, "of course, you could send for the district attorney and have him re-open the case, before the verdict is submitted, on the grounds of newly discovered evidence."

I answered him that I had no disposition to do such a thing; that I was too deep in the mire to get out by shoving others under me for a foundation.

At noon on the 24th the case was given to the jury and the court took a recess until three o'clock, when, upon reassembling, the jury returned into court and rendered their verdict of "not guilty." At this juncture Gen. Babcock arose and shook the hand of each juror with much warmth.

On the same night Gen. Babcock, in company with Judge Krum, as I have already stated, called on me at my strongly impregnated castle and we held a lengthy conversation privately. Among many other important things he told me during that interview, was the manner in which his case had been conducted, expressing great satisfaction with each of his attorneys. He asked me if I were

in need of money, and if so, he would give me all I
required.

I replied to him that I had then in my cell about
$12,000, and therefore, all that I needed was the
true friendship of himself and the President.

He was profuse in his assurances that no one
could be more appreciative of a high personal service than was the President for the self-sacrificing
position I had assumed, and that immediately upon
his return to Washington my pardon should be
issued. He further remarked that Mrs. Grant had
expressed her gratitude for the manner in which I
had silenced public criticism by avowing that I had
sold the fine team of trotters, with the buggy and
paraphernalia, to the President, instead of confirm-
ing the truth of current report that they were a
gift, and that he there conveyed her thanks to me
as she requested.

After detailing the trouble he had experienced in
getting possession of the Hardaway letter, and also
asserting that he had paid a majority of the jurors
a round sum of money each, he made a strong appeal to me to deliver up to him all his private letters. He assured me that his confidence in my
fidelity was unbounded, but gave as a reason for
his request that the correspondence might by chance
fall into other hands without my knowledge, and
then become a source of serious trouble to him.

I refused, telling him that I could trust myself,
but that my own safety was dependent upon his
good faith, and that while I did not doubt him in
the least, yet duty to myself forbade my giving up
the least vestage of influence in my hands. He

then asked me how much of a moneyed consideration I would require for the return of the letters.

My reply was that it would take a vast sum to
buy them. He urged me to fix the amount, saying
that anything I should ask he would agree to pay.

My refusal was them peremptory, and I assured
him that no promise or money would ever get them
out of my possession.

He then told me that my pardon would be sent
on at once after his return, and that I could come
to Washington where he would make good all my
expenses from the time of my indictment.

We then talked over the political situation during which he explained that since his acquittal the
President was relieved of suspicion and that Bristow and the other enemies of the administration
would be dismissed ; that the public would regard
Bristow's active participation in the prosecution as
a persecution of the President and that the consequence would be the re-nomination and re-election
of Grant; that in this effect matters would be so
arranged that I could hold any position I desired
and at the same time be fully relieved from any official stain.

On the next day C. W. Babcock, a brother of the
General's, in company with P. M. Schaurte, a postal agent, at St. Louis, called upon Thomas F.
Walsh,—formerly my chief clerk, and also assistant
postmaster of St. Louis for the period of twelve
years, but now assistant purchasing agent for the
Iron Mountain railroad company,—and told him
that they understood he was the custodian of the
letters Gen. Babcock had written to me; that they

B

wanted the correspondence, and were willing to pay him $5,000 if he would return it to them.

Mr. Walsh did not have the letters but he realized at once the object of his callers. He replied to them that whatever correspondence he had belonging to Gen. McDonald would remain as private as it had ever been and that he had no authority to dispose of a single letter.

On the day following they paid Mr. Walsh a second visit, during which they agreed to give him $10,000 and any reasonable position in the government he might want, for the return of the letters, but his reply was the same as before. Mr. Schaurte then assumed a different attitude by saying that they must have the correspondence; that it was to the personal interest of Mr. Walsh to deliver it to them, for if he positively refused it was at the risk of personal danger, and intimated that his house might be burned over his head.

Of course these threats produced no effect but when Mr. Walsh informed me of the facts I was thoroughly convinced that in those letters alone consisted all my influence and my hopes for an early pardon.

Gen. Babcock left for Washington on the evening of the 25th or 26th, but before leaving St. Louis he was serenaded by a government band, and a purse of $10,000 was made up for him by his friends to defray all his expenses incurred during the trial. But, though he went out of court with a very fulsome display, the verdict of the public was that he had been guilty of everything charged in the indictment. I will not attack the Court here because I have no reasonable grounds for so doing, but I cannot neglect to mention the almost universal opinion, boldly expressed at the time, that Judge Dillon's instructions to the jury was framed with remarkable partiality and virtually instructed the jury to acquit. In this connection I will quote the public declaration of John M. Keithley, of St. Charles, Mo., who was one of the jurymen, and who made the statement with the full knowledge of its intended publication. The report is copied from the St. Louis *Times:*

"Mr. Keithley says he never served with a jury who regarded the responsibility resting upon them with such indifference as that which declared Babcock not guilty. He says they felt the irksomeness of their confinement in the court-room keenly and looked forward to adjournment with the same pleasure that school-boys regard recess. At the hotel they gave themselves up entirely to such pleasure as they could command. Each evening was passed in card playing, and with one or two exceptions, the jurors did not seem to realize that they were to decide one of the most important cases ever tried in the history of this country.

One of the number, D. W. Taintor, of Gasconade County, was in the habit of wondering off at will, but where he went his fellow-jurors never knew. Frequently, in the evening, the bailiff would discover that Taintor was missing, but nobody could tell where he had gone. The bailiff would search the hotel in vain and generally Mr. Taintor would make his appearance, after one or two hours absence, and explain that he was walking about. He would also insist upon reading the papers; every day he managed by some means to get possession of the St. Louis papers, and while the bailiff's back was turned, he would inform himself of the contents.

Mr. Keithley declares very positively his belief in Babcock's guilt; he says he believed him guilty when he heard the evidence and up to the time of the charge of Judge Dillon had regarded it as his sworn duty to render a verdict in accordance with that belief. The charge, he says, converted what would have been a hung jury into an acquittal. Up to the time it was delivered a majority of the jury were for conviction, while several were undecided and two were for acquittal. Under the charge those who believed him guilty had to surrender that opinion in obedience to the law expounded by the Court.

Immediately after the jury were discharged one of them remarked, 'I believe him (Babcock) as innocent a man as ever lived,' to which Mr. Keithley replied, 'I believe him as guilty a man as ever lived.'"

CHAPTER IX.

Action of Congress on Babcock's Acquittal—Investigations by a Special Committee—Testimony of District Attorney Dyer—of John B. Henderson—of Attorney General Pierrepont—All Declare that Grant was Kept Informed of the Secrets of the Grand Jury by Fox—Bell's Testimony—How He was Hired by Babcock, with Grant's Knowledge, to Steal Evidence—The Belknap Scandal—Babcock's Second Indictment—Babcock Continues to Act as Private Secretary to the President—Sentence of McKee—Avery's Pardon, and How it Was Obtained—Avery's History of the Ring.

In March, Congress took action respecting the manner in which testimony had been purchased, witnesses suborned, Government officers stultified and the President's pet acquitted in the face of overwhelming evidence. The Judiciary Committee was given power to conduct an investigation, which conferred the right to send for papers and witnesses. In response to the Committee's summons, Col. Dyer, Gen. Henderson, and Messrs. Bliss, Peddrick, and Eaton, arrived in Washington on the morning of March 31st, and gave testimony before the Committee. Col. Dyer swore that Grand Juryman E. W. Fox, of St. Louis, kept the President informed of the proceedings in regard to Babcock's indictment, the nature of the testimony against him, etc. These secret communications were received by Grant, with a full knowledge that Fox had violated his oath,

thus making himself a party to an outrage upon
the law which he had sworn to see faithfully
executed.

The testimony of Gen. Henderson was as follows:
He stated, among other things, that in conversation
with Secretary Bristow in January, 1876, the Secretary admitted to him that he thought Gen. Porter,
formerly the President's private secretary, and
Gen. Babcock, or one of them, had access to the
Grand Jury evidence in the Attorney General's
office, and thereby ascertained what there was
against Babcock; and, said Gen. Henderson, "when
I came here to testify before the committee, I had
a conversation with the Attorney General himself,
when I stated to the Attorney General frankly
what I had heard from Secretary Bristow; that
the Attorney General said he did not purposely or
designedly let Babcock or Porter have access to the
files of his office, but he had frequently communicated what evidence he had against Babcock to the
President himself; *but he invariably found that the
President knew more about it than he did.* In explanation of this, the Attorney General stated that
a member of the Grand Jury, at St. Louis, E. W.
Fox, came to Washington in December, 1875, and
remained to the last of February, and he believed
Fox had communicated to the President all the material facts in the case, by giving what appeared
before the Grand Jury. The Attorney General had
no doubt the President came into possession of the
facts in that way."

Following is Pierrepot's testimony before the
committee as reported by the Associated Press:

WASHINGTON, March 23d, 1876.

Pierrepont's explanation of his circular letter to District Attorneys, as made before the Clymer committee, is that the President was very much disturbed at the constant receipt of newspaper slips and letters and personal statements, giving information of attempts on the part of Government officials in the West, to compromise fraud on the revenue, and that the President spoke to him on five or six different occasions, expressing his fear that such things, if allowed, would bring scandal on the administration. Pierrepont himself, was rather inclined to treat these statements as exaggerations, and did not believe that District Attorneys or special counsel of the government would be guilty of anything improper in the matter. He had, therefore, rather warded off the President's advances until finally the President suggested that the Attorney General had better write to District Attorneys on the subject. Pierrepont had therefore prepared and forwarded letters couched, as he said, in terms that were rather tame—nobody had made or suggested a draught of this letter and he had not submitted it to the President. In fact, the President knew nothing of it for three or four days afterwards, when he asked Pierrepont whether he had taken any action in the matter and then he told him he had written this letter and sent him a copy of it. A couple of days afterwards, on discovering that the letter had been published in the Chicago papers on the first of February, himself and Mr. Bristow expressed indignation in presence of the President, at the gross impropriety of giving publicity to it, and then the President, who did not manifest any feeling whatever on the subject, remarked that he never read the letter.

Mr. Pierrepont further stated that General Babcock admitted to him on the 3d of March, that he was instrumental in giving publicity to the letter, and defended himself on the ground that they were trying to destroy him, and that he had the right to defend himself. He, (Pierrepont) called the President's attention next day to Babcock's admission.

He stated that the letter was written without any reference to Babcock's case ; that he wrote it reluctantly and not until the President had repeatedly urged him to do so. He thought at first, when the letter appeared in print, that it had been given out by Dyer, and so said to Bristow, with whom he went to the White House, where both told the President their opinion on the subject in a very emphatic manner. The President, much to their surprise, regarded their indignation stolidly and with no signs of anger on his part at the publication.

Following is the testimony of Charles S. Bell, a detective, given before the committee, as reported by the associated press. The truth of his statements is well attested not only by one of Babcock's letters, but by the officers of the government at St. Louis. This testimony taken in connection with Babcock's letter of July 14th, 1875, signed " B. F." (bull finch), on page 186, is given to the reader for a moment's reflection :

WASHINGTON, May 31, 1876.

Before the Clymer Committee to-day, Mr. C. S. Bell, after testifying that he was appointed a secret agent of the Pension Office, at the recommendation of President Grant and Mr. Luckey, in February, 1876, at a salary of $2,200 and travelling expenses, reluctantly admitted that he was engaged as a detective in the Babcock trial under the employ of Luckey. Luckey told him to consult A. C. Bradley, and to do what he was told by Bradley. Bradley told him to get the evidence against Babcock from District-Attorney Dyer's office in St. Louis, in order to destroy it. He thought this was going rather too far, and would not do it; but he got hold of all the evidence surreptitiously from the lawyers and others of Dyer's office, and from Dyer himself, who did not know that he was in Babcock's employ, and then told Luckey that the case against Babcock was weak. He was to be appointed special agent of the Attorney-General's office, to be sent to St. Louis, but he was not appointed. That was on the 13th of December. The Attorney-General delayed the appointment, and finally told him that Dyer understood the object of his going there. He was then appointed a special agent in the Interior Department. He submitted a cypher between him and Luckey, in which he (Bell) was to communicate with Luckey while at St. Louis.

The President knew that he was to be sent to St. Louis as an officer of the Attorney-General to find out the evidence, and told him if Babcock was guilty he wanted to see him punished. He (Bell) first thought that it was a prosecution against Grant, but when he got hold of the evidence he made up his mind that Babcock was guilty. He tried to inform the President personally of Babcock's guilt, but as he could not see him he made this fact known to him by giving to the *Herald* the cipher between him (Bell) and Luckey, and mailed a copy to the President which he had reason to believe the President received. Three days after this he was dismissed. He met Babcock here several times, and when he told him that Bradley wanted him to get hold of the evidence, Babcock said if he did not get hold of the whole of it it would be of no use. Babcock said if he got the evidence he would be well rewarded, and that there were papers and telegrams in existence which if Dyer got hold of he should never be able to explain or get over (sensation). Mr. Pierrepont was averse to his going to St. Louis to play the spy for Dyer, and told him that a high Treasury official, whom he took to be Bristow, had found out what he was going to St. Louis for, and that it was therefore of no use for him to go. The President told Bell that he wanted him to secure all the evidence he could, whether any attempt was being made to manufacture evidence against Babcock, or whether Babcock was really guilty. He, therefore, gave him a card to Pierrepont, so that the latter should employ him to go to St. Louis as a secret officer. Under the guise of this appointment he was to be used by Bradley, Luckey and Babcock, to get the evidence and destroy it. He abstracted some telegrams and papers from Dyer's office on

the 14th of July.   When he returned to St. Louis he explained
to Dyer that he had been commissioned to steal the evidence
and destroy it.   This warned Dyer against Roger M. Sherman,
who was sent there by District Attorney Bliss, of New York, to
do the same.   He was told particularly to get hold of any
telegrams signed B. Finch or Bullfinch ; but subsequently
Babcock told him he did not think telegrams under such signatures had been sent in that quarter, but wished it to be particularly understood he only acted for Babcock as long as he
believed him innocent, but that when he became convinced
that he was guilty he "threw up the sponge."   He regarded
Babcock's prosecution at first as a political intrigue against
Grant, for whom he had been a scout during the war, and his
main interest was to serve the President.   Babcock wanted all
the evidence to destroy it.

Almost immediately upon the arrival of Gen.
Babcock in Washington, upon his return from St.
Louis, the Belknap scandal, showing his sales of
post-suttlership, etc., was made public, and the disgrace of the War Secretary reflected so much upon
the administration that Gen. Babcock wrote to
Judge Chester H. Krum, asking him to see me at
once and obtain my consent to wait my pardon un-
till the public excitement over the Belknap expos-
use should subside.   My interest and faith in the
President decided me to give consent to the request.
I therefore, uncomplainingly abided my time until
the 13th of April, when W. O. Avery and myself were
called into court and sentence passed upon us, his
being two years in the penitentiary and a fine of
$1,000, and mine three years in the penitentiary and
a fine of $5,000.   About this time I told Judge
Krum I should like to avoid going to the penitentiary, and thought my pardon should issue before

such a climax of punishment was reached. But
the Belknap scandal had not ceased to excite the
public when Babcock was again thrown into the
toils of an indictment. Suspicion, furnished upon
the statements of confederates, had implicated him
in the safe burglary which the House Judiciary
Committee was investigating in March and April,
1876. The result of this investigation was the
indictment of Babcock by the Grand Jury on the
16th of April, charging him with complicity in the
safe burglary conspiracy, and he was compelled to
give $10,000 bonds for his appearance to answer.

The administration was as deeply interested in
Babcock during the pendency of this indictment as
when he was before the St. Louis court answering
to the charge of conspiracy to defraud the government. So again a most courteous request came to
me to await until the excitement over this latter
indictment had disappeared. Again I consented to
await, and on the morning of April 16th, being the
same day on which Babcock was indicted for complicity in the safe burglary conspiracy, I left for
Jefferson City to enter upon my term of imprisonment in the penitentiary.

Perhaps another month had elapsed before I
again called for the pardon that was promised me.
This time there was a different excuse given for
postponing it. The President and Gen. Babcock
both appealed to me to wait until after the presidential nomination was made; they reminded me
of the effect my pardon might have; that as I was
in jail, the Democracy could not charge the administration with carrying out a sham reform, for the

results were satisfactory to the public. They further assured me that if I continued patiently considering the best interests of the Republican party, that Grant would certainly be re-nominated and re-elected, after which my reward would be a handsome recompense for my fidelity and sacrifice.

In the meantime, while it had been reported that Gen. Babcock had resigned his position as secretary to the President, before leaving Washington to enter upon his trial at St. Louis, he had, nevertheless, resumed his same duties after his acquittal. The public was well settled in the belief that the evidence was sufficient to convict him of conspiracy with myself and others to defraud the government, and when the President, regardless of public opinion, received the disgraced secretary with open arms of confidence and undiminished regard, he became the subject of much adverse criticism.

Gen. Babcock continued to perform the duties of secretary until his indictment for complicity in the safe burglary, when the demand for his dismissal came with such irrepressible force that the President was forced to accept his resignation.

On the 28th of April Wm. McKee and Col. Con. Maguire were brought into court to receive sentence. McKee was sentenced to imprisonment in the county jail for a period of two years and to pay a fine of $10,000. A suspension was granted in Maguire's case for several weeks, when at length the nominal sentence of six months' imprisonment in the county jail was passed upon him.

On the 17th of May following, McKee was committed to jail, but the period of his imprisonment was one of almost constant reception. He spent the day in company with his friends who called, and almost every night he was allowed the privilege, on the responsibility of the jailor, of visiting his family, returning to the jail usually just at break of day, so that the fact of his freedom might not be discovered. In six months from the time of his commitment he was pardoned and his fine remitted by the President. Maguire was liberated about the same time.

On the 17th of November, 1876, Col. W. O. Avery was pardoned by the President, his early release having been accomplished by the threats of his wife to make public the Babcock correspondence with her husband. The period of his imprisonment was just six months and one day.

On the 22d of November a lengthy article appeared in the New York *Sun* from the pen of Mr. Gibson, the Washington correspondent. Gibson resided in Washington, and for many years had been a next door neighbor to W. O. Avery, with whom he held a most intimate and confidential acquaintance. Upon Avery's return to Washington from his incarceration at Jefferson City, Gibson elicited from him his story of the Whiskey Ring and its operations. I have included it here because the article may be accepted as Avery's statement, colored slightly, perhaps, in his own favor, but, excepting the implied claims of his own innocence, the statement is a true one. It is as follows:

WASHINGTON, Nov. 21.—The pardon of William O. Avery, who was convicted on the charge of conspiring with McDonald, Joyce, and others to defraud the United States of the revenue from whiskey manufactured at St. Louis, enables me

to give a part of the inside history of the Whiskey Ring prosecutions, and the political complications growing out of them
which I have not been at liberty heretofore to disclose. In
order that the general public may properly understand these
disclosures, it is necessary to briefly review the prosecutions
of the St. Louis Whiskey Ring conspirators.

The investigations which led to the discovery of the existence
of a wide-spread conspiracy to defraud the Government by the
manufacture and disposal of illicit spirits in St. Louis, Chicago
and Milwaukee, began about the middle of February, 1875.
Mr. Bristow, then Secretary of the Treasury, had had some
experience in carrying out reforms, and fully appreciated the
opposition he would have to encounter in this last and greatest
undertaking. Although but six months in office, he had
learned how serious a matter it was to attempt to eradicate
corruption and purify an administration with the great bulk of
the leaders of his party in opposition, while he was constantly
in doubt respecting the intentions of his official chief.

The difficulties he had encountered satisfied Secretary Bristow that he could only depend upon the negative support of
the President in his contests with official plunderers, and he
was only sure of it when he was fortified with conclusive
proofs. Therefore he determined that the President should
know nothing of his operations against the Whiskey Ring
until he had obtained evidence to prove the conspiracy and
was ready to strike. He did not suspect until long after the
commencement of the investigation that any member of the
President's official household would be implicated. He was
aware of the intimacy between Supervisor McDonald and the
President, but attributed it to old time acquaintance. He
doubtless knew that Babcock also was intimate with McDonald,
but very naturally thought this was the result of the latter's
cordial relations with the President. Of the intimacy between
Joyce and Babcock he had no knowledge whatever. His
determination, therefor, to withhold all information of his
operations against the Whiskey Ring from the President, until

the culmination was reached, was not prompted either by suspicion or ambition. He had experienced trouble heretofore in regard to internal revenue matters, for when he had got the President to consent to a change of Supervisors, McDonald came forthwith to Washington and rallied sufficient political influence to have the order revoked. Baffled in his first move on the enemy's works, the Secretary was determined to take no one into his confidence in the second campaign whom he could not personally trust, and then, if any secrets were betrayed, he would have none but his own subordinates to blame.

All the details of the investigation were left to Solicitor Wilson, and, by the first week in March last, the work of ferreting out the frauds was fairly commenced. For six weeks but little progress was made, and the final result was often problematic; but about the middle of April the idea of comparing the returns of the gaugers with the records of the wholesale dealer's receipts and sales was suggested, and then the difficult problem was speedily solved.   The serial numbers on the ˙stamps enabled each barrel to be traced through all its various manipulations, and by the first of May, sufficient evidence had been obtained to warrant the raid, which took place on Monday, May 10th.   Up to the 15th or 16th of April the Secretary had not informed the President of the investigations he was prosecuting. At or about this time, however, the evidence obtained by the comparison above alluded to, or of the gauger's returns with the wholesale dealers' books in the various Eastern cities was amply sufficient to convict the distillers and minor revenue officers in St. Louis of conspiracy, and then, for the first time, the President was made acquainted with some of the facts. According to the testimony of Solicitor Wilson, this occurred about the time the President left Washington to attend the anniversary ceremonies at Lexington, Mass.

But a short time had elapsed, and before the President had returned, when Supervisor McDonald turned up in Washington. He had interviews with the Secretary and the Solicitor, and admitted that he knew the frauds had been detected, although he was not in possession of any of the details. The information which the Secretary had given the President a few days previous was general, save as to one particular case, that of shipments of illicits spirits by **Bevis & Fraser**, distillers of St. Louis to Wilmington, N. C., although **without entering** into any particulars. Mr. Bristow had **said that sufficient** evidence had been accumulated to convict the **revenue** officers and distillers of conspiracy. There **was no** other source from which McDonald could have received his **information** than through the White House, and, moreover, **what he** knew tallied with what the Secretary had told the President, so that the suspicions of the former were excited thereby. He questioned McDonald closely as to the source of his information, **but could not draw him out.** McDonald was satisfied that he had been caught, **and proposed to** make the distillers pay the tax on all illicit spirits disposed of, and, **moreover, to pay any** reasonable penalties. He begged for mercy, **and promised** fidelity hereafter if left undisturbed in office, and spoke **of his** ability to render good service to the party and administration. But these appeals and representations fell on deaf ears.

On May 7th, being the Friday **before the** seizures **were to be made,** according to preconcert in St. Louis, Chicago and Milwaukee, the Secretary and Solicitor called **upon the President,** and for the first time placed him in possession **of all the** details after the work was accomplished. After the **seizures,** there yet remained the more difficult task of **tracing the conspiracy** to the fountain **head** and bringing the guilty parties **to justice.** The conspirators, certain of powerful political influence **to support them, were** confident, **for** a season, of their ability **to defeat the Secretary of** the Treasury, but they **soon** discovered **that they had reckoned** without their host. Bristow had succeeded in accomplishing the retirement of Attorney-General Williams, **while his successor, Mr.** Pierrepont, in his ambition to win a share of the popular praise then bestowed on the Secretary of the Treasury, was willing, nay, anxious, to back up Bristow. This enabled Bristow to manage the legal as well as the detective machinery employed against the Ring, and all went swimmingly till it was determined to overhaul the telegraph office at St. Louis.

When the Grand Jury was convened in July, 1875, a *subpœna duces tecum* was served on the manager of the telegraph office in St. Louis to produce all messages to Joyce and McDonald, or sent by them. Now I quote the testimony of District Attorney Dyer before the select committee of the House of Representatives to investigate the Whiskey frauds. Mr. Dyer testified as follows :

"In July, during the investigation by the Grand Jury, I had a *subœna duces tecum* issued for the production of certain telegrams. That was toward the latter part of the session of the Grand Jury. In answer to that we not only gathered the correspondence of McDonald and Joyce, which passed between them when they were separated, one at Washington and the other at St. Louis, but we gathered also the dispatches of William O. Avery, as Magrue had testified about Avery being in the arrangement. In the course of that examination during July, I came across a batch of these dispatches that I felt it my duty to send to the Secretary of the Treasury. Mr. Avery, being then in the department as chief clerk of the Treasury, of course those that they sent from here I could only get copies of at the other end, the originals being here at the Washington office, and I had no means of determining who a dispatch was written by, even if I knew the handwriting. I sent the dispatches, including one signed "Sylph," supposing at the time that I sent it to the Secretary of the Treasury, that it was one of Avery's dispatches, and I never knew any better until I received a letter from the Secretary of the Treasury, in which he said that he had examined the dispatches, including this one signed " Sylph," and he was satisfied that the " Sylph," dispatch was not in the handwriting of Avery. I came

here and it was at the time of my visit here in August, after
the adjournment of the Grand Jury, that I first discovered or
learned that the dispatch signed "Sylph" was a dispatch
sent by Gen. Babcock."

Thus it seems that the "Sylph" dispatch, which first directed
suspicion to Babcock, was not found till the latter part of
July, and was not discovered to be in his handwriting till some
time during the fore part of August. The testimony of Dyer
in regard to these dates is corroborated by that of Ex-Senator
Henderson and Solicitor Wilson. Their importance will appear hereafter.

Indictments were found by the St. Louis Grand Jury at the
July term against McDonald, Joyce, Avery, all the distillers
and rectifiers and a great number of subordinate revenue officers. The evidence against Avery was confined to the testimony of Megrue and the telegrams to Joyce. Megrue had
been, during some fourteen months, the go-between of the
distillers and the revenue officials, and had attended to the
collection and distribution of the money. He did not testify
to the payment of money to Avery, but swore that in his settlements with revenue officers at St. Louis, they required so
much for themselves and so much for their friends in Washington ; and that on several occasions Fitzroy and Joyce had
mentioned Avery's name as one of the parties to whom they
had to pay money.

The facts in regard to Avery's case seem to be about as follows : He furnished information to McDonald and Joyce as to
the movements of revenue officers, and kept them informed
of the intentions of the department about sending special
agents to look after the St. Louis distilleries. This is proved
by his telegram to Joyce, and this he never denied. But none
of these telegrams bare date later than 1873, while Megrue's
connection with the Ring terminated several months before.
I have been acquainted with Avery, and have had good opportunities to observe his manner of living during the period he
was charged with being the recipient of several hundred dol-

S

lars a month from the Whiskey Ring, and I know the exact condition in which his family was left when he was taken to the penitentiary. He owned a modest little house, on which there was a mortgage of $3,600, two-thirds of its cost. The house was neatly, not extravagantly, furnished, and his manner of living indicated nothing not in keeping with the position he occupied and the salary he received. The expenses of his trial and the fees paid his attorneys were about $1,500 and this consumed every dollar he could raise, and when he was taken to the penitentiary in April last his wife had not enough money to buy a meal for herself and little girl, and for weeks thereafter she was compelled to accept the charity of her neighbors. Avery was, like the average government clerk, a man of barely sufficient capacity to fill the position he occupied. Without any intellectual independence, he was, like the great majority of the office-holding class, susceptible to flattery, and fond of the recognition of his superiors. Naturally an obliging officer, he disliked exceedingly to refuse any one a favor. Joyce and he had been intimately acquainted when Joyce was a clerk along with him in the Internal Revenue Bureau, and after they both married, their wives became intimate friends also. Joyce was always on terms of intimacy at the White House, and was suggested by Babcock as a suitable person to act as McDonald's chief clerk, when that individual, very unexpectedly to the politicians of St. Louis, became Supervisor of Internal Revenue for the District of Missouri, Arkansas and the Indian Territory.

Joyce is a bright, clever fellow, and became a politician of some importance in Missouri. He wrote cleverly, and at times furnished editorials for a considerable part of the Republican country press of that State. He kept up a constant correspondence with Babcock, and when he came to Washington was always a welcome visitor at the White House. Whenever Avery met Babcock, the latter invariably inquired after Joyce and McDonald, always familiarly as "how are the boys getting along at St. Louis?" Levi P. Luckey, another of the President's private secretaries, was also a friend of Avery's and an acquaintance of Joyce. Luckey is of no particular importance, but was used by Babcock for his own purposes. He received less salary than Avery, but lived faster and more extravagantly, and all the circumstances point to his connection with the Whiskey Ring along with Babcock. At various times Babcock used his influence with the President to secure small favors for Avery. He had him sent to Europe along with Luckey on Syndicate business, and also exerted his influence with Boss Shepherd to oblige one or two friends of Avery who wanted contracts from the Board of Public Works. It was important to the Whiskey Ring to have a complacent tool in close official relations with Secretary Bristow, and, accordingly, Babcock and Luckey had Avery made Chief Clerk of the Treasury Department, although Bristow preferred another man, but, of course, would not refuse the request of the President in Avery's behalf.

In this situation of affairs, it does not seem unnatural that Avery should feel under obligations to do anything he could for the friends who had manifested so much zeal in his behalf. He says that Joyce was continually appealing to him to furnish him with information in regard to the visits of revenue agents to St. Louis, putting it on the ground that McDonald was an irascible fellow who was hard to manage, and possessed an extravagant notion of his rights as Supervisor, and who was always giving a great deal of trouble whenever special agents came there without his knowledge. If he knew of their coming, argued Joyce, he could manage everything to the satisfaction of all parties, and much more to his own personal comfort. Avery knew that McDonald and Joyce were favorites at the White House, and he never suspected anything wrong about them ; still, he hated to furnish them with the information they requested. Joyce wrote to him repeatedly, urging it, and always insisted upon it personally when in Washington, but Avery avers that he declined on the ground that it would not be compatible with the public interests, and that it would not be right to do this in one case and not in another, although he did not believe then that the information was wanted for unlawful purposes. Finally, after many solicitations and repeated refusals, Joyce wrote him in the usual strain, and after the same old arguments had been urged anew, said : "If you have any doubt of the propriety of sending this information, see Gen. Babcock ; if he is not in the city, see G." This letter Avery sent to the White House, and in due time it came back with the following endorsment : "*Joyce and McDonald are reliable and trustworthy—Let them have the information they want.*"

U. S. GRANT.

After this, Avery gave himself no further trouble about the matter, but furnished whatever information Joyce and McDonald called for. This was during the time he was chief clerk of the Internal Revenue Bureau, and in a position to know everything that occurred in regard to revenue matters .After he was promoted at the particular request of the President, to be chief clerk of the department, it appears that he seldom communicated with the conspirators. Frequently, during McDonald's visits to Washington, Avery says McDonald would go to the White House, and drive up to the north front of the Treasury in the President's carriage, and while the President waited for him, would come into the department to make inquiries about the movements of special agents. On one of these occasions he requested Avery to write a telegram to Joyce, giving him information of his success in stopping a contemplated raid ; that he wrote the dispatch and signed it with his own name, not suspecting anything wrong. He was a little slow, and McDonald said, "Hurry up, the 'old man' is wating for me," and sure enough, when McDonald left, Avery saw him get in the President's carriage and the two were driven away together.

When Avery was notified on July 26th, that an indictment had been found against him, he realized the danger he was in. He had been apprehensive for several weeks, because he knew his telegrams to Joyce and McDonald had been found. Moreover, he knew that all the distillers and subordinate officers who had been indicted, were manifesting a disposition to turn state's evidence. He was, moreover, uncertain about McDonald and Joyce, and accordingly in this frame of mind, he wrote to Gen. Babcock, who was at Long Branch, telling him his apprehensions and doubts. To this, he received the following reply:

LONG BRANCH, July 22d, 1875.

MY DEAR AVERY:

I cannot believe that Joyce and McDonald have done any such thing as you refer to. I believe them both to be good, reliable officers. I will do anything in my power to aid you. Let me know all you see and hear—*keep cool ;* you may depend upon me. I do not believe they could be used against anybody. Now find out *if they can* be used as witnesses. I do not forward this, for I saw Scott Smith's notice in the *Post* last night. If you want to send anything to Joyce or McDonald, direct to them and enclose to Major E. B. Grimes, Assistant Quartermaster, St. Louis, Mo., with a simple remark, "Please send to Gen. McDonald and oblige one of his friends." You need add no more ; it will reach him. I see no objection to sending it ; undoubtedly these people act under legal counsel and write to no one. The Secretary, (Bristow) has not been here, and has not seen the President since his wife sailed—not that I can find out. See Luckey, and confide in him. Luckey is a true friend, and has excellent sense. Trust to his judgment, and tell him everything, and he will see you through— keep cool—give the telegrams that you *sent those parties* and what they were signed, and those which they accused you of sending. I may be able to see something. If an actual indictment should come, get a good, clear-headed lawyer, and make a square fight. I will do all I can. I repeat, *keep cool* as you can. Excuse haste.

O. E. BABCOCK.

P. S.—Keep memorandum of all you write those parties.

O. E. B.

There are a few important facts to note in connection with this letter. Up to this date, July 2d, Babcock did not know that the Sylph telegram had been found. That he feared it had is shown by the passage in his letter to Avery, where he says: "Give the telegrams (to Luckey) that you sent those parties, and what they were signed, and those which they accused you of sending." By reference to the testimony of District Attorney Dyer, heretofore quoted, it will be seen that, until sometime in August, it was supposed that Avery sent the Sylph dispatch. Bluford Wilson, in his testimony on this point says: "In August we discovered at the Treasury Department the celebrated Sylph telegram to be in the handwriting of the President's private secretary, Orville E. Babcock." There were various rumors, however, that the leading spirits of the Whiskey Ring in St. Louis were openly boasting that the prosecutions would not be pressed to the bitter end, because if they were they would reach the White House. In the famous letter written by W. D. W. Barnard, of St. Louis, to the President, the following passage occurs: "Col. Normile, prosecuting circuit attorney, McDonald and Joyce's confidential friend, asked me Saturday how far matters were going to be pushed towards them. I said I thought until the last man made restitution to his utmost ability to pay, and punished to the extent of the law, if local officers done their duty. He replied that both had told him that day, when seeking bail, that you could not give them up or Babcock was lost."

This letter was written on July 19th, and Grant's famous endorsement, "Let no guilty man escape if it can be avoided," was made on July 29th. Neither the President nor Babcock at that date knew of the discovery of the "Sylph" dispatch. Babcock was, nevertheless, ill at ease, and his letter to Avery plainly indicates the state of his mind. He, doubtless, felt secure of the fidelity of McDonald and Joyce, but he trembled lest Avery should weaken under the manipulation of Bristow and Wilson; hence his repeated assurances that he would stand by him and see him through. But that he might have a trusty friend constantly near him to encourage and report the state of his mind, he recommended Avery to write to Joyce, and find out if McDonald and Joyce were standing solid, and if they could "be used as witnesses." Against whom? Babcock, of course. And he was to send the letter enclosed to McDonald, and this enclosed to Maj. E. B. Grimes, Assistant Quartermaster at St. Louis.

This was before any suspicions had been directed against Babcock, and only a few days after McDonald's indictment, and yet he had arrangements made with Quartermaster Grimes through which he could safely communicate with the Whiskey Ring conspirators. It is also important to notice here the testimony of Grimes in the Babcock trial. He was called by the prosecution to prove the fact of the secret correspondence through him between Babcock and McDonald. He did not tell the whole truth, as will be seen by his testimony, because he fixes the date at which Babcock made this arrangement for the clandestine communication late in the fall, after Grant had left Long Branch, and was in St. Louis, accompanied by Babcock, attending the State Fair. Grimes testified as follows:

'I saw him in 1874 at the fair and the hotel; saw him last fall at the hotel and at my office, and rode out with him to Shaw's garden. I have always considered him as my best friend. I had a conversation with him during his visit here in 1875 at the Lindell Hotel in reference to his sending me packages or letters for other parties.'

Ques.—What was the conversation, as you recollect, had between you and Gen. Babcock at that time?

Ans.—I think, as near as I can recollect, Gen. Babcock said to me: I will probably want to send you some packages or letters, for some other parties, to deliver to some other parties.

Ques.—What else did he say to you in that conversation?

Ans.—Nothing in regard to that.

Ques.—To whom did he say he desired to send the packages or letters?

Ans.—He did not say. That was all the conversation that I had with him in reference to it. After that, if I recollect aright, he sent three letters to me; that is, I suppose he sent them—I am not certain that he did. The letter I got was enclosed in another letter that was addressed to me. I destroyed it as I destroy numbers of private letters that I receive weekly and monthly. I got a letter from Gen. Babcock saying, " Please deliver enclosed letter to Gen. McDonald." I am not certain when this was, but think it was after he was here.

The letter to Avery of July 22d, above given, shows that long before the date fixed by Grimes, there was an understanding between himself and Babcock in regard to correspondence with McDonald. This is important, because it shows that, before the Sylph dispatch was found, before suspicion was directed toward him by the developments made by the Grand Jury, Babcock had thought it prudent to arrange for a secret correspondence with the head and front of the Whiskey Ring thieves.

Now I return to the Avery case. Immediately after the receipt of Babcock's letter, which, as will be observed from its text, was not forwarded by mail, Luckey began to visit Avery constantly, and encouraged him to stand firm. Through this go-between Babcock held constant correspondence with Avery and inspired him with confidence in the final result. In the meantime it was arranged that Avery should employ Judge Krum of St. Louis as his attorney—Krum had been elected Circuit Judge, of St. Louis County, an honorable and lucrative position, but had resigned in order to become the attorney of the Whiskey Ring conspirators. He was retained by McDonald, Joyce, and all the principal distillers and revenue officials. All the store-keepers and gaugers who were indicted were told to retain Krum, and if they said they were without money to pay the retainer, $100, it was funished them. Krum had long been the particular friend of Grant, and had attended to his business in St. Louis, even driving out once every week or ten

days to look after his farm, which is distant about nine miles
from the city.   Avery wanted Ben. Butler, and so did his wife,
but both Babcock and Luckey advised against it, and said
Krum was sufficient; that there was no case against him; that
it would only be an additional and useless expense to retain
another lawyer.   Still, at the earnest solicitation of his wife,
Avery raised $500 and retained Gen. Butler; but when the
trial came on Butler, although furnished with a ticket and
sleeping car pass to St. Louis, failed to put in an appearance,
very much to his unfortunate client's regret.

Up to the very time of the trial, Luckey kept at Avery's
ear to encourage and hold out false hopes.   A day or two before Avery's trial commenced, Luckey came to St. Louis and
remained there till after Avery was convicted, and all the time
was in constant communication by cypher telegrams with Babcock.   Avery trusted Krum entirely, and placed all the letters
he had received from Joyce, McDonald and Babcock, in his
hands, to be used in his defense if it became necessary.   They
would, with corroborating testimony, have proved a perfect
defence, because they would have shown conclusively that he
had steadily and persistently refused to give the information
which the conspirators wanted till he was instructed by the
President of the United States to do so.

But Judge Krum was anxious above all to protect the President and Babcock.   After the telegrams of Joyce and Babcock
and the Sylph dispatch had been put in evidence in his case by
Henderson, Avery was urged by his wife to insist on the use of
the Joyce and Babcock letters, but Judge Krum only placed
three of the unimportant Joyce letters in evidence, carefully
witholding along with the rest the one endorsed by Grant.
The request which Avery had made was communicated by
Krum to Luckey, and of course he was alarmed.   They re-
assured Avery by telling him that he would get a new trial,
and then the excitement having died out somewhat, certainly
he would be acquitted.   But from that hour Luckey and Babcock began work upon Avery to induce him to destroy all letters

in his possession.   The following letter from Luckey is a specimen of the communications almost daily addressed to Avery after his conviction:

EXECUTIVE MANSION 9 a. m., Dec. 3, 1875.

DEAR BILLEY:

I have not yet met a man who says there is any earthly show of a case against you.   I saw Bradley (one of Babcock's lawyers) last night.   I don't anticipate any unfavorable results.   The ship should never be given up, no matter what the storm may be; no one knows what may come up to set the worst thing straight.   Keep no letters or memorandums, or *any thing* that might fall into the hands of anybody.   Keep nothing about you which in a moment of trepidation had better been destroyed; I am very earnest about this, and shall never lose my affection for you.   LEVI (LUCKEY.)

On Nov. 29th, 1875, District Attorney Dyer had informed the Attorney General that he had "sufficient evidence to convict Babcock with the conspiracy to defraud the revenue," and that an indictment would be prepared and laid before the Grand Jury for action thereon.   Naturally, therefore, Babcock and Luckey were "very earnest" in desiring Avery "to keep no letters or memorandums that might fall into the hands of anybody," because they knew that he had sufficient evidence to convict them both, and, as he had not been sentenced, he was still a competent witness.   By holding out delusive hopes to him, Avery was induced to pass quiet, and with the active interference of the President and the Attorney-General, Babcock was in due time acquitted.   The application for a new trial in Avery's case was refused, and the order for his arrest came, and he was thrown into the District of Columbia jail to await the arrival of the officers who were to carry him to the Jefferson City penitentiary.

All hope was now gone, but still one or two faithful friends stood by him, and, together with his wife, urged him to go before the select committee of the House of Representatives and make a clean breast of it.   A member of the committee was notified and a *subpœna* issued. He appeared before the committee an April 11th, 1876, but, unfortunately, it was in secret session, and there was no person present who knew what questions to propound in order to bring out the story. He would not volunteer, and after a few moments examination he was discharged, and went to the penitentiary with his lips sealed.

All the efforts of Babcock and Luckey were now directed to persuade his, Avery's, wife to destroy whatever letters and papers her husband had left in her care. They were at her house night and day, and brought their wives with them to make their appeals more irresistible. They promised a speedy pardon for her husband and protection for herself and child; and finally she consented, or feigned to consent, and neatly made copies of several letters which were, in the presence of Luckey, consigned to the flames. Assured now that they were at last safe, these precious scoundrels lost all interest in Avery and his destitute family, and the house was about to be sold over her head when a gentleman who had secured contracts from Boss Shepherd came to her rescue and lifted the mortgage and set about forcing a pardon for her husband.

All the letters from Joyce, Babcock, and Luckey were placed in his possession, and with this arsenal of solid shot to back the demand, negotiations were opened. At first there was a disposition to turn the cold shoulder, but an exhibition of a few of the documents to Attorney General Pierrepont brought a promise of a respectful consideration, and soon thereafter came the promise of a pardon—after the election.

It only remains now to refer to one other matter. I have shown conclusively that at the time Grant made his famous endorsement, "Let no guilty man escape if it can be avoided," on the Barnard letter, he did not know that Babcock's connection with the Whiskey Ring had been discovered. Shortly after this endorsement was made, the President was informed of the Sylph dispatch, and that it was in Babcock's handwriting. In this category I quote again from Gen. Boynton's article in the October number of the *North American Review* :

"The various forces of the opposition were at this time closing in upon the Secretary. While the President recognized the propriety of the general policy suggested by Mr. Bristow, the latter saw how obstacle after obstacle was placed in his way by the secret influence exerted upon the President. There was delay when the greatest promptness was demanded; and often where changes were to be made the new appointments were improperly controlled by manipulations to which the President was insensible. The endorsement came to the Secretary as a relief force to a garrison about to be overcome. To make it effective its publication was deemed of the greatest importance, and the Secretary wrote the President asking permission to give it to the press. The fact that this note remained unanswered caused much uneasiness. At the same time the "Sylph" dispatch was adding serious difficulties to the situation. This telegram was to Joyce, and read: "I have succeeded. They will not go;" and the evidence collected showed, beyond reasonable doubt, that it was to notify the Ring that he had succeeded in preventing two revenue agents, who had been ordered to investigate affairs at St. Louis, from going there. Gen. Babcock was early apprised of it. His explanation, when taken in connection with other points of the evidence, was regarded as worse than useless at the department. The President, however, accepted it, and from this time his interest in the prosecutions perceptibly diminished, and the attention he gave to all points which the Ring presented became a serious obstacle and the cause of grave embarrassment."

The following is from Solicitor Wilson's testimony before the Select Committee on Whiskey Frauds:

" I was asked yesterday whether the President consented willingly to the publication of the endorsement on the Barnard letter which has been so often referred to. By reference to a letter addressed to me by Gen. Bristow, under date of August 7th, written in the Treasury Department, I find that the Secretary of the Treasury had addressed an official communi-

cation to the President asking him for permission to publish
that endorsement, and at that date (Aug. 7) he had received
no response."

The following letter from Mr. Bristow was at this point
placed in evidence by Solicitor Wilson:

New York, Aug. 9th, 1875.

My Dear Wilson:

Your letter of yesterday with enclosure is received. The
time is very near at hand when I must make a square issue
with the thieves and scoundrels who have combined to destroy
me. I *must* be supported cordially and earnestly, or I *must*
and *will* break. I fear that the complications are such that
the former cannot be done, and the latter *must*. You can't be
too careful about talking to *anybody*. I have heard here that
the matter about the Sylph dispatch and our having seen it in
connection with Pierrepont, is fully known to P. & B., (meaning Porter and Babcock) and they are greatly disturbed.
Don't suffer yourself to talk to *anybody* about it. Of course
this is not meant for censure, but caution. I suppose I must
make up my mind to bear the abuse of the "Ring" papers,
hard as it is to do. They are fighting to keep their friends out
of prison, and to save themselves from exposure; and of course
will seek to destroy anybody who stands in the way. Well, as
for myself, I cannot turn back, nor will I stop to parley with
thieves. I have no ambition to serve, and no purpose to accomplish but enforcement of the law and an honest collection of the
revenue. I will compromise on nothing short of this, but on
this issue I am ready to be sacrificed any day.

B. H. Bristow.

More than a week elapsed after this letter was written, and
still the President gave no response to the Secretary's request
for permission to publish the endorsement on the Barnard letter.
Finally, on August 15th, the Secretary went to Long Branch,
determined to have the President's sanction to the publication
or to tender his resignation. What took place at this interview is known to but few persons, and for the present the

details of the scene cannot be given to the public.   However,
a reluctant permission to publish was obtained, and on August
16th the endorsement was given to the press.   In regard to
what occurred between the President and Bristow at this
interview at Long Branch, Solicitor Wilson testified as follows:

Ques.—Do you know whether the President of the United
States was willing that letter should be published?

Ans.—As to that I cannot say, but I am bound to presume
from the fact that Gen. Bristow directed me to give it to the
public that he was willing.

Ques.—Do you know, of your own knowledge, or from conversations with the Secretary of the Treasury upon his return
from Long Branch, whether he met with any opposition from
the President when he proposed to make the letter public?

Ans.—In response to that question, it is evident that whatever I should have to say to this committee would be hearsay,
and in view of the important issues which from time to time
arise between the Secretary of the Treasury and the President,
I must decline to repeat what was said to me.   Gen. Bristow
and the President of the United States are themselves the best
witnesses on that point, and while they refuse to answer, I positively will not answer.

It is certain, however, that whatever was the nature of that
interview between Bristow and the President, no cordial understanding was reached, and by the 1st of September the
Secretary had again determined to retire in disgust from the
Cabinet.   On this point, I quote from a letter written at this
time by Solicitor Wilson to a friend:

"I cannot in this letter go into details, but will say that the
Sylph telegram; the retention of incompetent, dishonest or
disloyal officers at St. Louis, Chicago and Milwaukee; the lack
of hearty sympathy and support from the President; the certainty of constant misrepresentation of his motives and acts
by "Sylph;" the delay in the Delano affair, and the revival of
the third-term insanity, all combine to make an honest man
uncomfortable, and in Bristow's case, to disgust him with pub-

lic life.   His eyes are fully open.   He means to walk out of the
Cabinet and politics at the same time."

This was the turning point in the career of Mr. Bristow.   If
he had adhered to his first purpose of resigning and frankly
stating his reasons, his political future would have been
assured.   But he faltered, and finally consented to patch up a
half-hearted, hollow truce with the President, who was shrewd
enough to see that to force Bristow out of his Cabinet at this
juncture would certainly make the Kentuckian the next President of the United States.   It was not possible, under the
circumstances, that cordial relations could exist between the
Secretary and the President, and the prosecutions of the
Whiskey Ring conspirators be followed to their legitimate end.
The ruptures were frequent.   Again and again Bristow had to
threaten his resignation, first, to prevent the removal of Solicitor Wilson, who was accused by the President of setting spies
to watch him when he and Babcock visited St. Louis in September; and again when it was determined to stop legal proceedings against Babcock at St. Louis and direct the District
Attorney to turn over all the evidence in his possession to the
Military Court at Chicago.   It was not the President's desire
to force Bristow out, and so he would yield when the square
issue was made, but, nevertheless, the whole power of his administration was exerted to save Babcock.   The secrets of the
prosecution were betrayed to his lawyers while the Attorney
General was employed to intimidate the District Attorney and
manufacture public sentiment in Babcock's interest.   After
Babcock's acquittal the country was disappointed that there
was not an open rupture between the President and Bristow.
The rupture would have occurred had not the President feared
it might prove to Bristow's advantage at Cincinnati.   He sup-
pressed his animosity, knowing that if Bristow was defeated
there, his retirement from the Cabinet would create scarce a
riffle of excitement in the public mind.

This letter, unlike a great many emanating from
the   Nation's   Capital,   bristles   with   important

facts, surmises and deductions having no influence or needful part in the purposes of the writer.

Avery obtained his pardon just as the correspondent has stated, through threats of exposure, and had I pursued the same course I need never have entered the jail. But I was loyal to the President and my promises, and ever mindful of the best interests of the Republican party. A thousand times, while chafing under the punishment I was undergoing, my tongue seemed determined to break the seal of secrecy; then a second thought would arise and make my resolution to remain silent stronger than ever. How could I fail to realize the fact that my confessions would defeat Grant and destroy the Republican party; how could I forget those promises of the President's, that were so full of the honey of exalted ambition; so ripe with the results which my desire it was to attain. In the success of Grant and the party, and the vindication and laudation of his administration all my hopes were centered, for in such a consummation lay my pardon, and honors which I was assured would shine with such lustre as would cause oblivion to hide the disgrace of my position. Ambition robbed me of my judgment and, like a silly moth that is flattered by the deadly lamp, I hung about these promises, and waited as one who knocks at the castle of his imagination and then sits down in the airy portal and waits an answer from dame fortune.

CHAPTER X.

In the following December, Hayes having been
elected President, I could see no further reason for
remaining in prison, and I determined to procure
my release. During the fall I had been very sick
and on two occasions the attending physician had
pronounced my case hopeless; but I still lingered,
in a semi-living condition, until a number of my
friends, without my co-oporation or request, interested themselves in my behalf, by obtaining a nu-
merously signed petition, together with a recommendation from the prison surgeon, praying the
President to grant me a pardon. This request having been refused the result so embittered me that I
decided at once, like Samson of old, to pull down

the pillars which supported the temple of official
iniquity and, if necessary, perish with Grant and
Babcock in the ruins. Accordingly I instructed
Thos. F. Walsh to write a strong letter to Babcock
and to tell him frankly that I was determined to remain in prison no longer; that he had been false to
his promises and that I proposed to hurt the White
House if something was not done for me very soon.
In proof of this I herewith submit an extract from
Walsh's letter replying to the one containing the
instructions referred to.

St. Louis, Iron Mountain & Southern Ry., Co.,
General Office,
St. Louis, Dec. 19th, 1876.

Dear General:

Yours of the 13th inst., just came to hand.

There is nothing now to be said only this: I wrote a nice
long letter to your friend (Babcock) in the east * * *
When the party east gets my letter I'll bet a new hat that
something will be done at once; and yet I said nothing except that which you instructed me to say, but I strung it out
elaborately, and gave considerable emphasis to certain vital
interests at stake.

* * * * * * * * *

Yours Truly
Walsh.

I concluded to push matters further and show my
determination, to do which I wrote another letter
to Walsh in which I instructed him to inform
Judge Krum that if my pardon was not forthcoming that I would place myself in communication
with Proctor Knott—whose committee was then in
session investigating the whiskey cases—and give
to him the facts connecting President Grant and
Gen. Babcock with the whiskey conspiracy. This

determined act of mine excited Gen. Babcock, who
was then in Chicago, and to whom Judge Krum
telegraphed **my** threat. Following is the reply I
received :

J. M. & C. H. Krum,

ATTORNEYS AT LAW.

307 Olive Street.

St. Louis, Dec. 27th, 1876.

Dear General :

Bliss has returned from Washington and has brought back
with him the papers in your case.

I am informed that the Attorney General opposes your pardon. This **much has been** indicated by Bliss **and** he has accordingly brought the application back with **him** without
action. He was willing to recommend favorable action but
upon receiving the above intimation concluded he had **better**
do nothing **at** present.

Now what I **write you is in** the strictest confidence. I do
not **want you to confer with** anyone **as to** this ; not even
Joyce.

I *know* that at headquarters the inclination is favorable to
your immediate pardon. I shall write to-day and endeavor to
have the proper intimation conveyed to the Attorney General,
so that Bliss can act favorably, as soon as possible. Your
friend in Washington has done all within his power to assist
you. I had a note from him to-day, from Chicago. **He** will
be at home again on Friday. He was confidant, **when he left**
home, that all was right.

I suggest again that you authorize me to employ Col. Cook
to look after the application in Washington. I do not think
his fee would be large. At all events an inquiry **of** him, as to
what it would **be,** could do no harm. Some **one** to represent
you as attorney, should **be employed, so that the** application
could be pushed along. **It is too** much to expect that the pardon will be granted as a matter of course ; but with some one
to represent the matter before **the Attorney** General, to satisfy

him that the certificates are from responsible **physicians, and**
to answer any objection which he may make, I cannot conceive
that there can be any serious obstacle.

    *   *   *   *   *   *   *   *   *

Now, **I want** you to write me yourself, and give me your
views fully, and while I feel that your patience must be nearly
exhausted, yet I hope that you will not give way to anything
like resentment or ill-feeling against any friend in Washington. No good can be done in that way.

You understand now that the obstacle in the way of your
pardon is in the Attorney General's office. That obstacle can,
I believe, be removed. All friends, upon being advised of it,
will help to that end. But I say again some one should represent you in Washington.

Destroy this letter but **answer** it yourself.

Very truly yours,

CHESTER H. KRUM.

[A fac-simile of this letter occurs on the subsequent pages.]

Upon receipt of this letter, on December 29th, I
at once wrote him a reply covering four pages of
legal-cap paper, in which I made a general statement of the promises made to me by Grant and
Babcock and the manner in which they has de-
ceived me; I also reminded him of the disgrace and
suffering I had borne for the the sake of these two
officials, and concluded the letter by declaring that
if my pardon was not granted by the middle of January, 1877, that I should expose every unpunished
member of the Whiskey Ring, and procure Grant's
impeachment.

Ex-Gov. Thos. C. Fletcher, of St. Louis, whose
name I have not mentioned before in this book because none of **his acts** up to this **time** had made it

J. M. & C. H. KRUM,
ATTORNEYS AT LAW,
207 OLIVE STREET,

St. Louis, December 27 1876

Dear General:

Bliss has returned from Washington and has brought back with him the papers in your case.

I am informed that the Attorney General opposes your pardon. This much has been indicated to Bliss and he has accordingly brought the application back with him, without action. He was willing to recommend favorable action, but upon receiving the above intimation concluded, that he had better do nothing at present.

Now, what I write you is in the strictest confidence. I do not want you to confer with anyone as to this — at even Joyce.

I know, that at Head Quarters the inclination is favorable to your immediate pardon. I shall wait to-day, and endeavor to have the proper intimation conveyed to the Attorney General, so that Blis can act favorably as soon as possible. Your friend in Washington has done all within his power to assist you. I had a note from him to-day, from Chicago. He will be at home again on Friday. He was confident, when he left home that all was right

I suggest again, that you authorize me to employ, Col. Cook to look after the application in Washington. I do not think his fee would be large. At all even an inquiry of him, as to what would be, could do no harm. Someone - to represent you as attorney - should be employed, so that the application could be pushed along.

It is too much to expect, that the pardon will be granted as a matter of course; but, with some one to represent the matter before the Attorney General, to satisfy him that tho certificates are from responsible physicians, and to answer any objection which he may make, I cannot conceive that there can be any serious obstacle.

* * * * * * * * * * * *

Now, I want you to write me yourself, * * and give me your views freely.

* * * * * * * * * * * *

The *fac simile* of this page was defaced in printing. Will appear in Second Edition.

And while I feel, that your patience must be nearly exhausted, yet I hope that you will not give way to any thing like resentment or ill feeling against any friend in Washington. No good can be done in that way.

You understand, now, that the obstacle in the way of your pardon is in the Attorney General's office. That obstacle can, I believe, be removed. All friends, upon being advised of it, will help to that end. But I say again. Someone should represent you in Washington. Destroy this letter, but answer it yourself.

Very truly yours

Chester H Krum

necessary, was employed by me to look after my interests in Washington. On the 11th of December, Gov. F., visited me in Jefferson City, when, upon his arrival, in company with Col. Joyce, we repaired to my room at the hospital, where we talked freely upon the manner in which Col. Joyce and I had been treated by the President. I told him that Col. Joyce had prepared a statement for me which I had decided to send to Proctor Knott if my pardon was delayed beyond the middle of January. I then handed him the statement and told him that I intended to swear to it, and that Col. Joyce would also attach his affidavit to the truth of every declaration it contained. This statement is as follows:

To HON. PROCTOR KNOTT, Chairman of the Special Committee on the Whiskey Trials, Washington, D. C.

SIR:—In the spring of 1872, I was Supervisor of Internal Revenue for the District of Missouri, Kansas, Arkansas, Indian Territory, New Mexico and Texas, with my head quarters at St. Louis. Through the winters of 1871, and 1872 I had personal interviews with President U. S. Grant, O. E. Babcock, Hon. Columbus Delano, Hon. W. W. Belknap, Hon. Geo. S. Boutwell, and Hon. J. W. Douglass, Commissioner of Internal Revenue. The object of my appointment and official action in the main I find to be the re-nomination and re-election of the President. I was picked out as a plucky man to do the desperate political work for my superiors in office, and I was given to understand that any means I took for the re-election of Gen. U. S. Grant would find favor and be justified.

In the spring of 1872, I had a private interview with the President and I told him my plans for the campaign, to control the conventions in Missouri and other states. It was well known among business politicians of the Democratic party that the

"Andy Johnson Whiskey Ring," had raised large sums in 1868 for the benefit of themselves and Chief, and the Republican politicians in Washington told me that I could pattern after the same thing and raise a fund to run the political machine in the interest of Grant. I told the President the proposed plan and asked his advice in the matter. He listened attentively to my loyalty to his administration and referred me to Gen. O. E. Babcock, and said whatever I did with him was satisfactory all round. I therefore raised a fund and put it into the political campaign of 1872. I told the President on one occasion that certain Republican and other newspapers had to be bought up in his interest, to which he consented, and I fixed the editors and proprietors, who were the most pliant and voracious tools in the camp. Gen. Babcock knew the details of the fraud, and kept me constantly posted as to the movement of revenue detectives through my district. Col. Avery rendered me all the assistance in his power while chief of the Internal Revenue Bureau and Treasury Department, and did all he could to further the political conspiracy. I told Commissioner Douglass all about the matter and he consented to everything, only saying that he did not care to hear the details. He wanted to be kept pure and shut his eyes to the conspiracy, so that when the storm came he could fizzle out into safety and obscurity and leave me to hold the bag. Deputy Commissioner Rogers knew of the conspiracy, and his particular friend, Revenue Agent Hogue, was a tool in the premises.

I have only to tell the true history of the team, wagon and equipments to show the peculiarly selfish character of the President. In the fall of 1874, General Grant, Babcock, Secretary Borie, and family were visiting the fair at St. Louis. At the time, I had a pair of fast horses and tendered them to President Grant while he remained in the city. Mr. Harkness the stable keeper will recollect that the President used them. I was with Grant on several occasions while in St. Louis, and he was greatly pleased with the team. Being a subordinate officer and wishing to ingratiate myself into the good graces of His Excellency, and knowing his weakness for fine horse-flesh, I told him I would present him with the team, but in such a way that it would appear as if he had purchased them. I had the bills for the wagon, harness and equipments made out in the name of the President and had the team taken to Washington by Nat Carlin, the Superintendent of the President's farm. The first week in December, 1874, I dropped in at the White House, the very day Congress assembled, and saw the President in his office. He had used the team for some time and was delighted with them. I told him that I had a bill of sale made out, with minor bills attached, amounting in all to about seventeen hundred and fifty dollars, if my memory serves me rightly. The bill was receipted and signed before I started from St. Louis. I asked him with a smile to hand me a few dollars. He pulled out a fifty dollar bill, threw it at me, and asked if that would do. I told him it was too much and threw it back. Then the President gave me a ten dollar bill, and I took out of my vest pocket a five dollar bill and a two dollar bill, which I gave to him in change, thus leaving me *three dollars* for the team!

When I closed the team transaction with the President, I expressed a desire to see the horses, and he said, "I have just ordered the team, let us go down and look at them." We went to the front portico of the White House, and after comments on the condition of the outfit, the President said, "step in and take a ride with me." I did so. We passed out New York Avenue to the Bladensburg road, and after a two hours' drive returned to the White House, where I was brushed by the porter, after which I took a drive to the floral gardens and hot houses in the private carriage of General Babcock.

In the morning before the team transaction, I was in General Babcock's office and conversed with him on business matters, and while at his official desk I paid him five thousand dollars ($5,000), part of the slush secured in aid of the political conspiracy. At another time, in April, 1875, I paid Gen-

Babcock the sum of five thousand dollars ($5,000) at his private residence in a top back room, which he was fitting up for a library. I took dinner the same day at his house, and General Horace Porter was a companion guest at the same time. General Belknap came in during the meal, and with wine and loud talk we had a high old time. Just before General Babcock sent the "Sylph dispatch," I had enclosed to him in the center of a fine box of cigars the sum of one thousand dollars ($1,000), and sent the package by Adams Express. Babcock acknowledged the receipt of the box and said, "the flavor of the cigars is fine and highly appreciated."

In the fall of 1874, while the President and his party were at the St. Louis Fair, more than ten days, I paid their bill at the Lindell Hotel, receiving back, however, a part of this amount through contributions from a few of the President's private friends. The bill was made out in the President's name, but the cash came out of private pockets.

I went east during the canvass of 1872, and secured the services of Hon. Geo. S. Boutwell and Hon. C. Delano to come into Missouri and speak to the people on the pending issue. I saw Boutwell at the Continental Hotel in Philadelphia, while the President was there, and made the necessary arrangements. When Mr. Delano and Mr. Kirk came to Missouri I travelled with them through the state and paid all expenses. In company with Hon. Henry. T. Blow, chairman of the Republican Central Committee, and other men, I assisted in raising several thousand dollars as a Grant fund to be used for special emergency—I subscribed to this fund $1,000, and Col. Joyce paid $500. I was at the bottom of organizing what was known as the Missouri Club, with Geo. Bain as President and Chauncy I. Filley as Executive officer, while Col. Joyce was corresponding secretary and general manipulator for the concern, as well as being a member of the Republican State Central Committee. I understood that some of the money raised in Missouri was sent to Senator Morton to aid in carrying Indiana. The foregoing statemets are the main milestones in the political conspiracy to re-elect President Grant, yet there are many details, secret meetings and presents, that can be brought to bear to corroborate the full truth thereof; letters, papers and telegrams can be also produced to sustain what I allege. This terrible exposure would never perhaps have been made had Grant and Babcock treated me with the fairness they promised. I willingly came to the penitentiary to save these officers and the nation from scandal, and gave up certain letters to Babcock to aid him in his trial. I acted in good faith. They did not. Then to, after all the whiskey defendants in Indiana, Illinois Wisconsin and Missouri, have been pardoned and released from prison, I am left to die in the gloomy walls by the very men who got the benefit of my manipulations. Patience and silence must cease and the world shall know the bottom facts of the conspiracey. Thus shall every man bear his part in the fearful exposure, and even-handed justice at last prevail. Truth is eternal and ingratitude and treachery must ever receive a just retribution.

I have done more than my share, and suffered more than impartial justice demands. Now let my superior officers come down to the level of my situation, and taste of the bitter dregs prepared for my consumption.

When Gov. Fletcher finished reading the statement he advised Col. Joyce and I not to act rashly; that we had shown our manhood and fidelity to the President thus far, and that it would be exceedingly impolitic for us to do anything now which would bring the disaster so long averted. He said that when the President learned of the course we had adopted that he would pardon us, and thus it would be unnecessary to take action which would make the secrets of Grant's and Babcock's crime public.

When Gov. Fletcher returned to St. Louis he talked to many of my friends and told them how bitter and determined I had become. Judge Krum informed the President and Gen. Babcock, and frankly told them that something would have to be done speedily or that an exposure would certainly follow. I was urged to remain patient a very short time, that the only cause for delaying my pardon was because of the recent appointment of Judge Tafft as Attorney-General whom it would be very unwise to let know the relationship existing between them and myself; that every thing was fixed for my liberation in a few days. This is the tenor of Judge Krum's letter, which reflects the wishes of Gen. Babcock.

On the 30th of December I received a letter from Walsh in which he advises me: "Upon no account act rashly; go a little slow now, and in a *very* short time all will be well."

Gov. Fletcher was actively engaged in my interest for several months; while never a participant in the illicit whiskey conspiracy he was, nevertheless, acquainted with the details, and who composed the membership, shortly after the exposure of the Ring. He had advised me repeatedly not to criminate Grant and Babcock until the last extremity had been exhausted.

The following letter which I recived through Dr. Thompson, the surgeon at the penitentiary, will furnish the proof for my statement respecting Gov. Fletcher's position:

St. Louis, Jan. 8th, 1877.

DEAR SIR:

I cannot be in Washington before the 12th (next Friday). I have been consolidating and getting into shape the influences and machinery for the work and if I mistake not I can now

lay off my coat and wade in and pull your matter through. I
am going at it in a manner that will admit of no failure; at all
events I can and will, in three days after I get there (at most)
have a final, square and *distinct* decision from the head of the
mess himself.

*   *   *   *   *   *   *   *

I do not intend that your papers shall go to the Attorney
General, but will take them myself direct to the President.
The Attorney General told Bliss that he was opposed to doing
anything in your case. Hold on till the 15th and on that day
if you do not hear from me then I have nothing more to say,
and then let her rip if you see proper, but wait till then.

Yours Truly,
FLETCHER.

The full import of this letter is too apparent to
require explanation. In giving me his sanction to
" let her rip," means that he will not oppose my
exposure of Grant if by the 15th of January my pardon is not granted.

On the 13th of January I received the following
letter.

WASHINGTON, Jan. 10th, 1877.

DEAR GENERAL:

I just learn it is only a question of a few days—it is determined upon. Your friends have been active and watchful.
Bliss returned your papers yesterday. At the General's (Babcock's) instance have watched the case closely—would send
particulars but learn that contents of letters to you and Joyce
have, somehow, been made known outside. I hope such is
not the case, although I have written nothing that I fear anyone to know. Please write as to whether your letters are read
and contents exposed. I had thought better of the gentleman
whom I had met when at Jefferson.

*   *   *   *   *   *

You will hear from me again in a few days. Be assured

the matter is settled.   When I write again I will enclose letter I had written but laid aside to substitute this.

Very truly your friend,

JNO. F. CLEMENTS,

916 F. St., N. W., Washington.

P. S.—When we meet will tell you all.

The writer of this letter was a confidant of Gen.
Babcock's, whom the latter had employed early in
1876 to work up evidence and furnish jurymen in
Babcock's interest, so as to provide for the trial the
means for an acquittal.   He was at one time a pension agent and editor at Macon, Mo., sharing the
former office with a Mrs. Boggs, as a compromise.

District Attorney Dyer has admitted that during
the trial of Babcock, Clements was a source of much
annoyance by his insinuating efforts to approach the
jury.   The letter just quoted might as well have
been signed by Babcock himself, as it was written
at the latter's request and dictation.

Six days after the date of his first letter, Clements wrote me again deploring the delay in my pardon, and declaring that within ten days, and perhaps in less than one week, the pardon would be
granted beyond question.   He begged me to keep
my courage and discretion and in the end I would
find reason to be thankful for having taken his
advice.

The pardon remained in suspension, with daily
assurances from friends and officials, that it would
be issued at once, until the 26th day of January
when the President granted me an unconditional
pardon, and on the 29th I walked from out the
shadows of the prison walls a free man.

U

Upon the return of Gov. Fletcher from Washington where he had remained until my pardon was issued, he told me that while at the White House and in the company of Gen. Babcock, he met Mrs. Grant, wife of the President, and that he saw her reading the letter I wrote to Judge Krum on December 29th, demanding my pardon under threats of preferring charges that would procure the impeachment of President Grant, as already referred to.

Within ten days after my release I went to Washington in the interest of Col. Joyce, to urge his pardon. While there I had my quarters at the Ebbett House, and remained until after Grant's term of office expired (March 3d). Nearly every day during my stay in Washington Gen. Babcock called on me and in response to my request for Joyce's pardon he always assured me that the President would sign the pardon before going out of office, but that owing to the troubles then agitating the country as to the installation of Hayes or Tilden, that the President thought it would be judicious to postpone the pardon until that matter was settled or, until the last day of his official life.

On the 3d of March (the 4th occurring on Sunday) I was in the marble room of the Senate waiting with anxiety for the issuing of Joyce's pardon. When the gavel sounded the hour of 12, when Grant was no longer President, I met Gen. Babcock as he was issuing from the President's room. I stopped him and enquired if the pardon had been signed. With some manifestation of embarrassment he replied that, owing to

the extraordinary pressure of business at the close,
it had not, but he said that Hayes would grant the
pardon speedily.

Said I: Gen. Babcock, you and Grant have made
me promises from one day to another, ever since I
consented to shield you from disgrace; you have
lied to me without consci°nce; have trampled upon
my friendship, and now from this day we are enemies, and I shall seek my own good time to hold
your villainies up for the world to gaze upon.

He appealed to me to harbor no ill feeling against
the President or himself; that they both regarded
me with the highest consideration and that they
were now, in common with myself citizens, whose
friendships should be as strong as in the earlier
years of our acquaintance, when we made our
interests mutual.

I contradicted his assertion that we were citizens
alike, and reminded him that he had a life position
and that Grant went out of office burdened with the
honors of a profitable presidency, and that this was
because Joyce and I had protected him and Grant
from the calumny which would have thrown them
into cells of infamy, if we had opened our lips against
them. I reminded him that he had disarmed Joyce
by procuring, through false promises, the tell-tale
letters which, during the operation of the Whiskey
Ring, he (Babcock) had written him (Joyce), but
that there would be a day of reckoning nevertheless,
when he and Grant would both wish they had never
been born.

This was the last meeting I ever had with Babcock, and although pressing invitations were given

me to visit Grant up to the day he went out of office
yet I never had or sought a meeting with him after
this trip to Washington.

Before leaving the Capital, I received the following letter from Col. Joyce:

JEFFERSON CITY, March 28th, 1877.

DEAR GENERAL:

I have not written you for the reason that I expected you to
be west 'ere this; but thinking you may yet be in Washington,
I drop a line to say that I am in fine health and brave spirits.

I presume that you have learned that Judge Krekel has recommended me, and that the legislature, irrespective of party,
has sent on a petition.

*It is hard to think that the men we helped and saved, went back
on us, but it is just like the world.*

Your Friend,

JOHN.

This letter filled me with emotion and bitterness;
never before had I seen such an exhibition of cow-
ardly ingratitude, as was mirrored by the highest
officer in the government.   History paints the deeds
of Nero and Caligula, as the embodiments of ancient
injustice and cruel despotism, but is is reserved for
me to pick up the character of Grant and Babcock,
and with the strong arm of the press hold them high
before modern civilization, that the eyes of the dis-
criminate public may gaze upon their putrid villainies
and compounded crimes, and smell the festering
odors of the foul ingratitude of these two ineffaceable
stains upon creation itself.   Joyce's letter, written
in a criminal's cell, brought back the memory of our
sacrifice and the empty reward paid for our devotion;
how honors may ride upon the back of crime, and
the blackest heart and smallest soul may be hidden

by official power and patronage. Joyce was a man whose traits were unselfish friendship and broadest charity, and yet so noble a character was forced to pay obedience and humble itself before the greatest ingrate since the days of Judas.

When this exposure of crime shall go out upon its mission of information, these monstrocities of villainy and corruption, (Grant and his confederates,) will exert their remaining influence to deflect the eye of public censure from the evidences of their thefts and prostitution of the Republic, by shouting like the priests of Baal, and pointing to me as a confessed criminal. Well, I can afford to let them prick me with their stings, for there is no drop of poison on them now to give me pain. I not only place the impress of my oath and honor on every statement I have made herein, but have produced the written confessions of Grant and Babcock; I have them fast in the trammel net of their own letters and the testimony of their own acts. I can afford therefore to bear their attacks, conscious that there is not one of my readers who can, by any argument hereafter, be made to doubt the full guilt of those I have condemned, and that•truth being mighty, justice, in the way of some commiseration for the part I have acted in the whiskey frauds, will some day be accorded me.

It is hardly necessary to inform the reader that I have not exhausted my store of evidence against Grant and Babcock, since our relations and correspondence extended through a period of more than five years. The fact is, I have not used a tithe of the condemnatory letters which I have in my possession, as to have included them all would have

very greatly enlarged this book without adding anything to the weight of evidence, which is already too
great for a Titan to bear.

On the 13th of July, 1877, Col. Joyce was taken
out of prison upon a writ of *habeas corpus*, having
served two years, and his sentence being cumulative,
the question of the legality of the sentence was
raised. While the writ was before the Supreme
Court of the United States, President Hays granted
Joyce an unconditional pardon, and thus the last
sacrifice for Grant was completed.

CONCLUSION.

In the preceding chapters I have briefly sketched, in a hurried manner, the principal facts proving the connection of President U. S. Grant, Gen. O. E. Babcock, Commissioner J. W. Douglass, Judge Chester H. Krum, etc., with the conspiracy organized in 1870 to defraud the Government out of the revenue on distilled spirits. The extent of this robbery I believe has never been estimated, and while the public has ever regarded the amount as almost inestimable, yet I dare say the true figures will, nevertheless, prove appalling. During the first two years of the Ring's existence the Government tax on proof spirits was fifty cents per gallon, but in 1872 the tax was increased to seventy cents per proof gallon.

Although my district embraced a very large extent of territory, there were only eight distilleries in the district that turned out illicit whiskey in the interest of the Ring; seven of these were located in St. Louis and one in St. Joseph. The average daily capacity of these distilleries aggregated about 9,600 proof gallons. But there were so many interferences from agents, and other causes which frequently originated among members of the Ring, that it is perhaps proper to estimate that the distilleries ran only about half the time, and the distillers reported to the Government only one-half of the whiskey they manufactured. Basing the calculation upon this estimate, the Government was defrauded out of revenue amounting to $2,786,000, in my district alone, in six years.

While I made frequent reference in my narrative to amounts paid to Babcock, McKee, and others, yet I did not mention a tithe of the remittances that were made. McKee's interest approximated $300,000, with which money he purchased the *Missouri Democrat*. In this connection I will recite a fact which I omitted in the earlier and proper part of this book: When the *Globe* was started in 1872 people marveled greatly at the immense circulation which it so quickly developed. When the circumstances are explained, however, all wonder will give place to contempt. The reader is already familiar with the reason why McKee abandoned the Liberal movement and returned to the staunch support of President Grant, and after the compact bringing about this result was sealed by the organization of the Whiskey Ring, we felt a mutual interest in extending the circulation of the *Globe*. To accomplish this speedily I sent a notice to the ten thousand revenue officials in my district asking them each to subscribe for at least one copy of the daily *Globe*, and also to use their influence in increasing its circulation. The result of this was that in one month after the paper issued its initial number, its circulation was over 16,000 copies. This stroke of policy was very gratifying, not only to McKee himself, but to the President as well, for the *Globe* was the administration organ and its influence became thus pronounced in the beginning.

Gen. Babcock did not receive more than $25,000 of the Ring money directly, but he was the recipient of many valuable presents purchased with assessments made on the distillers.

The position of President Grant rendered him an anomalous or honorary member of the Whiskey Ring, though he may have divided the allowances made to Babcock, but I do not wish to make the President a victim of inference. He was one of the projectors of the Ring, however, and actually stood god-father to its christening. Grant was ambitious, and, the power of the organization which could collect money to advance his aspirations to a second and third term of the presidency, furnished him with emoluments sufficient for his iniquity. He knew that in politics money is more essential to success than brains; he knew that campaigns meant a bestrewal of wealth in his pathway which would toll the voting rabble after him like hogs that are coaxed to their pens by sprinkling corn in that direction. Assessments upon employes of the Government was not enough, besides there were other aspirants to the presidency within the Republican ranks, so he seized upon the opportunity of providing campaign resources by defrauding the Government through a confederacy of members, all of whom had declared their allegiance to him. I was selected because of a capacity for managing which Grant believed me to possess, and in turn I chose subordinates calculated to perform their duties with becoming discretion. When the funds from illicit distilling begun to accumulate we applied them to organizing committees, and, through these, wards and districts, in the interest of the Republican party and President Grant especially. In addition to this we were almost weekly giving him costly presents and reporting to him how the illicit whiskey, or campaign fund was being distributed, and this constituted a portion as liberal to him as the payments of money were to us. I cannot deny the fact that I was a member and a beneficiary of the Whiskey Ring, and I have no wish to shield myself behind the behests of my superiors; but while I have defined Grant's position with all the charity that circumstances will permit, I also ask the indulgence and impartiality of the public in regard to my own.

When I was made Supervisor of Internal Revenue, at a salary of $3,000 per annum, I was the owner in fee simple of property valued at $150,000. At the same time I had over $8,000,000 of business in my hands — Government claims for collection — in which I could have made annually more than ten times the salary of a Supervisor.

But I was a Republican, and politics always possessed for me a great facination, besides, the arrangements I had with Grant were prospective of liberal emoluments. During all of Grant's visits to St. Louis, while I was Supervisor, I paid all his hotel bills as well, also, as those who composed his party. In the game season I furnished the White House with the choicest birds that were brought into the market, at a weekly expense of nearly $100, and in addition to this I paid out of my own pocket for the frequent entertainment of prominent Washington officials, and in all respects became the source from whence the Republican candidates in St. Louis derived their monetary assistance during campaigns. The result of all this was that I was constantly draining my accumulation, and daily becoming poorer. When, at length, the exposures came, I retained the sum of $5,000 from the assessments made on the distillers and rectifiers to pay the expenses of my trial. This amount, I can conscientiously say, was all the money I ever derived from the Whiskey Ring which I devoted to my own individual use. But no better proof of this can be furnished than the fact that when I was pardoned out of the penitentiary not a vestage of my fortune remained, and to-day I am the victim of improvidence as well as being made the sin offering of Grant and Babcock. In other words, my fidelity and unparalleled devotion to these two men has cost me a fortune of more than $150,000, and the disgrace and misery consequent upon a term of seventeen months' imprisonment.

How many will there be to rise up at this juncture and enquire why I suffered this loss and submitted to such punishment if I could have prevented it by opening my lips? Well, it does seem strange to me now, when the light of subsequent events throws out so prominently the pamorama of false promises and hollow hearts. Doubtful Thomas, was ever your sympathy aroused by the plaintive story of female innocence, destroyed by the seductive declarations of one whose honeyed words fell upon the heart like nectar to the lips, and set its seal of love and confidence in her very soul? The circumstance is by no means a rare one; in fact, the world is full of false pretenses and man's perfidy. Do not, therefore, make a single and conspicious exception, and lay the faults of which I confess, and all the causes of my humiliation at the portal of my own conscience as self-inflicted stains. I ask no sympathy from any one, but I do ask justice; I am not dead to public opinion, having forfeited none of my own self-respect. I was sustained through all the phases of my punishment, not only by the golden promises of the President, in whose hands lay the power that could end the sacrifice I was making for him, but also by evidence in my possession to compell a fulfillment of those promises. My misfortunes were the result of that blind devotion which a gilded hope sometimes inspires. Had I been less faithful, and when the first lock was closed upon me, had cried out to the public as I do now, I would have been treated "as tenderly as a sucking dove," and perhaps to-day I would be holding some high and lucrative position, all comments upon my guilt having been counteracted by the strong will of my equally guilty superior. Or, had I acted as did many others, accepted the promises of the prosecuting attorneys for the government, and become an informer, how different would have been my fate. My fortune would still be ample; Babcock would have served a term in the penitentiary, and Grant would have been impeached, and if not imprisoned, would to-day be roaming in foreign lands as did

Gen. Arnold when he conspired with Maj. Andre to sell his country to the British—a disgraced Executive, unable to find a friend on the face of the earth—with the purple of his power changed into the tattered habiliments of contempt and impotency.

But mark you the facts which outline and disfigure the consequences of my action. Descending from the exalted position of Chief Magistrate of the Republic, it is still Gen. Grant clothed with the vestments of honor and influence; a visitor to foreign lands he receives the homage of potentates who bend their imperial knees to America's warrior and most distinguished citizen. Having exhausted the admiration and flattery of every civilization he returned to the shores of the country he had robbed and whose benedictions he had insulted, but the rabble, in whose pathway he scattered the money wrung from his countrymen through a conspiracy infamous as was Arnold's crime, greet his coming with acclaims of joy and bestrew his walks with flowers whose perfume might kill the oder of his iniquities. But this honor to the only president who, like Sylla of Rome, drew the life blood from the veins of his country to glut his own feast, did not cease with triumphal greetings and honors which drew the artisan from his workshop and the producer from his fields mellow with the incense of productive nature, but grew apace like riot when the conservators of peace are asleep; the unreasonable throng crowned crime with a laurel wreath and lent their voices in the impious cry for Grant's re-election. I cannot place a greater stigma upon America, and the history of the future will so record it, than to state the fact, that with all his infamies there was found three hnndred and six men, some of whom held offices of public trust in the government, who voted thirty-six times in a national convention for the re-nomination of Gen. U. S. Grant.

But, by whom was this most disgraceful act inaugurated, and who were the managers of this conspiracy against the honor of the nation? The first and most persistent outcry for this prostitution of the people was made by the *Globe-Democrat* of St. Louis, whose success and influence was procured through the conjunction and illicit aid of the criminal whom they doubly desired to re-exalt. Following in the trail of the serpent were those defaulting and polluted officials who had thriven by Grant's infamous coalition. "Dreadful cases require allœpathic doses," was the exclamation of those political marplots who, to break the force of that unwritten law which prohibits any man from occupying the presidency for more than two terms, conceived the scheme for sending Grant on a tour around the world. They were conscious of America's weakness for the dazzle and tinsel of hereditary rulers and believed that the ovations of titled potentates would, like the gaze of the serpent, charm the American people until they would forget the traditions of the past in the blinding incandescence of inperialism. This is how Grant's crime was atoned for by my sacrifice.

Gen. Babcock returned to Washington after his acquittal and those who, like Lazarus, were fed from the crumbs of his table, gave him their congratulations and testified to their undiminished confidence by making up a purse of $25,000 and presenting it to him as a memorial of their high consideration—for his services in assisting them to rob the Government.

To-day Gen. Babcock is Inspector of Light Houses, an ornamental and sinecure position, with pay as major of engineers. This position was given him by President Grant, and was one of the last acts of that most infamous administration.

Maj. E. B. Grimes is still Quarter Master at St. Louis.

Col. P. M. Schaurte is still Superintendent of Postal Service, with headquarters at St. Louis.

E. W. Fox's son is still U. S. Consul at Brunswick.

L. P. Luckey is occupying a lucrative position in the Interior Department.

H. C. Rogers is still deputy Commissioner of Internal Revenue.

Col. Holt is still in the Revenue service.

And so on through the list with the exception of Commissioner Douglass, Col. Joyce, Avery and myself. Douglass was dismissed, while three of us assumed the burden of guilt and paid the penalty of our crime and devotion. Those members of the Ring who became informers were released with a nominal punishment—one day's confinement.

I can hardly anticipate the inquiry here, "Why do you make this exposure now?" The reason has certainly been answered to the satisfaction of all my readers. Had President Grant fulfilled his promises and kept faith with me as I did with him no power on earth could have induced me to give the world the secrets of the Whiskey Ring; but, after immolating me upon the altar of his ambition; fearing to mention my name lest contumely might attack him, his actions have justified me in exposing his guilt to the people, without subjecting myself to the charge of ingratitude or false friendship. What I have given to the public in this book I declare to be true (in the sense it is represented) in every particular, without a prejudicial discoloring or the slightest exaggeration. I believe that all candid and honest men will have no hesitancy, after reading my statements and the documentary proofs which I here submit, in admitting that upon the evidence, in an impartial trial, both Grant and Babcock would be found guilty of " conspiracy to defraud the government out of the revenue on distilled spirits," the charge upon which I was convicted.

I am satisfied with my course; I kept the faith when Grant had most need for it, and while I suffered as few men have suffered, for my fidelity, the satisfaction of knowing that my action has saved the nation from an ineffaceable disgrace—an impeached and perhaps imprisoned Executive—is still left me as my reward.

GEN. JAS. A. GARFIELD.

A FRAGMENT FROM THE RECORD

OF THE

OFFICIAL LIFE

OF

JAMES A. GARFIELD.

HIS CORRUPT CONNECTION

WITH THE

CREDIT MOBILIER, DISTRICT OF COLUMBIA RING, AND DeGOLYER PAVING CO.

THE MISSING LINKS SUPPLIED BY THE ADMISSIONS OF GEN. O. E. BABCOCK.

SOME OF THE CORRUPT OFFICIAL ACTS OF JAMES A. GARFIELD.

THE CREDIT MOBILIER SCHEME.

I deem it appropriate to insert as an appendix to this work a few of the corrupt schemes made public, with which James A. Garfield of Ohio, who is now the nominee of the Republican party for the presidency, has been implicated. In this connection it may be stated that it was notorious about Washington that Garfield's influence, while he was a member of Congress, was an article of merchandise. That his connection with other corrupt schemes has never been made public is due to the fact that he has always been in the hands of shrewd middle men who have been equally interested in concealing their criminal complicity. The first corrupt measure that Gen. Garfield became connected with, which still stands against him on the records, was his implication with the notorious Oakes Ames, of Massachusett, in the Credit Mobilier of America, and the following verbatim evidence in this case, taken from the report of the Select Committee, appointed by the Forty-third Congress, gives the history of the part he played in that gigantic swindle.

GARFIELD'S STATEMENT.

WASHINGTON, Jan. 14th, 1873.

J. A. Garfield, a member of the United States House of Representatives from the State of Ohio, having been duly sworn, made the following statement:

"The first I ever heard of the Credit Mobilier was some time in 1866 or 1867. I cannot fix the date, when George Francis Train called on me and said he was organizing a company to be known as the Credit Mobilier of America, to be formed on the model of the Credit Mobilier of France; that the object of the company was to purchase lands and build houses along the line of the Pacific railroad at points where cities and villages were likely to spring up; that he had no doubt money thus invested would double or treble itself each year; that subscriptions were limited to $1,000 each, and he wished me to subscribe. He showed me a long list of subscribers, among them Mr. Oakes Ames, to whom he referred me for further information concerning the enterprise. I answered that I had not the money to spare, and if I had I would not subscribe without knowing more about the proposed organization. Mr. Train left me, saying he would hold a place open for me, and hoped I would yet conclude to subscribe. The same day I asked Mr. Ames what he thought of the enterprise. He expressed the opinion that the investment would be safe and profitable.

I heard nothing further on the subject for a year or more, and it was almost forgotten, when, some time, I should say, during the long session of 1868, Mr. Ames spoke of it again; said the company had organized, was doing well, and, he thought, would soon pay large dividends. He said that some of the stock had been left or was to be left in his hands to sell, and I could take the amount which Mr. Train had offered me by paying the $1,000 and the accrued interest. He said if I was not able to pay for it then, he would hold it for me till I could pay, or until some of the dividends were payable. I told him I would consider the matter, but would not agree to take any stock until I knew from an examination of the charter and the conditions of the subscription, the extent to which I would become pecuniarily liable. He said he was not sure, but thought that a stockholder would be liable only for the par value of his stock; that he had not the stock and papers with him, but would have them after awhile.

From the case as presented I probably should have taken the stock if I had been satisfied in regard to the extent of pecuniary liability. Thus the matter rested for some time. I think until the following year. During that interval I understood that there were dividends amounting to nearly three times the par value of the stock. But in the meantime I had heard that the company was involved in some controversy with the Pacific railroad, and that Mr. Ames' right to sell the stock was denied. When I next saw Mr. Ames I told him I had concluded not to take the stock.

There the matter ended, so far as I was concerned and I had no further knowledge of the company's operations until the subject began to be discussed in the newspapers last fall. Nothing was ever said to me by Mr. Train or Mr. Ames to indicate or imply that the Credit Mobilier was or could be in any way connected with the legislation of Congress for the Pacific railroad or for any other purpose. Mr. Ames never gave nor offered to give me any stock or other valuable thing as a gift. I once asked and obtained from him, and afterwards repaid to him, a loan of $300; that amount is the only valuable thing I ever received from or delivered to him. I never owned, received or agreed to receive any stock of the Credit Mobilier or of the Union Pacific railroad, nor any dividends or profits arising from either of them."

Following is the testimony of Oakes Ames which bears direct reference in its denial of the statements made by Mr. Garfield:

WASHINGTON, Jan. 22d, 1873.

Oakes Ames recalled and re-examined. By the chairman:

Ques.—In **regard to Mr.** Garfield, state to the Committee the details of **the transactions** between you and him in reference to Credit Mobilier stock?

Ans.—I got for Mr. Garfield ten shares of the Credit Mobilier stock, for which he paid par and interest.

Ques.—When did you agree with him for that?

Ans.—That agreement was in December, 1867, or January, 1868; about that time; about the time I had these conversations with all of them. It was all about the same time.

Ques.—State what grew out of it.

Ans.—Mr. Garfield did not **pay** me any money. I sold the bonds belonging to his $1,000 **of** stock at 97c, making $776. In June I received a dividend in cash on his stock of $600, which left a balance due him of $329, which I paid him. That is **all the** transaction between **us.** I did not deliver him any stock before or since. That is the only transaction, and the only **thing.**

Examined by **Mr. Merrick:**

Ques.—The $329 which you paid him was the surplus **of** earnings on the stock above the amount to **be** paid for it; par value?

Ans.—Yes, **sir;** he never **had** either his Credit Mobilier stock or Union Pacific railroad stock. The only thing he re-alized on the transaction was the $329.

Ques.—I see in this statement of the account with Géneral **Garfield** there is a charge **of $47 ; that** is interest from the July previous, is it?

Ans.—Yes, sir.

Ques.—And **the $776 on** the credit side of the account is the 80 per **cent. bond dividend sold** at $97?

Ans.—Yes, sir.

Ques.—And the $600 on the credit **side is** the money divi-dend?

Ans.—Yes, sir

Ques.—And after you had received these two sums, they in the aggregate overpaid the price of stock and interest $329, which you paid him?

Ans.—Yes, sir.

Ques.—How was that paid?

Ans.—Paid in money, I believe.

Ques.—Did you make a statement of this to Mr. Garfield?

Ans.—I presume so; I think I did with all of them; that is my impression.

Ques.—When you paid him this $329, did you understand it was the balance of his dividend after paying for his stock?

Ans.—I suppose so; I do not know what else he could suppose.

Ques.—You did not deliver the certificate of stock to him?

Ans.—No, sir; he said nothing about that.

Ques.—Why did he not receive his certificate?

Ans.—I do not know.

Ques.—Do you remember any conversation between you and him in the adjustment of these accounts?

Ans.—I do not.

Ques.—You understood that you were a holder of his ten shares?

Ans —Yes, sir.

Ques.—Did he so understand it?

Ans.—I presume so. It seems to have gone from his mind, however.

Ques.—Was this the only dealing you had with him in reference to any stock?

Ans.—I think so.

Ques.—Was it the only transaction of any kind?

Ans.—The only transaction.

Ques.—Has that $329 ever been paid to you?

Ans.—I have no recollection of it.

Ques.—Have you any belief that it ever has?

Ans.—No, sir.

Ques.—Did you ever loan General Garfield $300?

Ans.—Not to my knowledge ; except that he calls this a loan.

Ques.—You do not call it a loan?

Ans.—I did not at the time. I am willing it should go to suit him.

Ques.—What we want to get at is the exact truth?

Ans.—I have told the truth in my statement.

Ques.—When you paid him $329, did he understand that he borrowed that money from you?

Ans.—I do not suppose so.

Ques.—You regarded that money as belonging to him after the stock was paid for?

Ans.—Yes, sir.

Ques.—There were dividends of Union Pacific railroad stock on these ten shares?

Ans.—Yes, sir.

Ques.—Did General Garfield ever receive these?

Ans.—No, sir ; never has received but $329.

Ques.—And that he has received as his own money?

Ans.—I suppose so ; it did not belong to me. I should not have given it to him if it had not belonged to him.

Ques.—You did not understand it to belong to you as a loan; you never called for it and have never received it back?

Ans.—No, sir.

Ques.—Has there been any conversation between you and him in reference to the Pacific stock he was entitled to?

Ans.—No, sir.

Ques.—Has he ever called for it?

Ans.—No, sir.

Ques.—Have you ever offered it to him?

Ans.—No, sir.

Ques.—Has there been any conversation in relation to it?

Ans.—No, sir.

Ques.—Has there been anything said between you and him about rescinding the purchase of the ten shares of Credit Mobilier stock? Has there anything been said to you of its being thrown up or abandoned or surrendered?

Ans.—No, sir ; not until recently.

Ques.—How recently ?

Ans.—Since this matter came up.

Ques.—Since this investigation commenced?

Ans.—Yes, sir.

By Mr. Merrick.   Ques.—Did you consider at the commencement of this investigation that you held these other dividends,
which you said you did not pay to him, in his behalf? Did you
regard yourself as custodian of these dividends for him ?

Ans.—Yes, sir ; he paid for his stock and is entitled to his
dividends.

Ques.—Will the dividends come to him at any time on his
demand ?

Ans.—Yes, sir ; as soon as this suit is settled.

Ques.—You say that $329 was paid to him ; how was it paid?

Ans.—I presume by a check on the sargeant-at-arms. I find
there are some checks filed without any letters or initials indicating who they were for.

Ques.—Have you had any correspondence, since this dividend
was paid, with him in regard to this matter ?

Ans.—I do not know what matter you refer to.

Ques.—If there were any correspondence between you I
would like to see it.

Ans.—I have no copy of it.

Ques.—Have you the original?

Ans.—No, sir. Mr. Garfield showed me a letter which he
intended to enclose with some money sent me. I did not know
who the money came from. He showed me a letter which he
said he intended to have put in. I indorsed on the back of
that letter my reply. I just turned over the letter and wrote
my reply on the back of it and let him have it.

Ques.—Your answer indorsed on the back of the letter was
published in the newspapers ?

Ans.—Yes, sir; he published the letter I believe.

Ques.—As published, did they correspond with your recollection of the papers as written ?

Ans.—Yes, sir. I wrote it off hastily. He came to my room and said he had been accused of all kinds of crimes and misdemeanors. I told him I had made no such statement as he represented. He wanted me to say in writing that I had not. I took his letter, which he said he had intended to have enclosed with the money, and wrote on the back of it that I had made no such statement.

Ques.—Did he enclose the money?

Ans.—Some money came to me enclosed in an envelope which he said he had sent. I gave it back to him.

Ques.—How much money was in that envelope?

Ans.—Four hundred dollars.

The following memorandum referred to by witness as a statement of his account with Mr. Garfield, was placed in evidence:

	J. A. G.		Dr.
1868—To 10 shares stock Credit Mobilier,	-	-	$1,000 00
Interest, - - - - - - -	-		47 00
June 19—To cash, - -	-	- -	329 00
Total, - - - - - -	-	-	$1,376 00
			Cr.
1868—By dividend bonds Union Pacific railroad,			
$1,000 at 80 per cent., less 3 per cent.	-	-	$ 776 00
June 17—By dividend collected for your account,			600 00
Total, - - - - - -	-	-	$1,376 00

WASHINGTON, January, 29th, 1873.— -examination of Oakes Ames. By the Chairman: Ques.—You may state whether, in conversation with you, Mr. Garfield claims, as he claimed before us, that the only transaction between you was borrowing $300?

Ans.—No, sir; he did not claim that with me.

Ques.—State how he does claim it with you; what was said?

Ans.—He states that when he came back from Europe, being in want of funds, he called on me to loan him a sum of money. He thought he had repaid it.

Ques.—What did you say to him in reference to that state of the case?

Ans.—I stated to him that he never asked me to lend him any money; that I never knew he wanted to borrow any. I did not know he was short. I made a statement to him showing the transaction and what there was due on it; that deducting the bond dividend and the cash dividend there was $329 due him, for which I had given him a check; that he had never asked me to loan him any money and I had never loaned him any.

Ques.—After you had made that statement, what did he state in reply?

Ans.—He wanted to have it go as a loan.

Ques.—Did he claim that it was in fact a loan?

Ans.—No, sir; I do not think he did. No he did not.

Ques.—How long after that transaction did he go to Europe?

Ans.—I believe it was a year or two.

Ques.—Did you have any conversation in reference to the influence this transaction would have upon the election last fall?

Ans.—Yes; he said it would be very injurious to him.

Ques.—State all you know in reference to it.

Ans.—I told him he knew very well that that was a dividend. I made out a statement and showed it to him at the time. In our conversation he admitted it and said, as near as I can remember, that there was $2,400 due him in stock and bonds. He made a little memorandum of $1,000 and $1,500, and as I recollect, said there was $1,000 of Union Pacific railroad stock, $1,000 of Credit Mobilier stocks and $400 of stock or bonds, I do not recollect which.

Ques.—When was that memorandum made?

Ans.—It was made in my room; I cannot remember the date. It was since this investigation commenced.

Ques.—Was it in that conversation that he referred to the influence this matter would have upon the election in his district?

Ans.—I do not recollect whether it was in that one or some other. I had two or three conversations with him.

Ques.—Tell us as nearly as you can, precisely the remarks he made in that conversation?

Ans.—It was that it would injure his reputation, that it was a cruel thing. He felt very bad, was in great distress, and hardly knew what he did say.

Ques.—Did he make any request of you to make no statement in reference to it?

Ans.—I am not positive about that.

Ques.—What is your best recollection in reference to it?

Ans.—My impression is that he wanted to say as little about it as he could, and to get of as easily as he could. That was about the conversation I had with him, about the long and short of it.

Ques.—Have you the memorandum that Mr. Garfield made?

Ans.—I have the figures that he made.

Paper shown the committee contain figures as follows:

$$\begin{array}{r} \text{``\$1,000} \\ 1,400 \\ \hline \$2,400.\text{''} \end{array}$$

Ques.—You say these figures were made by Mr. Garfield?

Ans.—Yes, sir.

Ques.—What do these sums represent? How did he put them down?

Ans.—$1,000 Union Pacific railroad stock, $1,000 Credit Mobilier stock and $400 which he could not remember whether it was to be in cash, stock or bonds.

Ques.—Is that what he received or what he was entitled to?

Ans.—What he was entitled to.

Ques.—That was his idea of what was coming to him?

Ans.—Yes, sir.

THE DeGOLYER BRIBERY.

His connection with the District of Columbia Ring was a notorious fact, and as soon as he filed his brief with the commissioners on behalf of the DeGolyer patent, "Boss Shepherd held it aloft in his hand and said: "This fixes Garfield for the future." In order that the reader may clearly understand his connection with that matter, I here insert the statement of Ex-Senator Doolittle. I copy from the Rochester (N. Y.) *Union and Advertiser* :

The respite of an hour for a criminial under sentence of death could not give the condemned more momentary relief than is found by the Republican newspapers in the error of the Washington correspondent of the New York *World,* attributing to Mr. Justice Swayne of the Supreme Court of the United States an opinion in the case of Chittenden vs. De Golyer and McClellan which he did not deliver. To the Rochester *Democrat* especially this, in itself trivial circumstance, furnishes a day of happiness such as it has not enjoyed since Garfield's nomination. But every intelligent man knows that whether Mr. Justice Swayne delivered an opinion in Mr. Garfield's particular case, or, as is the fact, in another and parallel case, laying down a general principle and giving a general interpretation of law applicable to all kindred cases, is of no consequence whatever. The chief significance attached to the erroneously reported passing of Judge Swayne upon Garfield's case was based upon the fact that he is a Republican and from Garfield's own State. The Republican newspapers are welcome to all the comfort they can extract from the *World's* error and our reproduction of it. We wish them every joy they can find in it. The *Union,* having been misled by its usually correct New York contemporary, takes great pleasure in making due correction. It can have no interest in misrepresenting any part of the history of the public career of Mr. Garfield, and has no desire to misrepresent it. It tells and relies wholly upon the truth as it stands upon the records of a Republican Congress, in the colums of the Republican press, and under the decisions of judicial tribunals. Opportunely and happily, at the very moment that the Republican newspapers are seeking to hide their diminished heads

in the *World's* error, we are in receipt of the full official statement of the case in the circuit court at Chicago, where the
plaintiff, Chittenden, was thrown out of court upon the ground
of his bribery of Garfield in the wood pavement contract matter.
For this statement we ten days ago wrote Hon. James R.
Doolittle, the counsel of DeGolyer and McClellan, whose
letter in reference to the Swayne matter the Rochester *Democrat* parades in such prominence this morning.   Judge Doolittle is a New Yorker, a graduate of Geneva college, a former
district attorney of Wyoming county, and well known to all
the old residents of Western New York.   He has been a Judge
of the Supreme Court of Wisconsin, was for twelve years a
Republican United States Senator from that State, and in 1866
was president of the National Union Convention, held at Philadelphia.   He is of the highest eminence as a public man and a
jurist.   His statement of the law case in which the bribe of
Garfield nonsuited the plaintiff, covers the whole ground and
is conclusive:

Following is Mr. Doolittle's statement :

CHICAGO, ILL., July 20, 1880.

DEAR SIR :—Your letter of the 14th inst. is duly received, in
in which you ask me to send you "the full text of the case " of
Chittenden vs. De Golyer and McClellan.   The declaration,
pleas, demurrer and brief on argument are quite voluminous.
They were not printed ; and it would be quite a labor to give
you a full copy.   With the assistance of my clerk I give you
an abstract of the case, and in quotation marks give you some
of the exact language of the pleas and the points submitted
to the court.   You will bear in mind this cause was decided
five years ago, and all I know of the facts came to me as attorney and counsel for the defendants.   But I shall only state
what appears upon the records, pleadings and proceedings in
court.

Respectfully yours,

J. R. DOOLITTLE.

The following is substantially a true abstract of the case, so far as it bears upon the action of Gen. Garfield :

May Term, 1875.—Before Farwell, Circuit Judge—No. 12,181.

State of Illinois, Cook County Circuit Court; George R. Chittenden vs. Robert McClellan, et al.:

The plaintiff, by E. A. Storrs, Esq., brought suit against the defendants upon a contract by which they agreed to pay him one-third of all the profits upon all paving contracts which he would obtain for DeGolyer and McClellan from boards of public works in eastern cities. The declarations alleged that he obtained a contract for paving 200,000 square yards from the Board of Public Works of the District of Columbia, at $1.50 per yard, when it would cost only $1,500 to lay it down. That the profits would be $300,000, and the plaintiff claimed the defendants should pay him $100,000, at least, and he claimed a judgment for that sum Besides the general issue—

The defendants pleaded in substance the following special pleas:

First—That the contract was void on its face.

Second—That it was obtained by the plaintiff by improper influences—against public policy, and therefore was void. Amongst other things the second special plea set out " that then and there, and while the matter was pending and undetermined before the said Board, he (the plaintiff) did pay to one Richard C. Parsons a large sum of money, to-wit, the sum of ten thousand dollars, he then and there being an officer of the United States, to-wit, Marshal of the Supreme Court, to apply to said Board, and the individual members of said Board, to obtain the award of said contract; and also then and there did employ, or caused to be employed, J. A. Garfield, then and there a member of the House of Representatives, and Chairman of the Committee on Appropriations of said House, to appear before the said Board, and before the individuals composing the same, to solicit and urge upon said Board the award of said contract, and in consideration of his said employment and

W

services and official influence then and there rendered the said plaintiff did pay, or caused to be paid, illegally, improperly and against public policy, a large sum of money, to-wit: the sum of five thousand dollars; and then and there, and in part by means thereof the said Board of Public Works were moved and induced illegally, improperly and against public policy to make the said award, which said award amongst other things contained the following clause or condition, viz:

"An additional amount of fifty thousand square yards will be awarded you, (the defendants meaning) so soon as the Board is reimbursed by the general government on account of expenditures around the public buildings and grounds, or you (the defendants meaning) will be allowed to lay it this season if you can wait until an appropriation is made for the purpose, (meaning an appropriation by Congress,) at three dollars and fifty cents per square yard. And the defendants aver that, then and there, and by the terms of the said award of said contract, fifty out of two hundred thousand yards so awarded were made to depend upon a future appropriation of money to be made by Congress; that then and there, by the usual course and practice of the House of Representatives, all bills for such appropriations would be referred to, and reported from, the Committee of Appropriations, of which the said Garfield was a member, and the Chairman thereof; the said plaintiff, and the said J. A. Garfield and the said Board of Public Works, severally, then and there well knowing that the said J. A. Garfield did, could and would, from his official position, exert a potent influence in procuring such appropriation by Congress for the purpose mentioned in said award; and that the defendants say that by means of the said premises the said award of contract mentioned in the said declaration was then and there illegal, improper, against public policy and void. And this the said defendants are ready to verify; wherefore they pray judgment if the said plaintiff ought to have or maintain his aforesaid action thereof against them."

Third—In another and further special plea, the defendants, amongst other things, alleged as follows:

"That some time in the latter part of May, 1872, and while the Congress of the United States was in session, and before any appropriations for that year had been made by that body for improvements to be made in the streets of Washington, in the District of Columbia, the plaintiff then and there represented to the said DeGolyer & McClellan, that through one R. Parsons (then Marshal of the Supreme Court of the United States) he had secured the influence of Gen. James A. Garfield (then a Representative in the House of Representatives in the Congress of the United States, and Chairman of the Committee on Appropriations of the said House of Representatives) to be used in behalf of the said DeGolyer & McClellan in the application for pavement contracts from the Board of Public Works of the District of Columbia; that by letter dated at the Arlington House, Washington, District of Columbia, addressed to said DeGolyer & McClellan at Chicago aforesaid, he stated among other things that Col. Parsons had arrived; that the influence of Gen. Garfield had been secured by yesterday, last night and to-day's labors; he carries the purse of the United States—the Chairman of the Committee on Appropriations, and is the strongest man in Congress and with our friends. My demand is to-day *not* less than one hundred thousand—two hundred thousand in all. Everything is in the best of shape—the connections complete, and I have reason to believe satisfactory. We want more books sent, 25 each, here.

"'The model is in Gen. Garfield's house—sent there last night; note, you will be ready to leave on the first train when telegraphed to. I can hardly realize that we have Gen. Garfield with us. It is rare—and very gratifying. All appropriations of the District come from him.'"

The plea then avers that Garfield appeared before said Board as set out in former plea, that the award of said contract with the conditions as set out in the other plea, was made, and goes on to aver:

"That then and there the said J. A. Garfield was a member

of the House of **Representatives, in** which all bills to appro-
priate money originate; **that he** was then **and** there Chairman
of the Committee on Appropriations of the House of Repre_
sentatives, to **which** Committee, by the rules and practice of
said House, all bills to appropriate money to be expended in
the said District of Columbia must be and are referred; that
then and there it was well known to the said Richard C. **Parsons, James** A. Garfield, Alexander R. Shepherd, the plaintiff,
and the said DeGolyer & McClellan, that the said J. A. Gar-
field, then and there and thereafter, in his official character as
member of said House of Representatives, and as Chairman
of said Committee, did, could and would exert and exercise a
potent influence in and upon the said Committee, and upon
the said House of Representatives, in reporting to and passing through said House, bills to appropriate moneys to be **ex-**
pended **in** the **said** District of Columbia, in **and** upon **the** said
pavements to be awarded by the said Board of Public Works.

"The defendants aver that then and thereby and by means
thereof, **the said A. R.** Shepherd as a member of said Board,
and the said Board of Public Works has moved and induced to
make and, in fact, did make the said award and contract above
set out and described in the declaration, and not otherwise.

"And these defendants further say that **afterwards, to-wit,**
on the 10th day of July, **1872,** at Chicago aforesaid, in consideration thereof, and **of the** services and official influence rendered and given as aforesaid by the said James A. Garfield,
and the said R. C. Parsons, the said DeGolyer & McClellan
made their certain draft for $10,000, and delivered the same to
the said Parsons, **at** Cleveland, which said draft was duly paid,
and then **and** there the one-half, or the **sum** of $5,000 was
paid to the said J. A. Garfield for his services and official
influence, etc.; that it was paid as **a** contingent fee and was
to be paid only upon the condition that the said award should
be granted by the said **Board of** Public Works, and not otherwise, **as was** then and **there** agreed between the said plaintiff
and the said Parsons for himself and for the said Garfield."

"And these defendants further say, that afterwards, at Washington aforesaid, the said Committee on Appropriations did recommend the passage and the House of Representatives did pass a bill appropriating large sums of money, which said bill passed Congress and was approved January 8th, 1876, for the sum of $1,241,920.92, out of which said sum said Board of Public Works were authorized to pay the said sum of money agreed to be paid by said contract and award."

"And the said defendants further aver that the award was, in fact, mainly procured by the official influence of the said Garfield alone."

"And the defendants say that by means of the premises the said award and contract were then and there illegal, improper, against public policy, and void, etc. And this the said defendants are ready to verify, etc., wherefore they pray judgment, etc."

When the matter came on to be heard, I, as counsel for the defendants, submitted a brief in writing, of which the fourth, fifth, and sixth points are as follows, viz:

Fourth.—"The pleas are good. They set out in substance that the contract was obtained by the plaintiff, of the Board of Public Works of the District of Columbia by improper influences; that the contract was in part to the amount of 50,000 squares, upon its face, contingent upon a future appropriation to be made by Congress; that the plaintiff employed James A. Garfield, then being a member of Congress and Chairman of the Committee on Appropriations of the House of Representatives, agreeing to pay him a contingent fee of $5,000 provided he would obtain the said contract of the Board of Public Works; that by his influence and persuasion he did procure the same, for which he received the sum of $5,000; that afterwards a bill was reported from the Committee of which he was Chairman, and did pass the House, and passed Congress and became a law, appropriating the sum of $1,241,000, out of which the pavement under said contract could be paid for by said Board of Public Works; that the plaintiff and the de-

fendant, and the said Garfield and the members of the said
Board of Public Works well knew, at the time of his said employment, and at the time of his service in procuring said
contract, that said Garfield, from his official position, did and
would have a potent influence in procuring the passage of
such appropriation to carry such contract into effect by said
Board of Public Works; and that by means of the premises
the said contract was, in fact, obtained by improper influences
against public policy, and is void."

Fifth.—" It is no sufficient answer to say that Garfield was
at the same time a member of the legal profession. His being
a member of Congress at the same time, any employment as
counsel upon a contingent fee or otherwise to obtain a contract from a board of public officers, dependent upon the
future action of Congress to fulfill, is against public policy and
is void."

Sixth.—"**That the plaintiff,** Chittenden, well knew and *intended* that the influence of Gen. Garfield, as a member of
Congress, was to be used in procuring the contract, rather
than his arguments as counsellor at law, is evident from his
letter to the defendants, set out in their special plea, in which
he says: ' The influence of Gen. Garfield has been secured by
yesterday, last night, and to-day's labors. **He** carries the purse
of the United States — the Chairman **of** the Committee **of**
Appropriations — and **is** the strongest man **in** Congress with
our friends. My demand is to-day not less than one hundred
thousand more—two hundred thousand in all. Everything is
in the best shape, the connections complete, and **I** have reason
to believe satisfactory. * * * **I** can hardly realize that we
have Gen. Garfield with us. It is rare, and very gratifying.
All the appropriations of the District come from him."

" In the recent case of Burke *vs.* Child, not yet reported,
(May, 1875) decided at the last October term of the Supreme
Court of the United States, Mr. Justice Swayne, in a very able
opinion, reviews all the cases and holds: That a contract
expressed or implied, for purely professional services is valid.

Within this category he includes drafting a petition, attendance on taking testimony, collecting facts, preparing arguments and submitting them, orally or in w...iting, to a committee or other proper authority.

"But such services are separated by a broad lane from personal solicitation and from official influence."

"The agreement with Gen. Garfield, a member of congress, to pay him $5,000 as a contingent fee for procuring a contract which was itself made to depend upon a future appropriation by Congress, which appropriation could only come from a committee of which he was chairman, was a sale of official influence which no veil can cover, against the plainest principles of public policy. No counsellor at law, while holding high office, has a right to put himself in a position of temptation ; and, under pretence of making a legal argument, exert his official influence upon public officers dependent upon his future action."

"Certainly the courts of justice will never lend themselves to enforce contracts obtained by such influences."

The court (Judge Farwell presiding) overruled the demurrer ; held the special pleas to be good ; and, that the contract was void as against public policy. That ended the case.

Respectfully yours,

J. R. DOOLITTLE.

THE DISTRICT OF COLUMBIA RING.

I have no disposition to add a word by way of comment upon the testimony given by Mr. Garfield and Mr. Ames or the exhaustive and convincing statements and arguments of Judge Doolittle.

But it is important that the secrets now in my possession, respecting the connection of Garfield with the District of Columbia Ring, should be made public through this medium.

In October, 1874, during my visit to Washington, for the purpose of ascertaining from the President the truth of certain rumors respecting the intentions of revenue agents, as reported in Chapter IV, I accepted an invitation to ride with Gen. Babcock, and during this drive I learned much regarding the operations of the District of Columbia Ring, gathered from a conversation with the General which was introduced in the following manner: As we drove over the old canal I was struck with the singular transformation which the old water-way had recently undergone. I had known it when there was but a semblance of an ancient canal, half-filled with stagnant water and sickening smelling garbage and mud. Now, behold, the wand of magic appeared to have been active, for out of the old, filthy canal, had arisen a beautiful avenue, handsomely paved, and clothed with the most luxurious, wide-spreading trees, in the branches of which the birds made merry sport and tropical music. Observing the marvelous change I asked the General how the money was obtained with which to make such extravagant improvements. Let me here inform the reader, who may never have visited the National Capital, that a greater part of Washington is the property of the Government. Not only the grounds occupied by the public buildings but also most of the picturesque sites overlooking the Potomac, the National Park,—and a large number of minor parks, —the ground on which stands the Washington monument, and many other fine, eligible locations, including all the triangular squares which have been made to bloom like beds of roses. By the application of vast sums of money all these places have been transformed from uninviting vacant spots into parks and gardens more beautifiul than the sylvan parterres of fairy-land.

Understanding these facts the reason for me addressing the General such an inquiry is readily apparent.

His reply to my question was: "Oh! we have got that matter all fixed; the Chairman of the Committee on Appropriations is our man."

I asked: Who is the Chairman?

He replied: "Gen. Garfield."

Said I: Why, I know Garfield; is he in the ring?

"No," he answered, "he is not exactly in the ring, but we have got him where we can use him all the same."

I enquired: You have to pay him, don't you?

He responded: "Well, you know Garfield is one of those easy, clever fellows who don't want much. We gave him an elegant residence on 'I' street, which we have furnished throughout very finely, and this seems to content him." Continuing his remarks further, the General said: "Besides, Garfield makes political capital out of the ring by obtaining good contracts for his friends. Garfield, too, is a good lawyer and we frequently have need for his services for which we pay him liberal fees. The fact is," warming up somewhat in the conversation, "Garfield is the coming man; when Grant gets tired of the presidency, as he will after one or two terms more, Garfield will be his successor and everything will remain lovely."

We talked some time, concerning improvements which could only be made out of the appropriations made by Congress. He explained the operations of the ring as follows: The ring was composed chiefly of government officials through whom heavy contractors were represented; certain influential members of Congress, chief of whom was Jas. A. Garfield, were admitted to the ring for their services in putting bills and appropriations through Congress. The next step was to have the contract for the work, provided for in the bills, let to contractors in the ring at exhorbitant prices.

Another scheme was to buy up all the property around an open tract, after which, through the influence of the ring, a bill would be passed providing for the improvement and ornamentation of the tract, and thus the ring would derive all the benefits of the improvements made at Government expense.

During the existence of this ring Babcock, in addition to occupying the position of private secretary to the President, was also Superintendent of Public Buildings, but for this service he received no salary, his compensation consisting entirely of perquisites—or his share of the ring money.

EARLY OPINIONS REGARDING GARFIELD.

To conclude the testimony establishing the venality of James A. Garfield, I herewith present a Republican address, issued by Mr. Garfield's first constituents, in the summer of 1876:

AN ADDRESS TO THE REPUBLICAN VOTERS OF THE NINE-
TEENTH (OHIO) CONGRESSIONAL DISTRICT.

FELLOW CITIZENS :—We, who address you, were appointed a committee for this purpose by an independent convention of Republicans, assembled for the purpose of putting in nomination a suitable **person as** candidate for Congress, in opposition to James A. Garfield.

The cause which impelled the calling of that convention, and inspired its actions, are set forth in the resolutions by it adopted and printed herewith. To the indictment contained **in these** resolutions, and the evidence submitted in support **thereof,** we respectfully call your attention and ask your candid consideration.

We have no grievances. We never sought favors at Mr. Garfield's hands, and have no personal quarrel with him. On the contrary, we have been among his warmest personal friends and supporters, and now only attack his acts and conduct in public life and the character he has thereby attained.

It is easier to flow with the tide than to row against it, and we regret the necessity that compels us to denounce him.

It is fitting that as true men we should seek the cause and remedy for this state of ruin, and we look not far nor long. Corruption in office and want of wisdom in legislation looms up before us. We review with pride our party history and achievements, but we now see fraud in high places eating at its vitals. Its revenue officers are found stealing and dividing with Whiskey Rings. Its secretaries sell post-traderships. Its Congressmen raise their own salaries and **make them retroac**tive; take great fees for argument on paving **jobs** before boards of their own creation, and pocket the dividends of great frauds like the Credit Mobilier. Corruption rides in $1,600 landaulets, purchased at government expense, and Congressmen build palaces at the **capital,** while the **people** toil and sweat under the burdens—they forget that **they are** the servants of the nation, and act as if they were its owners, seeking to wring from it the greatest possible number of dollars for **their own** purposes.

The Republican party has **done much** to purify itself within itself. Its Whiskey Ring revenue officers are convicted and imprisoned; Belknap is deposed and impeached, and only escapes conviction by a technicality. Its salary-stealing, Credit Mobilier, pavement-jobbing congressmen are mostly **retired.** James A. Garfield remains. Richard C. Parsons, his compeer as a great patent pavement lawyer, nominated without opposition in a district Republican last year by 6,500 majority, was buried at the polls by Henry B. Payne, a Democrat, by 2,500 majority. The office-holders nominated him, but the brave, honest people rebuked him.

James A. Garfield fell from 10,935 majority in 1872 to 2,529 majority in 1874. "Oh, what a fall was there, my countrymen." Rebuked, **shorn of character** for **truth** and integrity, **all** that is noble in manhood defeated, he stands a sad **and** blackened monument of avarice and greed.

By the arts of the orator and demagogue, of which he is a consummate master, he is striving and struggling, and may postpone the day of his final doom, but he wears upon his front the writing on the wall, "Mene, mene, tekel upharsin."

Flaming oratory upon the horrors of Andersonville and Libby, and the disordered condition of the South, are a poor compensation for want of integrity. The fools who believe that another great rebellion or payment of the rebel debt are imminent are only found in the post-offices and lunatic asylums. The people know better, and that cry of the demagogue to arouse their fears that he may get their votes ought to be of no avail.

G. N. TUTTLE,

P. BOSWORTH, **and**

H. H. HINE, of Lake County,

J. A. GIDDINGS, of Ashtabula,

L. E DURFEE, of Geauga,

L. D. BROWN, of Portage,

A. YOUMANS, of Trumbull.

September 10, 1876.

On the 9th day of September, 1876, the Republicans of the
Nineteenth Congressional District of Ohio opposed to the
return of James A. Garfield to Congress, met in convention at
Warren, Ohio, and organized by electing Dr. C. W. Ensign, of
Lake, for Chairman, and L. D. Brown, of Portage, and George
E. Paine, of Lake, Secretaries.

On motion, G. N. Tuttle and J. B. Burroughs, of Lake; B.
F. Perry, of Ashtabula; L. D. Brown, of Portage, and C. D.
Crary, of Lake, were chosen a committee on resolutions, and
H. H. Hine, William E. Hulett, P. Cosworth, and J. S. Case-
ment, B. F. Perry, and R. M. Murray were appointed a com-
mittee on conference for representative.

The Committee on Resolutions, after a long whereas, said:

Therefore, Be it by this independent convention of the
Republicans of the Nineteenth Congressional District of
Ohio—

1. *Resolved*, That dishonesty, fraud and corruption have
become so common, notorious, and obvious in the administration of our national government as to be not only humiliating
and disgraceful in the estimation of every honest and intelligent citizen, but to imperil the prosperity of the people, if
not the stability of the government itself.

2. *Resolved*, That this deplorable condition of the administration of our national government is largely due to the election to office and continuance therein of corrupt, dishonest,
venal men.

3. *Resolved*, That it is useless and hypocritical for any
political party to declare for reform in its platforms, papers'
and public addresses while it insists on returning to high
official place and power, men who have been notoriously connected with the very schemes of fraud which rendered reform
necessary and urgent; that to send those to enact reform who
themselves need reforming to make them honest, is worse than
setting the blind to lead the blind.

4. *Resolved*, That there is no man to-day officially connected
with the administration of our national Government against

whom are justly preferred more and graver charges of corruption than are publicly made and abundantly sustained against James A. Garfield, **the present** representative of this congressional district and the nominee of the Republican convention for re-election.

5. *Resolved,* **That since** he first entered Congress to this day there is scarcely an instance in which rings and monopolies have been arrayed against the interests of the people that he **has** not been found active in speech or **vote** upon the side of the latter, and in almost every case he has been the ready champion of the rings and monopolies.

6. *Resolved,* **That** we especially charge him with venality **and** cowardice in permitting Benjamin F. Butler to attach to the appropriation bill **of 1874** that ever-to-be-remembered infamy, the salary **steal,** and in speaking and voting for that **measure** upon its final passage; we also charge him with corrupt **disregard of the clearly expressed** demand of his constituents **that he should** vote for its repeal and with evading said demand by voting for **the Hutchinson amendment.**

6. *Resolved,* **That we** further arraign and denounce him for his corrupt connection with the Credit Mobilier, for his false denial, before his constituents ; for his perjured denials thereof before a committee of his peers in Congress ; for fraud upon his constituents in circulating among them a pamphlet purporting to set forth the findings **of** said committee and the evidence against him, when, in fact, material portions thereof **were** omitted and garbled.

8. Resolved, That **we** further **arraign** and charge him with **bribery in** selling his official influence as Chairman of the **Committee** on Appropriations, for $5,000, to the DeGolyer Paving Company, to aid them in securing a contract from the Board of Public Works of the District of Columbia; selling his influence to aid said ring in imposing upon the people of said district a pavement which is almost worthless, at a price three times its cost, as sworn to by one of the contractors; selling his influence to aid **said ring** in **procuring** a contract, to procure

which it corruptly paid $97,000 "for influence;" selling his influence in a matter that involved no question of law, upon the shallow pretext that he was acting as a lawyer; selling his influence in a manner so palpable and clear, as to be so found and declared by an important and competent court, upon an issue solemnly tried.

9. Resolved, that we arraign him for the fraudulent manner in which he attempted, in his speech delivered at Warren, on the 9th day of September, 1874, to shield himself from just censure in receiving the before named $5,000, by falsely representing, in said speech, that the Congress of the United States was not responsible for the acts of said Board, nor the United States liable for the debts created thereby, when in truth and in fact, as he then well knew, the said Board of Public Works and the officers of said district were but the agents and instruments of Congress, and the United States was responsible for the indebtedness by them created.

Republics, no less than kingdoms, are subject to the curses of unprincipled men whose cunning has exalted them to positions of great influence. Gen. Grant was one of those accidents which an earlier civilization would have pronounced "Divinely commissioned." But, like Judas, who, from the position of a faithful disciple, after years of well performed duty, his naturally corrupt nature at last gained the ascendancy, and from the pinnacle of fame's brightest chamber, he fell to those depths in which alone live the imps and foul creatures of infamy.

There never was a gang of robbers disbanded by the operations of the law without a repetition of bold effort; if a chief dies, or is deposed, another takes his place, whose reputation for bravery and available resource commends him. It is so with political parties, whose adroit flattery is admirably calculated to continue public deception, and, when a leader is stricken by the blight of unpopularity, a successor is provided who preserves the continuity of party principles, and at the same time endears himself to a discontented public by the unction of his avowals. Garfield occupies the position of public pacificator, with the old Grant crowd at his back, hiding all their corruption in his shadow.

Having been associated with those ring managers, whose relations with Garfield were in the nature of co-conspirators, I can appreciate what his candidacy for the presidency means. It is a continuation of the Grant policy in every essential particular, with its retinue of corruption, under a panoply of the most disgraceful national crimes. It means a subordination of public purity to the vitiated and remorseless taste of public greed; it provides for the Babcocks, Belknaps, Shepherds, and that long drawn out file of defrauders and official delinquents who, like poisonous ticks and chigres, have fastened their heads into the veins of the nation and from year to year glut themselves with public blood. Will the people suspend this infamous feast?

www.ingramcontent.com/pod-product-compliance
Lightning Source LLC
Chambersburg PA
CBHW030907270326
41929CB00008B/610